WAITING TO LAND

ALSO BY MARTIN DUBERMAN

WAITING
TO
LAND

A (MOSTLY) POLITICAL MEMOIR,
1985–2008

Martin Duberman

THE NEW PRESS

NEW YORK
LONDON

Requests for permission to reproduce selections from this book should be
mailed to: Permissions Department, The New Press, 38 Greene Street,
New York, NY 10013.

Published in the United States by The New Press, New York, 2009
Distributed by Perseus Distribution

LIBRARY OF CONGRESS CATALOGING-IN-PUBLICATION DATA

Duberman, Martin B.
  Waiting to land : a (mostly) political memoir, 1985–2008 / Martin Duberman.
    p. cm.
  Includes index.
  ISBN 978-1-59558-440-3 (hc.)
  1. Duberman, Martin B.   2. Gay men—United States—Biography.   I. Title.
  HQ75.8.D82A34 2009
  306.76'62092—dc22
  [B]
                                                                2009004830

The New Press was established in 1990 as a not-for-profit alternative to the
large, commercial publishing houses currently dominating the book publishing
industry. The New Press operates in the public interest rather than for private
gain, and is committed to publishing, in innovative ways, works of educational,
cultural, and community value that are often deemed insufficiently profitable.

www.thenewpress.com

Composition by NK Graphics
This book was set in Electra

Printed in the United States of America

10   9   8   7   6   5   4   3   2   1

For Naomi Weisstein,
the most courageous person I know

"'*Everything is biographical*,' Lucian Freud says. What we make, why it is made, how we draw a dog, who it is we are drawn to, why we cannot forget. Everything is collage, even genetics. There is the hidden presence of others in us, even those we have known briefly. We contain them for the rest of our lives, at every border we cross."

—Michael Ondaatje, *Divisadero*

Preface

Speaking truth about one's own life is nearly as difficult as speaking truth to power. Trying to combine the two is the equivalent of handing Sisyphus a second rock. As I've learned from writing two previous memoirs and from decades of involvement in left-wing politics, to achieve even the approximation of truth requires unwavering attention to known detail, the painful admission of inconvenient contradictions, and a humbling toleration for the elusive nature of presumed "facts" and seemingly rock-solid memories. Yet the maddening process of putting together even a rough approximation of "what really happened" remains an essential enterprise; no other counterweight exists to self-deception, or to public mendacity.

My first memoir, Cures (1992), attempted to describe my life through the year 1970. A second autobiographical book, Midlife Queer, published four years later, focused on the decade of the seventies. In this third volume, I carry the story up to the present day. Waiting to Land addresses issues that either hadn't arisen prior to 1980 (AIDS, say) or that hadn't yet become clarified (the disconnect between the Left and the LGBT (lesbian, gay, bisexual, and transgender) movement, as well as the now-solidified disillusion among gay left-wingers with the national LGBT organizations).

Waiting to Land is also different from the previous two memoirs in focusing far less on revelations about my private life. In Cures, I used my (very) personal history to illustrate a generational story: how I, like so many other gay men, internalized the then-current definition of homosexuality as pathology and—for those of us who could afford it—spent years in psychoanalysis attempting to change our sexual orientation. *Cures* ended with my leaving therapy and with my tentative entry into the worlds of gay culture and politics—themes I again explored through my own experience in *Midlife Queer*.

In this third memoir, the first-person voice is still dominant, but this time around I've kept my private life pretty much private. Some of my closest friends go unmentioned in the book. And my partner of nearly twenty-five years, Eli Zal, makes less than half a dozen brief appearances; though his centrality to my life can hardly be exaggerated, neither of us wanted to offer up our relationship for public scrutiny. My daily life these days has taken on the comfortably routine, subdued tones characteristic of most long-standing relationships and is far removed from the bachelor melodramas that filled the pages of *Cures* and *Midlife Queer*.

Waiting to Land concentrates on different realms: public engagement and political struggle—and the inevitable controversy both arouse. Over the past twenty-five years, my political involvement has continued on a number of fronts, with my radicalization deepening, not dissipating, through the years. During the same period, the national gay movement has simultaneously increased in strength and changed its focus to an assimilationist agenda (gay marriage, gays in the military, etc.). The movement's shift in priorities has disquieted many of its left-wing members, myself included.

The gradual evolution of the once radical gay movement of the early seventies into a more narrow conformity with mainstream values is part and parcel of the natural history of social justice movements in this country. The originators of a given protest often express intense opposition to the dominant culture and its power arrangements, but their radical perspectives give way in fairly short order to more centrist-minded leadership; the goal shifts from demanding structural change to demanding inclusion in the halls of power, the rhetoric from "Not me!" to "Me, too."

As assimilationist goals came increasingly to characterize the LGBT movement as a whole, many left-wing gays reinvested their energies in generalized ethnic, racial, and feminist concerns; engaged with specific issues such as poverty, education, housing, and health care; or formed small, underfunded local groups (like Queers for Economic Justice) that remained focused on the gay community but dealt with the needs of its least fortunate members (those living in shelters, the untrained and unemployed)—the very people ignored by the increasingly respectable and prosperous national gay organizations.

Ironically, those LGBT people who have maintained a left-wing perspective often fail to find allies, or even understanding, among leftists in general. The Left mouths the words of acceptance but avoids any awareness of its own considerable, buried homophobia. And when LGBT radicals suggest that gay people, given their different historical experience, have developed certain unique, transgressive perspectives that just might contain something of value for *heterosexuals*, the notion is usually met with astonishment—and dismissal. I myself, as I document many times over in this book, have experienced detached, patronizing tolerance far more often than concentrated curiosity from those straight people who proudly self-define as liberal or left-wing. I've come to realize that this isn't new; throughout its history, as I periodically reference in *Waiting to Land*, the Left has been marked by deafness to disenfranchised elements within its own ranks—thus, to give but one example, the indifference in the late 1960s of Students for a Democractic Society's male leadership to the mounting demand among its female members to share in decision-making.

To illustrate these assorted themes, I've drawn on various kinds of sources—primarily the voluminous diaries I kept during the period. But I've also included some private correspondence, as well as excerpts from essays I wrote during the years covered, interspersed with my 2008 comments, sometimes lengthy. This collage-like construction felt appropriate, a snug fit with the book's shifts in theme, fragmentary asides, and changes in mood and opinion.

A word more about my diaries. The entries included in *Waiting to Land* represent only a small portion (10 percent?) of the whole. Omitted entirely, as I've said, are the hundreds of entries about the evolution of my relationship with Eli (he says he has an equal number, God help me, in his own diaries). Also, my diary-keeping habits have varied. Sometimes I'd write daily, at other periods only every few weeks or so. Usually I'd write rapidly, even in a slapdash way, without pausing to reread until a much later time, or not at all. Oppositely, I'd sometimes expend considerable effort on a single entry, wanting to record as carefully as I could an event or reaction that held particular significance for me.

When I began *Waiting to Land*, I methodically read through all my diaries for the 1985–2008 period—and made some surprising discoveries. Two entries would have the same date, others no date at all. I occasionally had trouble making out my own meaning: my pen (or cortex) would have slipped, or I'd have written so rapidly that a word or phrase would be missing, or I'd confuse one person with another, mistaking who had said what. Diaries are no more trustworthy or well-groomed than other kinds of historical evidence (which is to say, experience).

I don't want to overstate the matter; the largest portion by far of my diary is legible and coherent, with the words suited to my feelings. But I did want to explain why, for this book, I sometimes had to clean up a given sentence, transpose a line, add a few words or even (though rarely) combine or shift the order of several short entries for the sake of narrative clarity. In some instances I (gleefully) threw probity to the winds and simply rewrote a particularly graceless sentence or incomplete thought; as every writer knows, morality plays second fiddle to craft.

Finally, I want to make explicit my awareness that many of the political issues *Waiting to Land* deals with—for example, trying to do cross-racial work—are tough and troubling, with reports from the front likely to be partial and one-sided. The perspective each of us brings to public questions is deeply inflected by our backgrounds— by everything from where we were born and the kinds of families we were born into, to our race, class, and gender. Our backgrounds haunt, perhaps even dictate, our adult reactions and choices. In this regard *Waiting to Land* is perhaps best read as one individual's attempt to come to grips with his entanglement over the years with a set of complex events, intricate personalities, and riven social movements.

The italicized portions of this book represent either excerpts from essays I wrote at the time or commentary by me written in 2008

Acknowledgments

My partner, Eli Zal, and my two noble friends, Terry Boggis and John Howard, read the manuscript for this book in its entirety. All three provided trenchant comments and even corrected spelling errors. I'm very grateful to them.

This is my second book with The New Press, and the experience has been as wonderful as the first. I've never worked with a more talented and congenial group of people. I particularly want to thank Ellen Adler, publisher of The New Press, for her brilliant critique of the manuscript; Maury Botton, for solving a number of production problems; Jyothi Natarajan, for solving everything else; and Bec Zajac, for being the most resourceful publicist I've ever known.

WAITING TO LAND

1980s

The moral bigots are citing "God's will"—i.e., punishment—in explaining the AIDS scourge and its concentrated incidence (in this country) among the gay male population.

Is the famine in Ethiopia, then, God's will?

The chemical explosion in Bhopal?

The Holocaust?

If so, God has a penchant for using savage weaponry to heap pain among those already heavily afflicted. If this is the definition of a "just God," it's time to topple divinity and redefine justice. If inclined to assist the moralists in this ethical dilemma of their own making, one might suggest a variant theology—the one ministers cite at the funeral of an angelic five year old. To whit: "We cannot know His inscrutable purposes." But to risk a guess—He strikes down the most innocent and promising among us in order to underscore His displeasure with the rest of us. By that variant interpretation, gay people would be elevated from the status of moral lepers to that of the Chosen—doomed saints of physical beauty, supernal gifts, psychic precocity.

Larry [*Mass; the doctor who first alerted the gay community to the potential catastrophe of the strange new virus*] tells me it's "certain" that today's 8,000 AIDS cases will be 16,000 in six months. Dear God what a tragedy, and what awful reverberations are yet to spin off from the primary disaster. The *Wall Street Journal* has raised a "bemused" question about the "curious" lack of public debate over possible quarantine measures—thereby helping to provoke such measures. All gay aliens are being detained—not merely deported—on the West Coast. The cry to *force* gay men to submit to the new blood test mounts.

The vote in Houston is 4–1 *against* a gay civil rights bill. Fear of the disease and the citizenry seem to be descending in tandem over the gay population.

FEBRUARY 13, 1985

Ed Greer [*my lawyer*] called to report on his first conference Monday with the FBI's representatives and lawyers. [*The FBI had turned down my request under the Freedom of Information Act to release the files of Paul Robeson, whose biography I was writing. I'd decided to go to court and sue for the release of the files. The case had been dragging on for some time.*] The meeting lasted 3 hours. Ed says they're intransigent and hard-nosed. They deny any taps on Robeson's phone, though admit to "overhears"—while refusing ("in the national interest," ho-hum) to name which "3rd party" phones *were* tapped. They announced that the 78 volumes of Robeson records in the NYC & Phil. offices are now 59 volumes—the others having "recently disappeared." Why press the suit into the ground if the FBI's going to destroy the crucial evidence as the case proceeds? Ed predicts a long and expensive fight. He asked for another $5,000 [*Greer was essentially working pro bono, but I'd agreed to cover costs*], and I sent it. I don't know how long my bank account can hold out—a consideration which the FBI is doubtless also aware of . . .

MARCH 25, 1985

A high-spirited session in today's class [*"The History of Sexuality"; I was teaching at the Lehman College branch of the City University of New York (CUNY)*] produced this raucous definition of pornography: "Anal sex with an armadillo—under 12."

APRIL 20, 1985

Bruce [*Voeller, founding executive director of the National Gay Task Force; he later died of* AIDS] called on his way home from the AIDS conference. He reports continuing horror—and indifference. Says Margaret Heckler [*secretary of health and human services*] gave a speech so overtly homophobic that the 300 (out of 2,500) openly gay participants caucused and submitted a formal protest. Bruce says no money is being made available for testing new drugs of *possibly* therapeutic value, and the Center for Disease Control is secretly sending (limited) funds to France in order to support the needed scientific work.

MAY 15, 1985

[*I'd been sitting on the New York Civil Liberties Union Board (NY-CLU) since 1981. At the time of my election, I'd written in my diary that I'd felt "glad for the opportunity to try to make some of those political connections (and alliances) between the gay community and other left-of-center groups. It's questionable, of course, just how 'left' the gay (male) mainstream is: discos, drugs and sex seem the subculture's true focal points . . . questionable, too, of course, whether the liberalism of the ACLU could accommodate itself to a social vision more radical than the traditional defense of civil rights (itself no slight task as the Reaganesque intolerance for 'deviation' deepens)—the social vision being tentatively constructed by some few gay men and a few more lesbian feminists."*]

Fractious meeting of NYCLU Board. A startling and frighteningly breezy dismissal (22–6) of a proposal to reconsider our connection with Bank Leumi because Israel is South Africa's second biggest customer. It's appropriate for "kids" to demand divestment, but not us realpolitick adults! Zooks!—if not the NYCLU, then who?

MAY 16, 1985

Paul [*Robeson Jr.*] has told Fran [*Frances Goldin, agent for the biography*]—yet again—that I'm out to destroy his father by revealing (not "inventing") his "gay side." I begin to think Paul—on a level not available to him—is the one bent on "destroying" his father. *He* invited a white, Jewish, gay male to do the biography. *He* first raised the issue — during our initial meeting in 1981 — of his father's "bisexuality" and his "affair" with Sergei Eisenstein. Three years of conscientiously responding to Paul's various false clues and accusations have left me with little more than accumulated stress, along with diverting needed energy from the book. I've got to distance myself — and get on with it.

JUNE 6, 1985

Tom [*Stoddard*] lost last night [*for the post of executive director of the New York Civil Liberties Union*] to Norman Siegel on the 2nd ballot, 19 to 14.

The Board meeting went from 3–10:30, without a food break. Tom, by general agreement, gave the best presentation and following it there seemed to be a groundswell toward him. But favorable references to his "magic" got converted by two speakers into snide deprecation of him as "a magical creature." BG then added a vicious characterization of him as "a whiner." Put together, those two code phrases did damage, and the groundswell never matured. A half dozen speakers finally buried it by reiterating the theme that in NYCLU's current state of disarray we (in JG's words) "must minimize the risk of making a mistake," must steer clear of an "unsafe" choice. And so the mediocre organization man wins out over the imaginative ("too emotional") one. I was dismayed to hear so much covert homophobia from members of the NYCLU Board, that presumed bastion of decency — though they'd furiously reject such a characterization of their remarks. That's part of the trouble with "sophisticated liberals": their rhetoric avoids the grosser forms of bigotry, assuming a form subtle enough to allow them to disguise *from themselves* the nature of their feelings. Tom was crushed; he had expected to win . . . [But he's] going to be okay: he's *angry*, not merely saddened.

JUNE 10, 1985

Ed Greer called to get my okay on a compromise he wants to present to the FBI: we'll settle for 50 summaries of "telephone overhears" involving Robeson. Ed persuaded me that *if* the FBI accepts, the compromise is the only positive outcome we're likely to get from the lawsuit. He thinks the chance is remote — it would be in the nature of a "freak" outcome — for Judge Broderick to order the release of any material secured with the help of foreign intelligence (like PR's status of health files). Indeed, the litigation could end in my getting nothing worthwhile (not even telephone overhears), at an additional cost of at least $20,000 in fees, and with the FBI deliberately withholding any ordered release until *after* my book comes out. Given Ed's diagnosis, I told him to push for the compromise.

JUNE 21, 1985

The FBI has turned Ed down. I've decided to continue the suit, though the odds aren't good & though I don't have any funds currently. Ed is willing to extend credit, which is generous of him, pending my eventual receipt, on delivery of the manuscript, of the final portion of the advance. I hate to commit all (foreseeable) future funds, but there's no other comfortable choice.

JUNE 24, 1985

Benefit at the Lesbian and Gay Community Center . . . The spectrum of organizations exhibiting at the booths was dazzling—from Eastern Orthodox Christians to Hikin' Dykes to gay police officers (humpy, of course). Thirteenth Street was roped off and guarded by the (straight) police for the occasion—13th Street, my old block! Who would have thought it 15 years ago, when I walked in fear of plainclothes entrapment?

JULY 18, 1985

I have an exclusive sexual but *not* primary affectional preference for people of my own gender. By the going definition, I'm only half-homosexual (not to be confused with bisexual). Time for a new liberation movement. The essence of gayness (and this applies to some heterosexuals and not to some homosexuals) is having grown up, or tried to, without the motivating and certifying power of established social norms—and hence skeptical of their validity. To be "gay" is to be a potential saboteur.

In June 1985 the Hetrick-Martin Institute—an agency that offered crisis intervention, shelter, and counseling to young gays and lesbians—got the approval of the New York City Board of Education to establish the Harvey Milk Academy as an off-site educational program for those who'd dropped out of the regular school system because of harassment. In 1985 the Board of Education operated thirty-nine off-site programs, all of them housed in community-based agencies serving young people with special needs (for example, those with drug-related problems). The New York Civil Liberties Union had never challenged any of those "segregated" facilities. But the Harvey Milk school proved an exception. The NYCLU board set up an eight-person committee, including myself, to determine whether the creation of the Harvey Milk school was a violation of civil liberties principles. The committee had two lengthy and stormy meetings during that summer. Throughout, I argued strenuously on behalf of the school's validity and necessity.

AUGUST 27, 1985 [THE 2ND NYCLU COMMITTEE MEETING]

By a 5–2–1 vote, the committee disbanded, having found "no violation of civil liberties in establishing the school." It had been a disheartening, difficult meeting, with W. and M. giving off more than a few whiffs of homophobia. The gist of their lofty argument was that although we should deplore the harassment of gay students, we should not sanction the "dangerous" practice of self-segregation.

Which is comparable to saying no Jews should be allowed to leave Nazi Germany until we solve the problem of anti-semitism there—an analogy I dulcetly offered the committee.

In its formal report to the full board, the committee made clear that it sanctioned the Harvey Milk Academy as "a transition program" only: the ultimate goal must be "the movement of students back into the mainstream" in order to avoid "a permanent system of segregated educational facilities." I had argued during the committee's discussions that for the school to prove transitional, New York City would have to take firm measures against expressions of homophobia in public education and provide a safe, nondiscriminatory environment for all students.

In its report the committee did call for "a genuine effort" in that regard but made no specific recommendations for achieving it—not even the creation of another committee to study the problem. Instead, it anchored its acceptance of the Academy entirely on it being a stopgap measure; should the school prove "non-transitional," the report emphasized, then it would "be in violation of civil liberties policy and the NYCLU would have to consider taking action to oppose the Academy."

The full NYCLU Board proved still less sympathetic. Meeting a month later, it rejected—by a two-thirds majority, no less—the assumption that no civil liberties issues were involved in even a transitional academy. All this in one of the country's few citadels of liberalism—so much, I was learning, for the limitations of liberalism. As I wrote in my diary, "the genteel homophobia exhibited by some [on the board] made me sweat." I would finally resign from the NYCLU board in December 1987.

NOVEMBER 1, 1985

The FBI has agreed to settle out of court, releasing 4 of the critical documents under contention. I didn't get all of what I wanted—and nothing from the crucial status-of-health files—but Ed thinks it's "a great victory," setting an important precedent for FOIA [*Freedom of Information Act*] litigation.

NOVEMBER 10, 1985

Discussing AIDS in my class on Thursday, the students split over the issue of whether to close down gay bars and baths, with some shocking venom expressed about the danger of gay people contaminating the general population. Then Friday [*the writer/psychologist*] Helen Singer Kaplan's letter to the *Times* rang a change on that theme: gay people somehow *owed* it to the general population to submit themselves for blood tests—with no awareness shown of the moral hypocrisy inherent in treating gay people like scum for generations and then demanding that they behave like saints, of the victims being told they should sacrifice themselves for the greater peace of mind of their oppressors. If any doubt remained of the malignity of the heterosexist vision of us, the last few issues of the *Post* have laid it to rest. Their inflammatory defamation sickened me. One article reported the trouble nurses are having in preventing AIDS patients in the hospitals from having sex. Another excoriated the gay bars for evading taxes. A third gleefully detailed the "sick" sex rituals of the Mine Shaft's [*the famed gay male orgy bar*] "animal" habitués. The last time the media felt entitled to use the term "animal" was in justifying the lynchings of blacks. . . .

DECEMBER (?), 1985

If conservatives were consistent in their dire view of human nature (man the predator) they would argue *for* government control of industry as a necessary means for protecting the public against the predictably rapacious habits of the untrammeled "entrepreneur."

The phrase "to *husband* one's energies" strikes me as an uncommon example of men admitting (through linguistic indirection) the greater fragility and inferior stamina over time of their gender.

At the heart of most personal antagonisms are irreconcilable similarities.

JANUARY 13, 1986

Dinner to celebrate Joyce's 55th birthday. Her psychiatrist son-in-law started in on the *cultural* (50 years ago it was the biological) barriers that prevent blacks from achieving. After an hour of going at it, he reluctantly admitted that *perhaps* racist barriers might also play a role in the lack of black advancement. His solution is to call on blacks to struggle harder—and to overcome their own "peculiar heritage." I told him that blacks have been "struggling hard" for some time, and many thousands (hundreds of thousands) already possess the strivers' values and credentials he advocates—*without* being allowed to practice their skills. He retreated to arguing the "innate" fear human beings have of differentness. I suggested that might be a learned cultural phenomenon—and could be unlearned. He laughed, as conservatives always do when up against the "hopeless romanticism" of radicals. . . .

Mayor Koch has today reprimanded gay radicals for their lack of respect in confronting Cardinal O'Connor over his opposition to the gay rights bill. And the Cardinal's "lack of respect" in working to deny basic civil liberties to gay people? Not a word of reprimand from our lackey "liberal" mayor.

JANUARY 19, 1986

A very friendly, helpful call from Benno [*Schmidt; president-designate of Yale and the then-husband of my close friend, the documentary filmmaker Helen Whitney*]. He takes well to my letter [*in which I'd offered to leave an endowment in my will for gay studies*] and has already sounded out Bart G. [*Giamatti, the outgoing Yale president, and future commissioner of baseball*] on preliminaries. Bart—predictably, given his anti-gay reputation—immediately objected to establishing an endowment devoted to "gay" anything: "gay," according to Bart, is an "advocacy" word. Benno says he hasn't yet made up his own mind on that issue. I drew the parallel with black studies. Would Yale insist on a center devoted to research about *colored* Americans, because some might regard "black" as an advocacy word? Don't people have a right to name themselves? Benno said that Bart suggested my money go instead to "the history of human sexuality." No, I said; along with the Kinsey Institute, there's plenty of grant money and research already devoted to that subject; there's none for gay studies. How about "the history of homosexuality," Benno suggested. No, I said, that's a clinical designation, loaded with moralistic implications. We dropped the subject of terminology for now. . . .

MARCH 19, 1986

George [*Chauncey*], Blanche [*Wiesen Cook*], Esther [*Newton*], John Boswell, Ralph Hexter [*gay classicist, Yale*] & Cory Friedlander [*head of GALA*] here this evening to discuss my idea for a Center for Gay Studies at Yale. A productive discussion. . . . We canvassed some rough models for the Center, the elements we need to concentrate on, the prospects for fundraising, candidates for an expanded governing board, 18 in total, 50% gay men and 50% lesbian—to have its first meeting on April 19. Expectations are high & eyes wide open as to the many roadblocks that lie ahead.

MARCH 21, 1986

I don't feel jubilant over the passage of the New York City gay civil rights bill. I don't feel like the supplicant who pleaded with the straight world to *grant* him his rights 15 years ago; I have them, self-decreed. I don't feel grateful to a City Council which acknowledges—by a split vote and within carefully defined limits—that I am a human being; I don't rely on their authority for my right to exist. I don't long to throw my arms around my cohorts in the antechambers of power and with them tearfully give thanks for a bill which explicitly denies that it sanctions the validity of my lifestyle and implicitly holds me at unequal arms length; I already feel superior to such patronization. I recognize, of course, that I'm able to hold such sentiments because I have a privileged, protected life; the bill *will* help some gay people save their apartments and jobs. And beyond that, it sends out a useful message to the rest of the country at a time when the momentum is against us.

APRIL 7, 1986

Fiftieth anniversary celebration of the Abraham Lincoln Brigade at Avery Fisher Hall. . . . The close, when the attending survivors—maybe 100 old folks in various stages of infirmity—mounted the stage to receive the crowd's plaudits, was memorably moving. I couldn't hold back the tears, crying for that "other America" which currently seems invisible. Finally, though, the particular kind of heroism which "knowingly" jeopardizes its own physical existence is foreign to me; and violence in the name of the best cause, frightening.

The lingering lyric connecting youth & death.

APRIL 8, 1986

Pretty much everyone asked to the April 19 meeting about the gay studies center has accepted enthusiastically . . . though many of the women are rightly leery of the male bastion Yale. It's a toss-up between attraction to Yale as a prestigious legitimizing agency & repugnance to it as a traditional dispenser of élite male privilege. . . . The primary goal is to gather a group of people and create the kind of structure that will serve *gay* people; to use the opportunity Benno's administration represents for *our* purposes. . . . If Yale should try to impose conditions—for example, requiring a high percentage of PhDs or actual professors on the Board—which would run counter to our vision of what is appropriate (in this instance, to those *without* "proper" academic credentials who have nonetheless made significant contributions to gay studies), then we would have to try to establish the center elsewhere.

APRIL 14, 1986

Did a cable TV interview with Arnold Rampersad on his Langston Hughes biography, due out in the fall. . . . Like his subject, Arnold is elegantly evasive regarding sexuality. I think I persuaded him (off camera) to put a "simpering man" in quotes and to remove "without evidence" from the galleys in stating his conclusion that Hughes was *not* gay. Arnold himself provides evidence in the book for an opposite conclusion; that is, if one associates homosexual acts with homosexual identity. While the two shouldn't be equated, the claim should not be made either that there is *no* relationship between them (as Arnold has it in the galleys).

APRIL 15, 1986

Reagan's bombing of Libya is sickening. Terrorism masquerading as a reproof to terrorism. Macho maniacs strutting over the corpses of children. And apparently the American public is offering Reagan overwhelming support for what, in this Alice-in-Wonderland world, is being called "an act of simple justice" (and Reagan, in the face of a summit cancellation & the opprobrium of our allies, is calling it an "overwhelming success"!).

APRIL 16, 1986

In his obit in today's *Times* on Jean Genet, Mel Gussow never once mentions his homosexuality! On & on it goes. . . .

APRIL 17, 1986

Benita's book [*Benita Eisler*, Private Lives: Men and Women of the Fifties] arrived today in the mail. In it she says twice that I was "one of the last of my generation to 'come out' as a gay man." Few of my generation have ever come out, and I was one of the first. How did she manage to get *that* reversed (using a tape recorder, no less)? She's grossly misread my activist history. Since I still don't doubt Benita's friendship, the actual casualty is the notion of being understood.

When I wrote Benita that I was "baffled" at how she'd gotten it so wrong, she responded that the comment was a "direct quote" from me. Unconvinced, I wrote her a second time: "It's inconceivable to me that I could have spoken words at absolute odds with my actual history," and I asked to see the page from the transcript where the sentence purportedly appeared. This time she phoned me. Having checked the transcript, she acknowledged that I hadn't said the offending line and was so apologetic that I started to make nice— "deliberately ignoring" (as I wrote in my diary) "the little voice in my ear whispering about the profundity of buried homophobia." That encouraged her to defend her misinterpretation as legitimate, given the "ambiguous" nature of my remarks on tape. No, I said, the transcript was not ambiguous: she had put her words in my mouth. Shifting again, she talked breezily about getting together soon for a drink. "Sure," I wrote in my diary, "One cyanide, and hurry."

APRIL 19, 1986

Thirteen of us gathered in my apartment—the "Organizing Committee" for the gay center as we have now designated ourselves. . . . On the whole it went well . . . though John Boswell [*the Yale historian, and author of the pioneering* Christianity, Social Tolerance, and Homosexuality] started huffy, "warning" us that Yale would insist, rightly in his view, on laying down essential guidelines for any Center sporting its name. Carole Vance [*coauthor of* Pleasure and Danger: Exploring Female Sexuality] issued an eloquent counter-warning that in the search for the legitimizing of gay studies, we have to remain vigilant that a rapprochement with traditional academia does not end in an accommodation to *its* norms. I sided with Carole, though I think Boswell's traditionalist values (shared by Ralph Hexter & Al Novick [*professor of biology at Yale*], but not by Tony Appiah [*then a professor of philosophy at Yale and the author of a number of important books, including* In My Father's House], will aggressively reassert themselves in what is bound to prove an ongoing struggle to maintain the integrity of gay differentness as we push for mainstream institutional affiliation. It's the old American story of balancing a radical vision against the urge to operate in a broader arena (the vision invariably diluting as dissemination spreads). . . .

MAY 12, 1986

Perhaps *the* reason—the one he'd be least able to acknowledge—Paul Jr. is throwing such a fit over the manuscript is that his father, a lousy parent, nonetheless *does* come off a hero. It was Paul after all who told me his father "had an affair" with Sergei Eisenstein and also who later told Fran that his father "had an affair" with Marc Blitzstein. Neither tale turns out to be true. So why did he tell them? Why indeed did he come to me, an openly gay man, in the first place? The answer seems inescapable: "gay" is *the* worst thing Paul thinks you can say about somebody; he planted the false rumors about his father in the (unconscious?) hope that I, a gay activist, would buy them—& thereby vicariously "destroy" his father for him.

JULY 3, 1986

. . . the Supreme Court decision [*Bowers v. Hardwick*] has given the states the right to police *private* relations between consenting gay adults. It's a shock & a major setback, especially coming on top of the Justice Dept. ruling that employers are free to fire people with AIDS. Apparently the depth of homophobia in the U.S. knows no current bounds. Tom [*Stoddard, then director of Lambda Legal Defense*] put it best—this is our Dred Scott decision. With the Congress voting aid to the contras in Nicaragua, and Rehnquist due to take office as Chief Justice, it's difficult to maintain optimism—even for a tempermental optimist like me, ever on the alert for signs of a national turnabout. The best (and possibly only) comfort available at the moment is the "long view"—battles are inevitably lost along the route to progressive change. Still, it's a rough moment. To think I've been arguing that acceptance of our privacy rights isn't sufficient—that it's a tolerance of difference only so long as we remain unseen; okay, says the Court, so now we'll take away your privacy rights. In justifying the ruling, the Court cites "history"—meaning, with typical American parochialism, history from the time of the 13 colonies forward—for proof that homosexuality has never been tolerated. (From that perspective we should also be clamoring for the restoration of slavery). Had the justices broadened the inquiry to include *human* history, the examples of classical Greece and much of the rest of the world would have dictated the exact opposite conclusion in regard to homosexuality. "History," as always, is used selectively to rationalize the prejudices of those currently in power.

JULY 4, 1986

I had planned to stay home. All morning the 21-gun salutes boomed from the harbor, the flight formations roared over the terrace. "What the Hell," I thought, "everybody loves a parade"— & took myself down to the dock. The images along the way restored my bah-humbug spirit: 2 homeless people trying to wash their hair in a water fountain; shouts from the women's prison on 19th Street; a couple trying to build a cardboard shelter in the crevice of a building. When I got down to the docks, they were closed off for private parties: ticket holders only. You need money to get close to Liberty. The rest of us were directed down to 14th Street where the crowd was allowed to view the passing ships through heavy metal fencing set several hundred yards back from the candy-coated tents on the docks. The

rechristened Horst Wessel led the ships up the harbor. The crowd neither applauded nor complained. One woman did lament the impos-
sibility of fitting her large camera lens through the fence openings. I
came back to the apartment to revise Robeson. He's needed.

JULY 9, 1986

Benno invited me up tonight to talk over prospects for the gay center. We spent less than two hours, and no more than half that time
was on the center, but a lot got said. Benno reiterated his enthusiasm
for a *research* center—in distinction to an undergraduate major in gay
studies or a policy-oriented public affairs institute. A research/archival/
think tank has in fact been the precise focus of our committee's
interests, so I had no trouble reassuring him that we were proceeding on parallel paths. (Benno is not naive: he fully recognizes—&
welcomes—the intrinsically *political* mission of any center devoted
to disseminating information—increasing understanding, changing
minds—about gay people). He expressed awareness that the alumni,
or segments of it, will likely chew his ass out for sanctioning even a
purer-than-Caeser's-wife scholarly think tank devoted to gay subject
matter, but seems prepared to face down that storm. I think he can
be taken at his word; he seems genuinely committed to the proposal.
He offered to appear at select fund-raising events as a further indica-
tion of his commitment.

That much "settled," he said he wanted my opinion on two other
matters he's currently wrestling with: how to handle the student suspended by a faculty committee for nailing up an anti-gay poster an
campus; and whether to throw his weight behind divestment for Yale
in South Africa. I see the poster episode as at heart a free speech
issue—gays are as legitimate subjects for satire as anyone else; the dividing line, *if* there is one (& I tend to be a 1st amendment purist)
would only come if physical harm to gays was being seriously advocated (something analogous to "yelling fire in a crowded theater").
These days, of course—in the face of the anti-gay backlash being

fueled by AIDS, in tandem with a hostile Supreme Court decision—
it could be argued that even benign satire could prove sufficiently inflammatory to warrant suppression. But given the danger of any form
of censorship, the threat, in my estimate, must still be "clear & present" (i.e., probably *never*). Benno seemed relieved at my opinion; his
own view coincides. As for divestment, I approached it on two levels:
even if it could be proven that the consequences will be disastrous for
blacks (& I don't think it can be), blacks themselves—or at least their
most morally attractive leaders, like Tutu—are asking for divestment. Can we declare that we know better than they do what is in
fact in their best interest? Here Benno & I did *not* coincide. He is *for*
sanctions but not divestment—though the lateness of the hour prevented him from spelling out his position.

JULY 13, 1986

Only secular societies are interested in the study of human history.
The rest are mystified—yes, that's the word—by such attention to
transient detail.

AUGUST 1, 1986

I arrived back two days ago from East Berlin. [*In 1963 Robeson had
been treated for acute depression at the German Democratic Repub-
lic's Buch Clinic; I'd gone to East Berlin for research and to do a set of
interviews.*] . . . I met many of Irene's [*a GDR citizen I'd met in New
York*] friends, mostly gay. A sweet bunch—quick to help, affectionate, serious, reliable. All I could manage by way of language was
Bach titles (*Eine Kleine Nachtmusik*) interspersed with the fragmentary recall of ancient school phrases (*Vielen dank fur die auskunft*).
This led to some hilarity, but for communication we relied on their
English. One of my first nights we went to a *state*-sponsored gay
disco. The costumes, music, décor—and even attitudes—were ser-
viceably New York. When I expressed astonishment at the official

recognition of gay life, Irene affected offhandedness: "I *told* you there was full acceptance of gay people. You didn't believe me." Discussion at Bert's apartment the final night of my stay produced a more rounded, far less euphoric view. In the GDR the laws are increasingly progressive & the Party seems committed to equal legal and social status for gay people (though as recently as two years ago, Klaus was expelled from membership in the Party for presenting a formal series of demands on behalf of gay people — & *not* restored since). The one-step-forward-one-step-back pattern is familiar enough from the USA: NYC finally passes a civil rights bill, while simultaneously the Supreme Court denies us privacy protection. But in the GDR the steps back seem more frightening than ours. Doerner (Humboldt Univ.) is apparently gaining support for his view that the "mistake" of same-gender sexual orientation occurs between the 3rd & 4th month of pregnancy and can be "corrected" through hormonal intervention. He claims entire success in his experiments with rats & is only awaiting official sanction to move the experiment on to humans. In Prague, meanwhile, Bert reports a still worse situation. His friends there tell of a "brain operation" being performed (voluntarily, so far) with some regularity to "destroy" interest in same-gender sex; since it succeeds in inducing epilepsy, it does tend to distract the mind. The same operation is being performed in Hamburg. As for the USSR, Bert reports (after a six-month stay in Moscow), that gay life decidedly exists but is officially against the law. The GDR, in sum, represents the best of a bad set of conditions in Eastern Europe; and that best, despite all our setbacks, is no match for the organizational vigor and assertiveness of gay life in the States.

As regards Robeson, the trip was a success. On arrival I was thoroughly grilled by Dr. Alfred Katzenstein [*Robeson's chief physician*] and having apparently passed muster, was then invited to spend a full day with him and his wife, complete with 5 hours of taping. He is thoughtful and earnest, and not a charlatan, but I was not impressed either with his general insight or his specific range of information about his own field (for example, he insisted that it was "highly unusual" to give more than 10 to 12 electric shock treatments [*Robeson had been given 54*] in the early '60s). Nor was I much impressed with any of the other "Robeson associates" I met (except for Ollie Harrington [*the African American illustrator and cartoonist*]—warm, witty and shrewd; talking with him was the highlight of the trip). The melancholy feeling grew in me that Paul was in the hands of medical second-raters. That was worth finding out. Additionally, the Robeson Archiv in Berlin had richer holdings than I'd been led to believe. . . . I ran into Bayard Rustin and his lover Walter Naegel on the plane back from London and they invited me over to watch a tape they've brought back of "Songs of Freedom," the BBC program on Robeson for which both Bayard and I were interviewed. The show was okay, not more, not less. We went out to dinner afterwards. . . . Bayard has scant interest in talking about the past, is cynically detached, not much concerned even with safeguarding his own image. . . . He was at his most animated when showing me the assorted, massed object d'art that clutter their apartment—"collecting" now seems his chief passion.

AUGUST 11, 1986

I read of Davey C.'s death from AIDS at 28. . . . He had so many qualities—was so physically beautiful, smart *and* politically hip. Plus he was a sweet and generous man; soon after I came out of the hospital following the heart attack [*1979*], he came to visit me. After we talked a while, he offered me a blow job—thought I "needed" it. I did, psychologically—some connection with the possibility of getting pleasure out of my body, out of life, again. He sucked me off on the couch, a gesture of generosity not lust. To my surprise, I came. We were both pleased. What is there left to say about this gruesome, senseless killer AIDS? Except that the wrong people are dying, those who gave themselves incautiously to experience, to life; the risk-takers, the inventive ones. The fearful ones who literally sat on their asses still sit.

Twenty members of the organizing committee met here this afternoon to thrash out the proposed by-laws. Thrash is the word. I didn't like the "Executive Committee" section proposed by the governance committee (chaired by Boswell) at all—I thought it set up a Yale (i.e., white male) EC at *odds* in composition, and therefore perspective vision, from the organizing committee that parented it. The women uniformly agreed, with Ruby [*Rich*], Carole [*Vance*] and Carroll [*Smith-Rosenberg*] leading the assault. Boswell caved in so precipitously—lapsing from contentious speechifying to total silence—that I knew he'd shifted tactics, not views. On the way out he told Larry [*Gross*], "I don't have time for this"; Larry purports to have "calmed him down," but time will tell.

*R*epresenting, as they put it, the "grass roots," "Jane" and "Don" have resigned from the organizing committee for the Center. Both have done pioneering work on gay and lesbian history, and without the usual perks that attend university affiliation. They feel understandably threatened, I suspect, at the prospect of "their baby" taking any steps out of their line of vision. But gay studies has not, in fact, been solely a grassroots phenomenon, as they claim; many of the early researchers into gay history (Boswell, for one) had academic credentials from the start. For a lot of the right reasons, Jane and Don detest academicians, but we tried (to no avail) to make it clear to them that as gay people we, too, are natural-born outsiders and hope to do it differently in setting up as a university-affiliated center.

After all, as I wrote to Don, ". . . from the very first meeting I've stressed the pre-eminent importance of two principles: (a) gender parity and (b) the significant inclusion of minorities and non-affiliated scholars. I've also stressed that these are non-negotiable principles—whether the negotiations be with Yale or any other institution. Yale historically has indubitably been a bastion of white male privilege; but so have most academic institutions. No risk-free option *is on the horizon. Would that there was. We can minimize the risks by adhering* rigidly *to our organizing principles." I suggested much more discussion at meetings, over lunch—wherever. But neither Jane nor Don expressed interest. They adhered to their own (in John's words) "favorite vision" of "an independent research institution, with a board of perhaps 6–8 decision makers on it, quite independent of any established academic institution." They never explained how this could happen without the "in-kind" perks (such as free office space) a university could provide, especially at a time when the AIDS crisis is absorbing much of the money the gay community itself might ordinarily supply.*

In the meantime, as I wrote in my diary, "my own desolating thought, as the rifting discourse swells, is: Are we struggling to institute what is in fact merely a passing phase in human identity? I've begun to wonder whether the whole emphasis on 'identity' (sexual and otherwise) isn't at bottom a strategy for de-limiting our options as human beings, part of the general plague of over-categorizing experience, of the endemic insistence that we choose, *that we agree to become* one thing *(gay or straight, male or female, etc.). The emphasis on establishing an* identity *may be necessary in forming a political movement— but comes at the expense of fluidity, a self-conception once preferred. . . . Still, we need to foster respect for identity differences as they exist* now *in order to lessen the suffering we currently see around us."*

SEPTEMBER 23, 1986

All the sophisticated theoretical turns, it seems to me, finally come down to one simple question: "How can we lessen human misery?" Conservatives aren't interested in the question. They excuse their indifference to suffering by claiming its inevitability: "The poor ye shall always have with you." And they try to discredit those who persist in raising the question as fuzzy-minded idealists who refuse to understand the "facts" of human existence. In today's climate even some minority members are prone to accept the truth of these "facts."

In seminar today, 35 year old Sam, Hispanic father of three, loudly denounced the "welfare cheats," using the instilled rhetoric of the Right to assail his own people, and smugly closing his ears to all the counter-evidence offered him.

SEPTEMBER 29, 1986

Boswell, it turns out, is not only prepared to resign from the center, but to destroy it. Today's letter from him—a copy of which he sent to Benno—effectively seals the prospects of negotiation. Benno feels he can't proceed without the support of Yale's "gay star." Since Boswell has characterized the Committee's deliberations as "unremittingly hostile" to Yale, Benno can be pardoned for foregoing an affiliation which promised in any case to bring him maximum trouble with the alumni. I'm shocked and angry at John's behavior; isolated at the last meeting, failing to secure control of the center for himself, he sets out to sabotage it—at Yale, anyway. . . . a now-consolidated organizing committee can at least *try* to set up shop elsewhere. . . .

OCTOBER 11, 1986

The feeling is growing in me that the center's now minimal chances might be increased if I move out from the central position, encouraging the others to a more collectivized responsibility for the center's fate. Oh I still want to control, but seeing that helps to confirm my sense that I should take additional steps to make sure I can *not*. No-one has hinted that they think I'm holding the reins too tightly, but *I* begin to think leadership responsibility ought to rotate more—I want the other committee members to view the center less as my project than as ours. The heightened commitment likely to follow from an "our" enterprise will in turn heighten the chance to push the center through—and particularly if we want to push for it being some place other than Yale, where my special entrée to Benno justified my prominent role. Sure, I'd like to head up the enterprise still—shit, lets face it, I want my name chipped in stone over the entrance—but since I can recognize, begrudgingly, that the center takes precedence over my ego, I have no excuse for confusing the two.

MARCH 22, 1987

. . . meeting of the center board/committee (we keep alternating terminology, forgetting that an organization that doesn't exist can't have a board). About 10 of us present. "Trish," new to the group, acts as if it had no prior history, throbbingly lectured us on the need to represent minorities—our announced intent and consistent commitment from the beginning. Her gushing self-righteousness consumed half the meeting. Lord, I weary of the eight-month-long parade of prima donnas who don't do scholarship and have been "activists" as of this year. Yet we did manage *some* movement toward opening up actual negotiations with the City University of New York (CUNY). . . .

APRIL 3, 1987

. . . Susan Weisfuse of the 92nd Street Y had called me several months back for help in presenting a proposal for a lecture series on "Homosexuality in Society" to the Y's planning committees. Two weeks ago she called back to say one committee had initially turned it down, the other had approved, and the two had finally negotiated a go-ahead. They want me to plan and moderate the entire series. I immediately said yes—it seems to me a rare opportunity to do outreach and education. . . .

APRIL 6, 1987

I went down to New Brunswick tonight to give a talk on gay history to the gay & lesbian group (the town, not the gown group). I figured it would be a pleasant outing. Well, sort of. But primarily I came away feeling *more* isolated—the rarefied nature of who I am & what

I do confirmed. Two people out of some forty had even heard of Magnus Hirschfeld and—this was the real shocker—no more than half the group had heard (not been there—*heard*) of Cherry Grove! Though 40 minutes from Manhattan, it was a true small-town gathering. The chief items on the agenda concerned a planned picnic on Sunday & a potential excursion to see a local production of Torch Song Trilogy. I suppose this *is* the stuff of most gay lives—& why not? Except it doesn't make for much of a political movement, & still leaves me feeling the perpetual outsider.

MAY 8, 1987

A wonderful outcome to our meeting today with Harold Proshansky [*president of the CUNY Graduate School*] about the center—he's for it, straightforwardly for it! He thinks the time is if anything overdue, thanked us for bringing it to CUNY (what a happy contrast to Benno's hesitations and retreats), and will work actively with us to prepare strategies for getting the Board of Trustees' approval . . . it was nice not to have to justify our lives for once, to have the legitimacy of who we are and what we're trying to do taken respectfully for granted. . . . Proshansky emphasized that a great deal of hard work lies ahead. He plans to approach Chancellor [*Joseph*] Murphy first (he's widely viewed as a great champion of minorities) and then to ask a select group of the campus presidents each to kick in $5,000 from their slush funds. That way, should our own fund-raising falter, we'll still have a minimal budget to get started with. . . .

MAY 11, 1987

Murphy has turned Proshansky down for money and forbidden him from approaching any of the campus presidents. Here we go again: a "radical" being radical on every issue but ours. . . . Well, the project hasn't been smooth up to now, so why should it suddenly become so? (Except that it seemed for a moment that it might). . . .

MAY 12, 1987

Proshansky called to fill me in. He summarized Murphy's reaction as "it's an item on the list and I can't respond to it now." [*Murphy later told him that (as quoted by Proshansky) he, Murphy, "would not publicly oppose the center, but would not lift a finger to help it."*] Unlike on Friday, Proshansky was brief to the point of abruptness, making only two points: (1) *we* had to find the money—$50,000 minimum to prove we're "viable", and (2) the center has to present itself as a pure research institute or it will never get clearance.

JUNE 24, 1987

The experts in nutrition acknowledge and encourage an "instinctive" human craving for dietary variety. We need to transfer that insight to the area of sex. Hands will of course fly to the American face in instant horror—"oh no! the *sexual* instinct is to mate with one partner, forever." But "instinct" shouldn't be invoked solely to confirm preexisting values. Especially since no one has yet successfully isolated and described our so-called "instinctive" needs.

JUNE 28, 1987

It's often said that a lesbian couple is more likely to stay together than a gay male one because as women, lesbians have been socialized to have lower expectations of their need for and entitlement to sexual variety. Put that way, radical liberationists are inclined to view the lesbian couple (or indeed any longterm couple) as an expression of defeat, a form of relating appropriate only to those with a truncated capacity for sexual adventuring & pleasure. But the matter can be put quite another way: lesbian women (like women generally) have been more encouraged to develop their capacities for loving than have gay men (or men in general). Even those women not trained to be indifferent to the pleasures of sexual variety recognize, in our single-option culture (especially for women) that they must sacrifice pleasure, or reduce its primacy, in order to preserve a loving partner-commitment. Gay male priorities—trained needs—are the opposite.

JULY 13, 1987

The Oliver North fan club is sweeping the country. Rogue boy scout shreds the Constitution and becomes national hero. It's his sex appeal. He combines some of our favorite mythic images: Jimmy Stewart twang, Huck Finn space between his teeth, Sgt. York "patriotism," Mel Gibson subdued swagger. How about North and Bernard Goetz [*subway vigilante*] for the national ticket? A sure winner.

AUGUST 7, 1987, FIRE ISLAND

I stopped in to see Larry [*Mass*], Arnie [*Kantrowitz*] and Vito [*Russo*]. Larry and Arnie were celebrating their 5th anniversary today and looking benign. Vito was not. He's in a rage over the smug attitude of Cherry Grovers towards AIDS, and his fiery letter to the *Fire Island Times* to that effect has caused "outrage" in the community. Good—the community deserves it, and more important, vented anger will help keep Vito [*who was HIV-positive*] alive.

AUGUST 8, 1987

I went with Eli [*Eli Zal, whom I'd met a few months before and with whom I still live*] to have dinner at the apartment of his friends Carl, Michael and Walter. A steaming East Side tenement on a steaming New York night. But my discomfort was soon put into perspective. Michael, ill with hepatitis and tuberculosis, his current AIDS-related maladies, could hardly sit at the table. Walter, who has already been hospitalized once and yesterday was told he has a T-cell count of 0, nonetheless looked fine and carried on in a cheerful, if spacey manner. The atmosphere in general was not only chatty and "up," but deeply supportive between the three men—who in varying combinations have been lovers for some 15 years. This kind of untheatrical bravery reduced me to near-silence. [*All three were soon dead.*]

AUGUST 13, 1987

Last night the committee gathered here for one of our least success-ful meetings to date. . . . I'm tired, after a year and a half, of these repetitive, inconclusive gab-fests. I've never been one for organiza-tional haggling and have stayed committed this time only because of the importance of the project. But I get angry at how everyone else complains to *me* about how busy they are, how incapable of inter-rupting their book, their vacation, their love affair, in order to make a phone call or write a letter on behalf of the center. Last night it was "Evelyn." She arrived grumpy and stayed that way. . . . She insisted we were trying to do too much too fast (fast??!!), and wanted our planned first public event on November 17 [*a panel on the history of gay people in New York City*] cancelled. I could tell it was time to back off and so agreed to postpone, though I think it's a mistake — we'll look like foot-draggers (or incompetents) to Proshansky, and our timing for a grant proposal to Chicago Resources Center could be jeopardized. . . .

SEPTEMBER 6, 1987

The public face-off with Paul Jr. yesterday at the SAS convention came off better than I could have anticipated. His formal speech did not, as expected, attack me — or even mention me. It was a dry, un-focused presentation, the gist being that his father should be under-stood first and foremost as a Black Nationalist. Clearly this is the line of attack he's preparing to discredit the uncomprehending white bi-ographer. Since Paul didn't directly discuss me, I dropped the few notes of response I'd prepared and kept my own speech focused on Robeson Sr. himself. There it stood after an hour & a half — a rather conventional academic gab-fest after all.

But then during the question period, a young woman asked us both if we'd been harassed by government agencies because of our involvement with Robeson Sr. No, I said, the only harassment I felt, and from the beginning, was the criticism leveled at me, a white man, for undertaking a black man's biography (I wasn't about to let the session end without *some* attempt to liven things up!). I went on to explain why, despite my skin color, I thought I *was* an appropriate choice as biographer, citing not only my experience in the world of theater, but the fact that as a gay man I was able to share Robeson's "outsider" perspective. I hadn't expected to say that & wasn't sure I should have, but Frances assured me afterwards that the comment had been appropriate & telling, & two men in the audience later came up to thank me, as gay men, for having revealed myself. Paul, looking anxious and angry, then said that in theory he saw no reason why a white person couldn't write about his father (never revealing that *he* had come to *me*), but that *this* white man had, in his reading of the manuscript, failed to do justice to his father. He later said he had had doubts about me from the beginning *on racial grounds*— which he had never hinted at before and which if true, would make his decision to offer me the book bizarre (a point I again refrained from making—though I'm not sure I should have).

Freda [*Diamond, Paul Sr.'s lover for many years*], to my great surprise, joined the debate twice from the audience—the second time with devastating effect on Paul's formal presentation. She recounted publicly the anecdote she'd already told me privately about Paul Sr. saying to her, on hearing that Paul Jr. had described him as a "black nationalist" on TV—"Oh, is he trying to cut me down to that size again?" Paul blanched, but recovered gracefully, saying something to the effect of "As you can see, my father's old friends still treat me like Paul *Jr.*" But he left her comment unchallenged, thereby leaving its full impact intact—& giving me the opportunity to use the anecdote in the book.

OCTOBER 13, 1987

Eli and I got back Sunday night from a 3-day trip to D.C. centered around the National March for Gay and Lesbian Rights. . . . We did a spot of museuming (the William Merritt Chase show was unexpectedly vivid), and then went to the Vietnam Monument. Half in the earth, it conjured up precipitous death; the lines of people eagerly pouring in conjured up their willing complicity in destruction, their own included, slowly swallowed by the onyx grave. . . .

The March on Sunday was *huge*. Waiting for hours at an assembly point in the Ellipse, the crowd seemed thin and I began to fear a meager turn-out. But then we spotted the actual march in the distance and left the Ellipse to watch it go by. It seemed so large that after 3 hours of viewing we still hadn't seen the end of it. The *Times* estimated the crowd at 200,000 but I think *Newsday* was closer to the mark in citing upwards of half a million. Miles and miles of marchers stepping past in interchangeable blue jeans, wool shirts and sneakers, making the strong visual point that "we are everywhere, and everybody." Watching the TV coverage that night of the simultaneous Columbus Day Parade in New York, with its paramilitary drill units and rifle clubs, I was glad that in *our* march no one brandished a single weapon; nor were any police needed to discipline the crowd; I saw only one bunch of angry, confrontational people—the Jesus freaks, carrying their hate-filled banners, screaming their violent slogans.

The AIDS quilt—central symbol of the march—lay spread out on the Mall near the Vietnam Monument and stood in eloquent contrast to it. The names of the Vietnam dead are carved into hard unyielding stone, each name appearing identical with every other. By contrast, gay men choose to memorialize their dead using a traditional woman's art form, choose soft, yielding bunting, colorful threads and deeply individualized panels that are by turns playful and melancholy. A *different* kind of male sensibility is at work on that quilt—a sensibility that epitomizes a feminized counter-culture and beckons us towards its saving grace.

e Marxists, mostly heterosexual, will have none of it.
d the feminist and gay liberation movements as the latest
ersonalistic" diversions that time and again in our history
have ɪately sapped the strength of movements for substantive social
change, detouring energy from the "proper" work of objective analysis and economic re-structuring into the illusory (and peculiarly
American) pursuit of individual "self-fulfillment." They deny that the
current assault on traditional definitions of gender will bring in train
the destruction of traditional arrangements of power. They scorn the
notion that the challenge to sex-role stereotyping and normative definitions of sexual morality could ever prove the cutting edge of a
broad social transformation that would destroy class distinctions and
re-distribute the wealth. Instead, they insist the feminist and gay
movements are indulgent dead-ends for a privileged few.

And they make their argument in a style that exemplifies a patriarchal vocabulary. The male Marxists I know will fight the establishment tooth and nail—yes, tooth and nail, the male style—on issues
relating to entrenched economic privilege, but share the oligarchy's
belief in the pre-eminent importance of hierarchy, reason, authority,
leadership, order, discipline—all traditional male values. Men in
general tend to over-rationalize experience, are impatient with personal idiosyncrasy—"subjectivism," the Marxists call it—and are inat-
tentive to emotional realities like intimacy that cannot be precisely
measured or threaten the priority of equilibrium. Left-wing men
want to destroy distinctions between the classes, but are wary of dis-
mantling those that separate the sexes. To oversimplify, one could argue that the main reason so many young males show a willingness to
go to war is because they've been raised as traditional males—follow
orders (or give them), even if that means taking life or surrendering
their own. If such blind destructiveness is ever to end, the beginning
may lie in giving testimony; in honestly bearing witness to the suffering in our own lives, we can begin to understand how cruelly the
world-as-structured treats us all.

OCTOBER 14, 1987

Epidemics always lay bare the rudimentary attitudes of the culture in which the epidemic occurs. The government and the public alike used the syphilis scourge of the early 20th century as an opportunity to reassert traditional values—just as with AIDS today. And in the U.S. no value is more traditional than being uptight about sex. As one moralist put it in regard to syphilis, "perfect inhibition is the only guarantor of perfect health and perfect morality." Just so today. The emphasis is being put on returning to monogamy, not succoring people attacked with a virus; on altering behavior and further stigmatizing the already marginalized rather than ameliorating their suffering.

OCTOBER 17, 1987

Tonight was the first of four 92nd St. Y evenings. From the point of view of reaching a mainstream Jewish/intellectual/straight audience—the original aim of the series—it proved a near-total washout. Judging visually, there weren't more than half a dozen non-gays in an audience of 150 (itself a low turnout in a hall that seats 300). Given the devotion of the Y's audiences to its programs, this amounts to an overt boycott. It makes me angry & disheartened. How *does* one reach straights with an affirmative gay point of view if not through the Y's prestigious auspices? Eli says to rest content in having sent 150 gay people home feeling better about themselves—& of course he's right.

OCTOBER 24, 1987

The second evening of the Y series. The topic was "Is There a Gay Sensibility?" which could be rephrased as "Are Gay People Different (other than in their sexual orientation)?" In my own remarks as moderator I recalled what *Village Voice* writer Jeff Weinstein once answered to the question: "No, there is no such thing as a gay sensibility, and yes, it has had an enormous influence on mainstream culture." During the Washington march two weeks ago, I saw one of the marchers carrying a sign which focuses the topic another way. The sign read: "I was a lesbian before I ever had sex."

As regards gay men, the question could be posed as: which of two recent entertainments should we take as the more accurate reflection of gay male life: *Torch Song Trilogy* or the German film *Taxi zum Klo*? *Torch Song* portrays a lifestyle which at its heart embodies the heterosexual values of hearth, home and family. *Taxi* focuses on anarchic, freewheeling relationships, casual sex and drug-taking, sex-role crossings and gender bending. The answer, of course, is that both are accurate portrayals of different segments of the gay male community, with perhaps most gay men sampling both at different points in their lives, along with several other variations (like a live-in primary relationship that from the beginning presumes a variety of outside sexual contacts).

Likewise, there's the range of what people mean when they speak of their "gay identity." An upwardly mobile gay white man in Manhattan hardly shares a self-definition anywhere close to that of a lesbian Chicana woman living in the Southwest and locked into poverty. Individuals have always sought to understand their place in the world, and to secure a sense of belonging, by describing themselves in terms of group affiliation—as members of a particular nationality, region and religion, and by asserting certain ethnic, racial or professional ties. But only in roughly the past two hundred years, and mostly in the West, have a growing number of people defined themselves in terms of their sexual orientation. What had once been a stigmatized category—the homosexual—is now adopted as a preferred way for organizing one's experience.

That, in turn, has given rise to the ongoing debate about whether that identity is biologically given or culturally acquired. Many believe their sexual (and gender) identity as adults is so powerful and their memory of its onset so early, that it *must* be biological in origin. Yet that's probably nothing more than a measure of the fullness of our socialization. An acquired identity comes to have all the force of a biological one because its acquisition is beyond the reach of our memory. We can't recover the steps by which we were acculturated and so we tend to convert a social process into a set of genetic givens. If we *could* trace the process of acculturation, we would not have been very securely socialized in the first place—since acculturation consists precisely in learning to accept as natural, normal and inevitable what is in fact a set of parochial and transient social conventions.

But if, as gay people, we can't be identified as genetically or hormonally different from the mainstream, it's still possible to say that we *are* different culturally. Even if a self-conscious "gay identity" has emerged only recently, it can still be argued that *now* at least a distinctive gay sensibility has evolved from a unique set of historical circumstances and experiences. The trouble comes in trying to spell out the distinctive features of that sensibility (it's the same kind of trouble that emerges when we try to define how "the Jewish novel" is a demonstrably different category of fiction; we know it is, but itemizing its distinctive features is difficult).

Many gay men and lesbians, like some African-Americans, don't believe in the first place that they differ in any significant way from mainstreamers in general, insisting instead that they're "just folks." But other gay people and blacks—and they tend to be the political radicals—argue otherwise. They claim that having had a different historical experience, they've developed a different view of the world. For protective coloration we may have learned to conform to mainstream norms of behavior, but inwardly we feel like outsiders, have double vision, are spies in the culture. Few blacks, of course, have the option of "passing" but many gays can—and for many generations did.

The subsequent two evenings at the Y during November ("The Politics of Discrimination" and "The Jewish Response") drew comparably decent-sized, enthusiastic audiences—but they remained almost entirely gay. "The Jewish Response"—the one evening insisted upon and arranged by the Y itself, not by me—did produce some animated discussion. One of the panelists, Rabbi Hershel Matt, represented the liberal wing of Judaism, and (as I later described the evening in an article) "spoke compassionately of the need to welcome Jewish homosexuals into the fold of Judaism." He said that he based his view on the fact that all the gay people he knew were just like everybody else — either searching for or involved in loving, supportive, monogamous relationships.

That brought me up short. Since the AIDS crisis began, many gay men have *drawn back from their previous erotic pattern of multiple sexual partners, but the more radical among them insist that they've done so from necessity, not because they now view sexual variety as "immature" or as inimical to a satisfying life; in other words, they've put a hold on the sexual revolution, neither rejecting it nor their own past histories as having been morally (or even medically) misguided.*

As moderator of the panel, I asked Rabbi Matt if he was aware of this attitude among some gay men, and asked too whether he knew that promiscuity (not monogamy) had *been a central feature of the lives of many gay men in the pre-AIDS years. I also asked whether he'd feel as welcoming toward gay men whose lifestyle was promiscuous as he said he felt toward those who shared his own (and mainstream America's) commitment to sexual values that stressed the centrality of lifetime monogamous pair-bonding. Matt blanched at my questions, honestly confessed that he did not personally know any homosexual men who fit the promiscuous pattern I described, and said he would "have to think further about all of that."*

When later reviewing the book Twice Blessed: On Being Lesbian, Gay and Jewish *for the magazine* Tikkun, *I did some further thinking on these issues myself: the essayists, I wrote, "want to be welcomed into the Jewish family in which they were raised; they want to win acceptance, find a home, end the marginal status of lesbians and gays. But they also stress that they wish to retain and deepen their affiliation with Judaism because they see it as having itself long been the preserve and refuge of outsiders; indeed, they see their gayness and their Jewishness as two parts of the same tradition: the struggle to broaden established notions of acceptability. . . . Tikkun olam — repairing the world — is cited by several of the essayists as simultaneously at the core* of their Jewish identity and *at the heart of their gay protest against 'things as they are.' Indeed, it can be argued that the fates of Jews and gays have paralleled each other throughout European history; in societies that have not tolerated religious diversity, sexual variations have also been suppressed; Jews and gays have been lumped together as threats to the social fabric—and the histories of both have been marked by resistance and survival against great odds. . . .*

"*Profound though the similarities are between gayness and Jewishness, the compatibility founders on questions of sexual ethics. The Jewish tradition assumes and demands that sexual desire be channeled into heterosexual marriage and procreation; historically, that tradition has shown no tolerance for same-gender eroticism and love. . . . The essayists insist, sometimes in a plaintive tone that attests to the argument's fragility, that their relationships, too, are marked by emotional intimacy and stability, mutual faithfulness and economic interdependence; that, like good Jews everywhere, they resist sexual expression outside the confines of the committed couple, dutifully suppressing any impulse toward erotic adventuring, vigilantly exercising sexual restraint. . . . No notion is more deeply seated in American life than the view that a committed, exclusive relationship is the only hope for a satisfying life and that to maintain such a relationship, the two individuals involved must curtail any impulse to pursue intimacy and erotic pleasure elsewhere. It is a view which, in the name of security and safety, places sustained partnership somewhat at odds with pleasure, and perhaps even with individual growth.*

"*But there is another tradition within the gay world that is strongly at odds with this philosophy, one not at all susceptible to reconciliation with mainstream mores, Jewish or otherwise. Radical gay men (and in recent years, some lesbians) continue to affirm, even in the face of AIDS, the rightness of a sexual revolution that insists human nature is not monogamous, that a variety of sexual experiences are essential to self-exploration, and that these experiences do not compromise and may even reinforce the emotional fidelity of a primary relationship. . . .*"

Nearly a decade later, Daniel Boyarin of the University of California at Berkeley published an immensely important book, Unheroic Conduct, *which extended the debate about Judaism and homosexuality to Judaism and gender roles. A towering figure in Talmudic Studies, Boyarin argued that traditional Ashkenazic Jewish culture produced, in opposition to the Roman model of masculinity that valorized warrior aggression, an ideal that stressed the overriding virtues of gentleness, nurturance, emotional warmth, nonviolence, inwardness, and studiousness. But by the nineteenth century this once-heralded figure of the "feminized" Jewish man had become, in the minds of many Jews, a roadblock to assimilation into Western culture. A successful effort (joined by Freud and Theodor Herzl, among others) was made to discredit the once-privileged model of a gentle, scholarly masculinity as either the pathological product of the Diaspora or a figment of the anti-Semitic imagination.*

Boyarin believes (and I agree) that the restoration of the earlier tradition—or at least knowledge of it—would greatly help to destabilize binary notions of gender, liberating both men and women from stereotypic roles that currently constrict human possibilities. As unlikely as the reestablishment of the earlier model is, Boyarin's recovery of a tradition that stresses nurturance and emotional connectedness in men wreaks havoc with simplistic biological claims that gender roles have been uniform through time and can therefore be considered innate.

One could argue that to the extent "Ashkenazic" masculinity exists in the modern world, it can primarily be located among gay men. There are, to be sure, enormous variations to be found among them in regard to how they view gender, sexuality, and relationships. But in general they do consistently score higher than straight men in studies that attempt to measure empathy and altruism; they volunteer more time to nonprofit organizations than their straight counterparts; and they are more likely to have friends across lines of color, gender, religion, and politics. It's telling that during the trial of Matthew Shepard's murderers, almost every leading gay organization came out publicly against applying the death penalty. Urban gay male life, in fact, is notable for the absence of community violence. The gay bar scene rarely spawns shouting matches, brawls or an exchange of blows. Dances, parades, political rallies, and marches are suffused with drama but nearly devoid of violence.

These differences from straight male life can easily be overdrawn. The public peaceableness of gay men (and lesbians) may derive from having been subjected for generations to gay-bashing and police brutality that taught us, out of prudence and fear, not to let our anger show in public. But it does come out in private: the rate of domestic violence among both gay men and lesbians comes close to the heterosexual mark.

Also, for decades now, the cohort of gay men who obsess over their gym-toned muscular bodies, imitative of stereotypical macho maleness, are, it can be argued, struggling to divest themselves of all traces of effeminacy, of the gender-discordant behavior that as boys led them to be taunted at school and berated at home (mostly by their fathers). In setting up muscular masculinity as an ideal, this segment of the gay male community reinforces, as Boyarin puts it, "the dimorphism of the gendered body and thus participates . . . in the general cultural standard of masculinity rather than resisting it."

In repudiating aspects of the self that could be read as feminine, these gay men (and their admirers) risk considerable psychic damage—deep injury to the affective life that includes the loss of emotional expressiveness and resilience, as well as the need to avoid relationships that might evoke any resurgence of "feminine" traits. Also, the fanatical pursuit of powerful bodies often seems yoked to an undernourished interest in the public arena—a form of self-absorption that minimizes the importance both of politics and the life of the mind. The snotty attitudinizing that pervades the summer watering hole of Fire Island Pines, gathering place for stud-bunnies and their sugar daddies, reflect an emphasis on physical beauty and consumerism that are light-years removed from any concern about the survival issues that dominate and defeat most of the planet's inhabitants—including most of its gay people.

Though no statistics are available, my anecdotal impression is that the majority of gay men still strive to appear not as supermen but as "normal" men—assimilation, not the assertion of differentness, is the goal both of individuals and of most of the national gay political organizations. And those queers who look and sound like "normal" people (or are at least able to fake it in public)—meaning, mostly, clean-cut white men and lipstick lesbians—are being welcomed into the American mainstream in mounting numbers. The armed guards at the gate, however, continue to bar admission to (as they might put it) overweight butch dykes, foul-mouthed black queers, dickless "men" and surgically created "women" delusionally convinced that they're part of some nonexistent group called the "transgendered." To those, in other words, who do assert and display their differentness.

But we need to be careful here. Vast generalizations don't hold. First of all, even before AIDS, only about 20 percent of the gay male population pursued erotic adventures in any sustained way—about the same percentage as those who choose celibacy. Still, it remains true that roughly three-quarters of long-term gay male couples define fidelity *in terms of emotional commitment rather than sexual faithfulness—a much higher percentage than is found among either lesbian or heterosexual couples. Certainly there's plenty of evidence to support the view that monogamy is comparatively rare among animal species. In their book* The Myth of Monogamy, *David Barash and Judith Eve Lipton offer a barrage of information to the effect that monogamy is "not natural" and certainly "not easy." But they also argue that no better alternative exists, "that open, unstructured, and non-restrictive sexual relationships" do not make people happier.*

In his 2002 book Can Love Last?, *the relational psychoanalyst Stephen Mitchell throws unsettling light on the notion—common among heterosexuals as well as homosexuals—that erotic excitement and domesticity cannot coexist for long. The usual explanation for their incompatibility is some version of "familiarity breeds boredom." But in Mitchell's view, turning off to our primary partner is essentially a function of risk management. We separate sex and love because otherwise the stakes would be too high—too likely to heighten depend-ency and vulnerability, too threatening to our (illusory) sense of being in control of our lives.*

I've long argued that the natural history of relationships means that erotic zest between two partners, no matter how loving, will dissi-pate within a few years. A new idea dawns: erotic zest weakens because the prospect of heightened closeness threatens. Most people can toler-ate only limited amounts of intimacy, and they throw up a wall around their sexuality after a time to prevent the further "invasion" of closeness.

This seems truer for men than women. The macho masculinity that we privilege in our culture is, Mitchell argues, "easily destabilized by dependency longings." Most men cannot risk monogamy. And we give them an easy way out: our cultural script tells men that for them (unlike women) sexuality is rapacious and indiscriminate; that the male libido demands adventure. Yet Mitchell reports that when his patients "complain of dead and lifeless marriages, it is often possible to show them how precious the deadness is to them, how carefully main-tained and insisted upon." Long-term partners "collapse their expecta-tions of each other in collusively arranged, choreographed routine."

We then relocate our sexual interest away from our primary part-ner, telling ourselves that he or she has become too familiar to ignite desire—whereas in fact we're fleeing the threat of deeper knowledge of the other and deeper exposure of ourselves. We refuse to acknowledge that our partner, far from having become wholly known or from being securely centered, is a mysterious multiplicity of selves. Armed with our denial of the other's (and our own) potential, we rush off to our one-night stands, threesomes, and orgies.

So when heralding, legitimately, the advances in self-understanding that sexual adventuring can provide, we'd do to well to remember that—at least for some of the adventurers—incessant sexual escapades may also be symptomatic of a flight from the psychic dangers repre-sented by prolonged, concentrated intimacy with one partner.

JANUARY 4, 1988

Chicago Resources Foundation has turned down our request for a grant to help launch the center. It was more of a shock because we'd been optimistic about our chances. Four other promising foundations have also turned us down out of hand. This is a serious blow. Proshansky can't/won't present us to the Graduate School Board of Trustees for formal accreditation as a Research Center until we have our first year's budget of $50,000 (his figure) in hand. As of now we have about $5,000 (part of it in pledges), with no major donor in sight. I guess it's going to be a struggle all the way—right down to nickel and diming it. I hope enough of our people remain enthusiastic to *allow* for a struggle.

*W*hen I met with the dean of the graduate school the following month, he confirmed that the Board of Trustees was unlikely to approve the Center for Lesbian and Gay Studies (CLAGS, as it came to be known) unless we raise the full $50,000—and then added two new stipulations: we had to have a higher percentage of CUNY graduate faculty on our board than currently, and we had to have an executive director in place who had a graduate school appointment. That left one person eligible—me. I'd been trying during the previous six months to step to the side, arguing that CLAGS had come to be seen as "Marty's project" rather than "our project." Under the gun in finishing the revision of my Robeson biography, I wanted to free up more time. I also thought it essential to hold to our founding principles, which included "gender parity" on all levels. But the board insisted that my "prestige" was needed if the center was to have any chance of approval; they did bow to my wish to have a female co-chair—even as we all recognized that, like it or not, I alone among the board members had a graduate school affiliation and would—according to the dean's stipulation—have to become the sole executive director should the center ever become established. ("My reluctant but needed contribution," as I wrote in my diary at the time.)

After I'd met with the dean and heard his steep new demands, I felt more relief than regret. After two years of petty riffs, I felt fed up with organization-building and infighting. I was burned out. And given the failure to date of our appeal to foundations, it seemed likely, in 1988, that we'd eventually have to throw in the towel. Yet I felt I had to continue to give it my best shot. I strongly believed that a center devoted to rigorous scholarship (not propaganda) on LGBT lives was essential to counteracting the demeaning myths about who we were—even as the center could establish that a gay subculture did exist and that its values and perspectives were not, on matters relating to sexuality, relationships, family, parenting and friendship, carbon copies of mainstream mores, and therefore had much to offer.

The 1980s were probably the first moment in time when an attempt could be made in this country to formalize LGBT studies within a university structure. (That had already happened in the Netherlands as early as 1981, but in no other country). Thanks to fifteen years of political activism; an AIDS crisis that in the public eye humanized (as well as demonized) gay people and created more sympathy for them; and the accumulation of a substantial body of work (by, among others, John Boswell, Alan Bray, Blanche Wiesen Cook, John D'Emilio, Lillian Faderman, Jonathan Ned Katz, Joan Nestle, and Leila Rupp), the time was at least potentially ripe.

   The ground had become fallow for lesbian and gay studies for reasons that go back even further. Major credit belongs to the advent, following the Stonewall riots, of an organized gay political movement (activism, as always, precedes academics). Behind that, in turn, was a whole series of developments in the 1960s: a counterculture that challenged traditional pieties and authorities; a black struggle that contained at its core ("black is beautiful") the assumption that it was fine—maybe better than fine—to be different; and a feminist movement that boldly confronted the inevitability and "naturalness" of orthodox gender roles. Had there not been this across-the-board assault on long-standing norms, the gay movement (and the emergence of gay studies that followed in train) would never have been possible.

Much of the new scholarship had been viewing LGBT lives through the prism of a historical, rather than the traditional psychological, perspective. Yet after the first dozen years of research into historical material, information regarding whole centuries and several national histories remained virtually nonexistent. And what preliminary findings we did have related mostly to the behavior of white men, and some white women. Efforts to reclaim the gay past, moreover, had thus far focused on two areas of research: biography and the history of repression. Since almost all the researchers into gay history were—and continue to be—scholars who are themselves gay, it's understandable that in the beginning the urge to rediscover and reclaim gay "heroes"— Walt Whitman, Willa Cather—proved irresistible.

As for the history of repression, Jonathan Ned Katz's two pioneering collections of documents (Gay American History, 1976, and Gay/ Lesbian Almanac, 1983) began the process of unearthing a tale of oppression as freshly appalling as it had been recently obscure. We now knew, for example, that as early as 1624 the colony of Virginia executed a ship's master for homosexuality, and the New Haven colony served up a notable first in world history when it prescribed the death penalty for lesbianism in 1656. For many decades the New England clergy debated "unnatural filthiness" (John Cotton's words), arguing about whether actual penetration had to have occurred before the death penalty was applied, or whether any "voluntary effusion of seed" caused by bodily contact, even without penetration, was itself sufficient grounds for execution. Opinion finally clustered towards the latter view—and a profusion of executions followed. During this same period, two heterosexual child-rapists got off with a fine and a whipping. By the time of the American Revolution, Thomas Jefferson and a group of "liberal" reformers proposed a revision of Virginia's law that would have eliminated the death penalty for sodomy and substituted instead—castration. This, as the world measured such matters, constituted progress.

By 1988, scholars of the gay past had moved the focus away from biography and the history of repression and more toward an analysis of how gay people have viewed themselves *through time. Here a polar-*

izing debate opened up, and in changing form continues to the present day. Essentially it recapitulates the ancient "nature versus nurture" argument. The gay community as a whole overwhelmingly opts—gay men more so than lesbians—for the "nature" explanation ("I was born this way") and is devoted to the notion that a consistent homosexual presence, personality, and patterns of behavior can be perceived through time and across cultures.

But the scholarly world has just as solidly come down on the opposite side, insistent on the contingent nature of erotic desire and sexual identity. Most lesbian and gay scholars deny that the categories "homosexual" and "heterosexual" are real and persistent aspects of the human psyche that can be identified historically. They argue that such binary distinctions, rather than being an innate, universal grammar, are not found through time and across cultures—nor are the taboos, judgments, and penalties attached to particular sexual acts.

Historically, homosexual behavior has been organized in many different ways—sometimes shaping itself around substantial differences in age or social class between the two partners, sometimes creating "third gender" figures, sometimes insisting that homosexual behavior be understood according to traditional gender roles (he who penetrates is "male"; he who gets penetrated is "female"). Our sexual behavior, as well as our sexual identity, is, like everything else about our humanness, a product of the particular society in which we live, a reflection of its time-specific norms and values. Queer theorists, moreover, have additionally complicated the picture by modifying the triumphalist emphasis since Stonewall on "proud to be gay" to include the melancholic effects that homophobia has had on gay lives: the shame produced by stigmatization has made a significant contribution to certain formative aspects of gay culture.

FEBRUARY 4, 1988

On the first page of its Metropolitan section, the *Times* has published an article by Jane Gross entitled "Homosexuals Detect New Signs of Friendliness Amid Bias." It features pictures of me and

Tom [*Stoddard, then executive director of Lambda Legal Defense*] —
two middle-class white men. I think the article is on the whole
nuanced, especially in describing how two counter-streams are currently at work—that is, both an increase in understanding and acceptance and an increase in homophobia. And as for myself, Gross
did quote me accurately enough (which is rare). But on a number of
other counts the article is seriously skewed, and the headline offensive (gay people have long since rejected the term "homosexual" as
clinically derived). Statistics from the New York Gay and Lesbian
Anti-Violence Project would give the lie to Gross's claim that anti-
gay violence has decreased. Worse, neither lesbians nor gay people
of color are ever discussed in the piece, thereby reinforcing the long-
standing invisibility of both. Poor Tom is catching hell for saying he
was afraid of walking hand in hand with his lover because of "fear of
disapproval." My guess is that Tom actually said something closer to
"fear of being attacked."

The book publishing world is doing better in providing something like equal time for lesbians—but thanks to independent lesbian
publishers, not mainstream houses. A whole new wave of women's
presses (like Firebrand and Kitchen Table) has come into being to
supplement the earlier houses, Naiad and Spinsters. Gay men have
been much more powerfully placed within trade houses than almost
all women, with the result that an increasing number of gay male titles are now appearing under the sponsorship of such major firms as
St. Martin's and New American Library. With more resources and
higher budgets, trade publishers can do much more with distribution and publicity than the independent presses can. As everywhere
else, lesbian writers are getting short-changed when compared with
their male counterparts—but at least they've taken matters into their
own hands and outlets for their work do now exist.

FEBRUARY 10, 1988

Tom's remark [*in the* Times] about "holding hands" may well have
been misguided, but not enough to warrant the vicious letter Daryl

Yates Rist [*the gay activist and writer*] has sent him (which Tom read to me). Rist is doing his usual self-righteous number, howling down, in the preacher tones of his fundamentalist youth, the deviation from Holy Writ. And so yet another round of gay internecine warfare commences. Why is it so difficult to acknowledge each other's efforts, even if they aren't the ones we ourselves might choose to make? Tom is marvelously equipped to go the mainstream route, working for gay civil rights within the system—and has been doing it marvelously well. Those rights neither are nor should be the *sine qua non* of the gay movement—but God knows they're worth having. Let others, differently equipped, make different contributions, be it acting up in the streets or writing gay novels, and let us all *try* to show a decent regard for each other's contributions, whatever they be.

FEBRUARY 20, 1988

. . . climactic meeting of the committee, with dissolution looming as one real possibility. In the upshot, the meeting proved restorative. Almost everyone talked earnestly, a few passionately, of their renewed sense of the importance of legitimizing gay/lesbian studies through university affiliation, of the potential beacon the center could become for stimulating work in the field. By the time we adjourned, I felt genuine commitment had been re-asserted, and my own mood much improved. Under the weight of the long-standing bickering within the committee, my spirits had sagged to a low point—along with my optimism (long sustained by a hair) about the center's ability to survive. I only hope today's avowals of commitment last.

MARCH 16, 1988

Today's seminar [*on "The History of Radical Protest in the U.S."*] got off on a tangent—heated and discouraging—about "welfare cheats." A lot of venomous anti–poor people sentiments expressed, along the tired "why don't they get up off their asses?" line. Discouraging, I thought, coming from students who are often from under-

privileged backgrounds. But then it dawned on me: They're venomous because they don't see *themselves* as special. They've gotten
so used to juggling family, work and college simultaneously—to putting in 16-hour days matter-of-factly—that they can't understand
why anybody can't do the same. They don't see themselves as unusually energetic and determined, though they are; they learn to take
their own heroism—it's nothing less—for granted, and scornfully assume anybody could take on the triple burden they do. Themselves
victims, they victimize others. Instead of their resentment getting
turned against the Lifestyles of the Rich and Famous, who live well
without working comparable hours (or at all), they denounce instead welfare recipients who don't (or often can't) work and live
badly. Thus the powers-that-be get their battles fought by a segment
of the underclass that itself suffers from the system's inequities (if less
than the single mothers penned in hotel rooms). I think I made a
dent today, mostly because I kept my voice down and fully expressed
my admiration for their own struggle for a better life.

*B*y the spring of 1988, the center had been turned down by two
more foundations, and was still nowhere near raising the $50,000
Proshansky had set as a start-up budget. As a result of passing the hat
at two public events we'd held—both of which drew standing-room-
only crowds—as well as small donations from individual contributors,
we did have nearly $10,000 in the bank. But that had taken us two
and a half years to raise. At that rate, we'd still be at it in the twenty-
first century.

We tried not to think about that, taking heart in the fact that here
and there a course or a conference relating to lesbian and gay studies
had started to surface. Nowhere in the country did a department or a
scholarly research center exist, and only rarely could a brave student
find even minimal fellowship money to pursue a topic in LGBT studies. On the few campuses where a course had been offered, it stood
alone, wasn't always repeated or had trouble finding students brave
enough to enroll.

As a still-fragile enterprise, the center also had to deal with an attempt by a covey of conservative gay professors in the CUNY system to cut us off at the knees. They went straight to Proshansky with the charge that "Duberman is a Communist sympathizer" and has packed the board with fellow left-wingers. In a formal reply to Wayne Dynes, lead saboteur, and professor of art history at Hunter College, Proshansky shrewdly wrote that he and his staff were "unequipped to resolve these problems." He suggested that Dynes take up his complaints directly with me and the center's board.

Proshansky cc'd me on his letter, thereby creating an opportunity to write Dynes myself. I reminded him that I'd written before, personally inviting him to participate in a CUNY-wide meeting specifically designed to discuss what principles and structure should guide the center. He had neither responded to my letter nor shown up for the meeting. Instead, I wrote him, "you go above our heads and, in essence, try to persuade Proshansky that we are not entitled to exist. . . . With such friends, gay studies hardly needs enemies." Dynes never responded to that letter, either. He and I did later manage a brief truce, but before long he and his cohort (all gay white men) were again sniping away at us from the sidelines.

With my biography of Robeson completed and due to be published in January 1989, I turned to writing up a proposal for my next book. It would be called Cures: A Gay Man's Odyssey. As the publisher of Paul Robeson, Knopf had the contractual right of "first refusal" on the new work. Knopf's editor-in-chief was—and is—Sonny Mehta.

JUNE 30, 1988

Sonny has *vehemently* turned down the proposal. He told Frances [*my agent*] "Martin should not be doing this book. This is not the next book by Martin that Knopf wants to publish"—in other words, garden variety homophobia.

JULY 9, 1988

Paul Jr. continues to denounce me. In asking me to take on the biography he seems to have hoped, unconsciously I believe, that I'd claim his father for gay liberation and thereby wreck retrospective revenge.

When I began the Robeson biography in 1981, the notion that he might be "gay" or bisexual never crossed my mind. I'd been forced to entertain those possibilities only because Paul Jr. himself dropped those false clues in my path. And early on. At our very first meeting, I'd expressed my surprise to Paul that he was inviting me to do the book. "You can see that I'm white," I said, "but do you also know that I'm a gay man who's been actively involved in the gay political movement for years?" "Of course I know," Paul had answered, with startling nonchalance. "I've had you thoroughly checked out." "Well," I said, "you're going to catch hell. But if you're willing to proceed, I certainly am."

We then talked for hours, ironing out details of what would be a formal, signed agreement between us. For me, there were two key elements: full and exclusive access to the vast Robeson Archives, which up to that point had been essentially closed to scholars; and a clause stating that Paul surrendered all control—I'd already heard from various sources that he could be "extremely difficult"—over what I ultimately decided to put in the book. Paul said he'd expected both demands and, affability itself, readily acceded to them.

Business done, we settled back into an easygoing chat. At one point Paul said (or words to that effect), "I'm not looking for a 'Saint Robeson' sort of biography but rather a tell-it-like-it-was account that would make my father an accessible human being rather than a pedestalized god. That's why you didn't have to be uneasy about the gay stuff. My parents were both entirely laid-back on the subject and had many gay friends. In fact my father had an affair with Serge Eisenstein." My agent Frances Goldin, who'd been present throughout, and I briefly exchanged a stunned look, as if to say "Did you just hear what

I heard?!" Turning to Paul I simply said, in as bland a tone as I could master, "No, I didn't know that. Very interesting . . ."

Ultimately I was able to track down Eisenstein's sister-in-law, Zina Voynow, as well as Monroe Wheeler (the longtime companion of novelist Glenway Wescott, both of whom had known Robeson in the 1920s), and a gay man who'd lived in Moscow during the 1930s and had gotten to know Paul Sr. All (and later on, several others as well) responded in essentially the same astonished way: "What?! That's absurd! Paul Robeson was the most rigorously heterosexual man I've ever known. Who fed you that nonsense about 'an affair with Serge Eisenstein?'"

A year later, finally satisfied that the tale was false, I told Paul Jr. that I'd failed to turn up any corroborating evidence whatsoever for the "affair" he'd mentioned. He wheeled on me angrily—"What the hell are you talking about? I never said any such thing!" Well, I replied, Frances was in the room so can we ask her about it. When I subsequently did, she entirely confirmed what Paul had said about his father and Eisenstein. She agreed to tell Paul as much, since he was currently in one of his periodic rages about my purported attempts "to claim" his father for "gay liberation." But when she did, he again denied having made the remark and refused to discuss the matter further.

That didn't prevent him, some time later, from casually remarking to Frances that his father had had an affair with the composer Marc Blitzstein. This time I wasn't in the room, but Frances phoned me: "Marty, sit down before I tell you this, and promise me that you will not, as with Eisenstein, attempt to prove or disapprove the matter." I withheld the promise, but did sit down. Later I talked to Blitzstein's biographer, Eric Gordon, who said he hadn't found a shred of evidence confirming the rumored affair.

Later still, when the Advocate, the leading gay publication, printed the claim that Robeson had "recently [been] revealed to have been gay," I protested the claim. (And in the biography itself, I wrote that "I had found absolutely no evidence of Robeson's erotic interest in men.") I couldn't resist telling Paul Jr. about the Unimpeachable Scholarly Integrity I'd demonstrated in rebutting the Advocate piece.

He stared at me stonily, hardly gratified by the news; after all, he'd been widely asserting that I'd been peddling the notion that his father had had affairs with men.

Beyond all that, I myself wondered from the beginning whether I was the appropriate biographer. I was still wondering about it a decade after the book was published and, as a way of sorting out my conflicted feelings, wrote an article for the Nation digging into the set of interlocking issues involved. Was this a case of bizarre miscasting, a grotesque mismatch of author and subject? I explored the matter at some length:

> What, after all, are the essential qualities in a given biographer that heighten the chances for understanding a given life? Who is best qualified to write about whom, and why? Are there certain unbreachable guidelines that must be followed, certain fundamental boundaries that must not be crossed? Do we want to argue, for example, that no man should attempt to write about a woman, no younger person about an older, no adult about a child, no straight person about a gay one, no white person about a person of color (or vice versa)?
>
> Even the most committed essentialist, I felt sure, would balk at strictures this severe: we've become too aware of how reductive the standard identity categories of gender, class, race and ethnicity are when trying to capture the actual complexities of a given personality. Paul Robeson cannot simply be summarized as 'a black man'—whatever spot on the diverse spectrum of black males we arbitrarily decide to hold up as the authentic one. Besides, many people have overlapping identities that compete for attention and shift in priority over time.
>
> But why is the assumption so widespread in the first place that a match-up between author and subject in regard to standard identity categories is the best guarantor of understanding? Indeed, why do we lazily assume that these categories are, in every case, the critical ones, while ignoring any number of

other commonalities between biographer and subject that might provide superior insight—matters such as having been raised in similar family, class or regional cultures or having shared similar psychologies of self, professional experience or religious affiliation?

Which of the links (or absence of links) between biographer and subject are likely to prove the most significant? Perhaps— heresy!—the answer is none, or none that can be presumed in advance to guarantee access to the deepest recesses of personality. Perhaps what will turn out to matter most is that which is least visible and hardest to define: something to do with an elusive empathy of spirit between biographer and subject, a shared if shadowy sense of how one should best navigate through life, treat other people, leave a mark and make a contribution. How one positions oneself in the world will always reflect to some degree the seminal experiences and indoctrinations of class, race and gender, but may also, perhaps even to a greater degree, float above them, wondrously unanchored in categorical imperatives, mysteriously untraceable in derivation.

To take as a given that no white person is able (or morally entitled) to write about someone black can itself be seen as a form of racism—a particularly simplistic form, for it's based on the insidious assumption that fellow-feeling hinges on the color of one's skin and that an individual's character and insight can be accurately prejudged on the basis of their membership in a particular group.

Since no biographer can duplicate in his or her person the full range of their subject's experience—or exactly duplicate any of it—every biographer will be found wanting in some areas. And yes, the disability can sometimes be directly linked to racial (or class or gender) dissonance. I don't doubt, for example, that as a white person I failed to capture some of the nuances of what it meant for Robeson to grow up in the black church (his father was a minister). Yet, oppositely, my own sometime career in the theater gave me a background few schol-

*ars (white or black) could bring to bear in evaluating Robeson's
stage experience. . . ."*

In his letter-to-the-editor response to my 1998 Nation piece,
Paul Jr. managed a whole whopper-set of distortions, contradictions,
and outright falsehoods that, in their recklessness, figuratively took my
breath away (see pages 248–251 for details). Among much else, Paul
Jr. insisted that I'd omitted from the book a "list" he'd given me of his
father's black lovers, even as he simultaneously insisted that he'd (his
words) "refused to give him the names of four black women with whom
my father had major affairs but who chose to remain anonymous."
That contradiction aside, I found it "amazing," as I wrote in my Nation reply to Paul's letter, "that the same Paul Robeson Jr., who told
me that Sergei Eisenstein and Marc Blitzstein had been his father's
lovers (in neither case true) would, out of a newly discovered respect for
privacy, withhold the names of Robeson Sr.'s four black female lovers."

What further set my head spinning, as I'd earlier written in my diary, was the information that Helen Rosen, Paul Sr.'s longtime lover
and confidante, conveyed to me after an hour-long conversation with
Paul Jr.: "He ranted on at considerable length," according to Helen,
about my refusal to acknowledge his father's black lovers—"Duberman has that list and is suppressing it." I do? The only black lovers
Paul Jr. brought up were Nina Mae McKinney and Ethel Waters.
McKinney possibly (the evidence is minuscule) had a brief, passing
affair with Robeson Sr.; there's no evidence at all that Waters had so
much as a single sexual encounter with him.

On several other sensitive matters—that Paul Sr. hadn't wanted
children and was a disinterested, even negligent parent—I also relied
heavily in the biography on the unanimous testimony of Helen Rosen
and two of his father's other closest friends over many years, Revels
Cayton, the well-known labor organizer and Paul Sr.'s most intimate
black male confidant for more than fifty years, and Freda Diamond
("After I played chess with him," Paul Sr. told Freda, "and discussed
football, then what am I supposed to do?"). Of the three other possible
contenders for "intimates," two (Ben Davis and Bob Rockmore) had

died by the time I began work on the book, and the third, Lloyd Brown, who'd helped Paul Sr. with his autobiography, Here I Stand, had publicly and bitterly denounced me for daring, as a homosexual, to undertake Paul Sr.'s biography. I was, according to Brown, "a sick writer."

During the spring and fall of 1988, when the biography was in press, Paul's calumnies against Helen, the actress Uta Hagen (who had also been Paul Sr.'s lover), and me hit the stratosphere. Allowed to read the manuscript—though legal opinion was divided as to whether he had any contractual right to do so—Paul submitted some seven hundred pages of typed commentary to Knopf denouncing me, in essence, as a racist and a red-baiter; from "the outset," as he was later to put it, he'd been "uneasy about [my] lack of sensitivity to African-American cultural traditions." But then why had he ever gone ahead and asked me to do the biography? Maybe my theory about his unacknowledged anger at his father is the bottom-line explanation.

Knopf's legal staff dutifully checked out whatever part of Paul's commentary might be called factual, and I myself wrote a detailed response. So many of Paul's charges were on their face transparently contradictory and bizarre that Knopf remained unshaken in its confidence in the biography. But as I read through his seven-hundred-page critique, my own outrage mounted, not simply because of his tendentious attack on me, but for his unjust attempt to smear Helen and Uta as well—the two people, of the many dozen I interviewed, who I'd found to be the most straightforward truth-tellers.

In the section of Paul's commentary that dealt with his father's 1942 Broadway "Othello" (to Hagen's "Desdemona"), he tried his best to destroy Uta's reputation. He suggested that her analysis of Paul Sr.'s performance—which had dared to suggest certain shortcomings—was a reflection of her "latent racism." On top of that, he belittled her as someone who "drank heavily," and who "attempted suicide" when Paul Sr. terminated his affair with her. I found no trace of evidence to support the charges of racism, excessive drinking, and attempted suicide.

Paul Jr. was even less restrained in attacking Helen Rosen. He tried to dismiss her as "an upperclass American WASP" (she was Jew-

ish) who didn't understand black people and who knew few of them. In fact Helen knew most of Paul Sr.'s black friends (on the East Coast, that is) and saw people like Ben Davis, William Patterson, and Viola Scott often (though she never met Paul Sr.'s friend Bumpy Johnson, the famous black gangster).

Paul Jr. also tried to cast special blame on Helen for the role she played during his father's breakdown in 1961 in London. Paul Sr.'s wife Essie had put in a frantic phone call to Helen (not to Paul Jr.) as the person her husband most trusted, asking her to come immediately to England, which she did at once. When she arrived, Paul Sr. was curled in a fetal position and hallucinating, and the decision had already been made by Essie, Paul's agent Harold Davison, and the latter's physician, for Paul to enter the Priory, a well-regarded psychiatric hospital. Helen had never heard of the place and had no hand in choosing it.

Yet Paul Jr., in his commentary, insisted that Helen was directly implicated in removing his father to the Priory and accused her of "panic, ignorance and stubborn egotism"—a character analysis wildly off the mark. Paul Jr. has always denied that his father suffered from bipolar or delusional depressive disorder and has ascribed (without ever producing believable evidence) his father's 1961 breakdown to his deliberate poisoning by the CIA or other governmental agencies. Similarly, he continues to insist that the electroconvulsive therapy (ECT) given Paul Sr. at the Priory was needless as well as suspiciously extensive. But the experts I consulted considered the protocol used a responsible one, given Paul Sr.'s acute symptoms and suffering. The arsenal of medications available today barely existed in 1961, and even today ECT remains the preferred treatment for relief of severe symptomatology that refuses to yield to medication.

In his commentary Paul Jr. further accused me of consistently underestimating his father's achievements and stature and overestimating his "negative traits." One example must suffice: starting in 1950, when the State Department lifted Paul Sr.'s passport—thus denying him the right to travel and perform abroad—he'd been subject to a series of body blows: the closing down of the magazine Freedom *and*

*the Council on African Affairs, both of which he'd been deeply in-
vested in; the U.S. black leadership's growing rejection of him; and
Khrushchev's 1956 speech revealing for the first time the magnitude of
Stalin's crimes—all these sharp disappointments culminated in an
emotional breakdown. Paul Jr. scoffed at my comment that his father,
like everyone, was susceptible to melancholy, "weariness, despon-
dency . . ." as "ludicrous," and my portrait of him in these years (he'd
had another breakdown in 1956) as a shaken and downcast man, simply the product of my own racism. It might be argued that Paul Jr.'s insistence that his father was far too strong ever to suffer from clinical
depression or succumb to it, is itself a form of racism: the black man as
Superfly, immune to the full range of human feelings and reactions.*

*Happily, no one else who read the manuscript shared Paul Jr.'s as-
sessment. And when the book was published in January 1989, nearly
all the prominent African-American scholars who reviewed it were
unanimous in their praise. Henry Louis Gates Jr. congratulated me on
"a job brilliantly realized." In the* Nation, *Harvard professor Nathan
Huggins hailed the book as "a magnificent biography, fully propor-
tionate to the dramatic, heroic and tragic dimensions of Robeson's
life." Arnold Rampersad in the* Washington Post *called the biography
"enthralling . . . a marvelous story marvelously told." In the* Boston
Globe, *Nell Irvin Painter wrote the review that Paul Jr. doubtless
hated most: "Duberman rates high marks for having seen much that
white biographers of African-American subjects frequently disregard,
notably anger and strategies for its management, without which no
black person can succeed in public life."*

*Nor, having denounced me for having insufficient sympathy for
the left, could Paul have been pleased with several reviews in the conservative press that took me to task for showing* excessive *sympathy.
In the* New Leader, *Barry Gewen characterized me as an "apologist"
for Robeson's "political obtuseness." Similarly, Harvey Klehr in* Commentary *emphasized how much I "strained" to explain Robeson's unyielding support of Communism. In the* Wall Street Journal, *Eric
Breindel claimed that I'd demonstrated "that Paul Robeson, at least
by the early 1950s, was well aware of the crimes of Stalin" [I'd demon-*

strated no such thing] and that I seemed in the biography "almost to regard Robeson's abject fealty to Stalinism as a virtue"—no, I'd tried to explain not judge his decision to remain silent at the revelations of Stalin's crimes, which I was at pains to differentiate from "abject fealty."

In February 1989, I'd been in San Francisco on the final leg of the book tour and had paid a return visit to Revels Cayton and his wife, Lee. Revels had greeted me at the door with a broad grin and a bear hug, effusive with congratulations for having "gotten it right." Later, over coffee, I told him about Paul Jr.'s formal statement to the press calling the book "prurient." Revels shook his head in disbelief, chuckling over what he called my "restrained version of Sr.'s sex life." "There was much more sex in the life than in the book," he added, and he reminisced about how, when he and Paul were young men, they'd go "whoring" night after night in Greenwich Village. Then he made a remark that startled me: "You know, I've been thinking about it and I believe that only a gay man could have understood Paul's sex life."

I never pressed him to explain what he meant, but his comment stayed in my head for a long time. When I came to write my Nation piece a decade later, I spelled out my own gloss:

> Most heterosexual scholars, a conservative breed not known for their erotic capers, would be likely to share the mainstream view that lifetime, monogamous pair-bonding is the optimal path to human happiness—not to say moral decency. That assumption, in turn, would incline them, when confronted with the unconventional erotic history of someone like Robeson to evade, minimize or condemn him for his robust sexuality. Legions of heterosexual scholars strenuously believe in their hearts, not merely in their public pronouncements, that sexual "restraint" is one of the admirable moral cornerstones of our national character. (It took DNA, remember, finally to break down their adamant denial of a sexual liaison between Thomas Jefferson and Sally Hemings.)

Confronted with Robeson's many sexual adventures, such scholars would most likely characterize them as "womanizing" or "Don Juanism." Additionally, they'd probably "explain" the fact that Robeson's most intense, long-lasting affairs were nearly all with white women by regurgitating hoary, simplistic formulas about his need to prove himself to the white world—or to work out his anger against it.

White conservatives, moreover—whether scholars or not—long since enraged at Robeson's political militancy, gleefully latch on to his erotic history as an additional weapon in portraying him as a "moral transgressor." And for white racists, Robeson's exuberant sexuality can usefully be made to play into the long-standing, vicious stereotype of the black man as a "rampaging lustful beast." That almost all of Robeson's major affairs were with white women, finally, has compromised his stature with some African-Americans who otherwise deeply admire his unyielding struggle against racism and colonialism—as well as with some older-generation white socialists who tend to be cultural conservatives and who experience discomfort over Robeson's troubled marriage and his frequent extramarital affairs.

But the biographer's job is to tell the truth—to the extent that gaps in the evidence and inevitably subjective interpretation will allow for it. The biographer isn't responsible for how others manipulate that truth in order to serve agendas of their own. I feel no obligation to address the discomfort of white racists and conservatives. But I do want to say something more to those on the left who share with the right the underlying assumption that monogamous, lifetime pair-bonding is, for everyone, the most defensible, natural, moral path.

How much sex is too much sex? Does the answer hinge on the number of different partners involved, the number of encounters with the same partner, particular configurations (three-way or group sex, say) or particular sexual acts (anal intercourse, say, or sadomasochism)? The answers will hinge on individual assumptions about what is "normal" or "healthy" *(and are bound to be inflected as well by how one defines the desirable obligations and boundaries of a primary relationship). In this country numbers alone are likely to settle the argument: The higher the figure, the more brows start to furrow—even though we're talking about consenting adults.*

What do people mean when they level the accusation "womanizer" against Robeson? Three definitions of the term currently predominate: A "womanizer" is someone whose self-regard hinges on frequent conquests; is someone incapable of love and, to disguise the fact (not least from himself) pursues multiple sexual encounters; and, finally, is someone who treats his partners as exploitable objects, to be used disdainfully and discarded cavalierly.

None of those definitions, I'd submit, apply to Paul Robeson. That's the overwhelming testimony of his psychiatrists as well as his lovers. Every woman I spoke to who'd been involved with Robeson for an extended period emphasized that he treated her as an equal, not a mere convenience or appendage. He could be difficult, neglectful and secretive, but was much more often tender, considerate and loving. As if in confirmation, one of Robeson's psychiatrists described him to me as a man whose "motivational spring was compassion, not ego." And so when I hear Robeson described as a "womanizer," I've learned to take it as a rule of thumb that I'm listening to someone who despises the man politically and wishes to discredit him—as nothing can do so more powerfully in our sex-negative culture than the accusation of "philanderer."

When non-gays credit anything of value in gay culture—and few do—they rightfully cite its iconoclasm, its suspicion of traditional social mores, especially in regard to gender and sexual behavior. When I was writing Robeson's biography, my iconoclasm stood me in good stead. Yet ultimately I came to feel that it was less important in helping me get beneath the layers of his personality than what I'd call our shared status as outsiders—outsiders who to a significant degree had been "let in," had been treated by the mainstream as respectable representatives of an otherwise despised group.

Here is how I ultimately summed it up for myself in a diary entry:

Like Robeson I know about the double-bind of being accepted and not accepted.

I know about the outsider's need to role-play (the uses of theater off-stage).

I know about the double-vision of the outsider who is let inside: about being a "spy" in the culture.

I know some of the strategies for concealing pain, including from oneself.

I know about the exuberant investment of hope in a "liberation" movement—and the attendant despair when it falls short.

I know about the seductive double-talk employed, when considered serviceable, by the white male power structure.

I know about the tensions of trying to be a "good" role model.

I know about the conflict between the yearnings of lust and the demands of a public image.

I know about the tug-of-war between the attractions of career and of doing "good works."

I know about the disjunction between the desire to be liked (and knowing one has the necessary social skills to accomplish that) and feeling disgust at the neediness of the desire.

I know about stubbornness—and about the need to sometimes play the supplicant.

I know about the counterpulls of feeling gregarious and longing for—requiring—solitude.

I know about concealment.

I know about buried anger.

I know about politeness substituting for anger, about anger eating up one's vitals, distorting one's judgment.

I know about loneliness.

To whatever extent my biography of Robeson does represent an empathy of the spirit, I believe the sensitizing factor of critical importance was, as Revels Cayton had suggested, precisely my homosexuality.

Of the three cover reviews today, [*Arnold*] Rampersad's in the *Washington Post* is the standout. He *gets* it: instead of blaming the victim, he squarely denounces the racist society that limited and distorted black political options; he knows that the generosity of Robeson's spirit got squeezed into an airtight container *because* he cared, & refused to settle for crumbs. . . . Since its reviewer failed to red-bait Robeson, the *Post* supplied an accompanying cartoon showing him with a hammer & sickle medal pinned to his chest, narcissistically carrying a pouting portrait of himself in his hand, and with a leering buffoon's grin on his face.

In L.A. two weeks ago, I had the proverbial "power lunch" with Tom Mount and Terry Nelson (both fronting for Sidney Poitier). The trio's movie offer for the book is stunningly good . . . plus the talk of integrity (who ever knows what the actuality would bring) in filming Robeson's life was impressive. Later, on the phone, Poitier emphasized to me his determination to tell Robeson's story in all its authentic, radical richness.

But now, a week later, the plan has unraveled—thanks to Paul Jr. [*In a burst of euphoric fellow-feeling at the start of the book project in 1981 I'd given Paul the contractual right to veto second serial deals; he not only turned down a slew of movie offers and foreign rights, but also the Book-of-the-Month Club.*] Poitier was on the phone with him for an hour. . . . It seems Jr. spent the first half hour insisting *he* would control the movie's contents entirely or would refuse consent, and the second half hour detailing his own hitherto unrecognized "genius." Poitier is certain Jr. can never put together the needed funding on his own nor get agreement to his absurd terms. [*And as of 2008 he hasn't.*]

*I*n its February 13, 1989, issue, the Nation *published Darrell Yates Rist's wildly controversial article "The AIDS Obsession" and invited various people, myself included, to respond to it. In his piece Rist denounced the gay community's single-minded focus in recent years on fighting the AIDS scourge, characterizing it as "fashionable hysteria" and theorizing that our "keening" reflected a "compulsive . . . need to partake in the drama of catastrophe."*

But the catastrophe, I wrote in response, was real "and the legions of the young in ACT-UP who have stationed themselves on the front lines deserve something better than being characterized [as Rist had] *as 'clones' and 'chic street protesters.'" If the straight world, I argued, had shown more than a modicum of concern and involvement, gay people would never have had to rely so entirely on their own resources—which they've marshaled with heroic determination.*

Rist had further denounced the ACT-UP demonstrators as "immoral because they are panic-mongering." To me that was a shocking mischaracterization of young men fighting for their lives, especially since Rist never paused to denounce a federal government whose indifference made such a fight mandatory. That was blaming the victim—and excusing the oppressor—with a vengeance.

"The paradox" I wrote, "is that as a result of the successful mobilization of our own people in the fight against AIDS, so many have for the first time discovered their anger at heterosexist oppression that we may emerge from this crisis with the needed legions—at last—militantly to insist on an end to our persecution."

APRIL 23, 1989

Feelings of marginality and of gender non-conformity are what separate lesbian feminists from straight feminists. The same feelings *connect* lesbians to gay men—despite all the recent insistence on how different the two cultures are. A natural psychic alliance does exist. What has prevented it from being recognized and from maturing is the gay male *denial* (particularly the white, middle-class gays who dominate the organized political movement) of marginality and gender non-conformity — indeed the counter-insistence that they are "just folks."

MAY 31, 1989

Out of the blue, the center has gotten a $20,000 bequest from a man [*David Clarke*] who recently died of AIDS in San Francisco. On top of that, at a meeting yesterday, the executive director of the Rapoport Foundation (the legacy of another gay man dead of AIDS) expressed real interest in funding us. In combination with the benefit Eli's planning for us in November, we may then be over the top ($50,000) and ready to apply for formal accreditation to the Board of Trustees.

JUNE 1, 1989

I spoke at the unveiling of "Stonewall Place" in Sheridan Square, spoke extemporaneously, since the hour I'd saved for preparation got eaten up in grid-locked taxis and delayed errands. . . . I mostly emphasized the need for the movement, as it looks beyond the 20th anniversary of the Stonewall riots, to reach back to its radical roots in GLF [*the Gay Liberation Front*] — to embrace the diversified minorities (and especially the drag queens who helped initiate resistance back in 1969) within our own community, and to combine with other oppressed minorities in order to wage a broad-gauged struggle against inequality. The crowd, to my surprise, cheered loudest at the most radical moments in the speech — leading Dave Wertheimer to wonder later (as if the reaction had been almost too good to be true) if they had actually understood what I'd been saying. I think they did; the large (500?) crowd seemed young, intense and decidedly activist. When Mayor Koch, who preceded me, tried to read the official proclamation, the "Koch is killing us" signs jabbed the sky and the catcalls were so loud not a word Koch was saying could be heard.

Hizzoner stood there, characteristically, with a smug, fixed grin—but at least knew enough, once his gig was up, to beat a hasty retreat. My opening line—"I take no pride in sharing a platform with Ed Koch, but I do take pride in the event for which we've gathered"—proved a crowd-pleaser.

SEPTEMBER 20, 1989

Lisa [*Duggan*] and Nan [*Hunter*] gave an interesting presentation at the center's first monthly colloquium of the season last night. They argued that lesbians experience their sexuality differently than do gay men—and thus the difficulties when the two try to work together politically. Women, in their view, come to their sexuality later, as a result of a process; see it as mutable over time (rather than feeling, as gay men do, that at a certain point they "discovered the truth," and until that point had "lived a false life"); and believe their orientation is related to choice, attached to the will.

The choice, moreover, hinges on gender solidarity rather than (gay male) genital arousal. Whereas gay men—like men in general—see their sexuality as animal, uncontrollable, lesbians see it embedded in social relations. Liberal gay male politics fits male experience, but not female, for whom politics descends from gender. This was less true during the early days of GLF—and of AIDS politics today. In those two cases the issues were not about an "ethnic" minority wanting its rights, but rather about control of the body by the state.

The ethnic model dominates the gay legal struggle—and probably must, since it carries the advantage of familiarity (tribal politics) for other Americans and is based on the comfortable notion of coalition politics, which everyone understands; this way we just add "sexual orientation" to an already long list of protected minority differences. But the anti-gay opposition understands, even if gay politicians chose not to, that gender dissent is the real issue at stake, the real cutting edge of rebellion—and thus fiercely lashes out at "gay marriage" or the idea of women participating in combat.

All this is extremely provocative, if (in my view) over-simplified.

Lisa and Nan, ironically, present the concept of lesbian sexual mutability as itself immutable, a truth forever fixed rather than one more transient cultural artifact. Also, I felt uneasily reminded of Erik Erikson's airtight categories and his notion of female "inner space"—an effort to present women as *innately* different, which (rightly) brought feminist wrath down on his head.

NOVEMBER 5, 1989

Yesterday's all-day center retreat came off better than I would have predicted . . . we started in with a review of our history which, as we recounted it, helped remind us that our real enemies were outside the room not in it—meaning not only institutional homophobia, but those in our own midst who (like Boswell and Dynes) do *not* believe in gender parity and those whose own power-hunger (like KG and MW) gets expressed in self-righteous hysteria. . . . I acknowledged that my own work drive makes me impatient of those less willing or able to accomplish as much as fast. . . . I don't mind working the hardest but I do mind getting back resentment for it . . . and I also can get impatient with people not doing the few chores they do volunteer for.

Jim [*Saslow*] and Seymour [*Kleinberg*] suggested that my commitment is greater than anyone else's because I'm the founder—it's my baby and I want it to survive. True enough. But as I said, my ego-investment in the center is not nearly as high as they presume. I tie my ego to my books not to institutional success, and I long for the day . . . when I can retire to my study to write them. And then it struck me—leave *now*. . . . That led to a good discussion. A number of people felt that the center would "collapse" without me, that I was "the glue and the motor." But others thought that after a period of transition . . . the organization would come through. . . . I pointed out that eventually the founder does have to step aside if an organization is to develop a personality and ongoing life. . . . I feel as if a huge burden has been lifted from me. It isn't at all clear that I'll be able to extricate quickly—or even that the center [*which we'd begun*

to refer to as CLAGS] will survive—but at the least I've made it clear
that push-come-to-shove I won't put up with excessive abuse, *don't*
want to control CLAGS as a one man operation, and *am* determined
to set it up and then leave it to others to run. [*It was finally agreed
that we'd revisit the question sometime soon, but as it turned out, I
wasn't able to get free of CLAGS until 1996.*]

NOVEMBER 19, 1989

Eli's benefit for CLAGS was a great success: 350–400 people;
$17,000 gross (about $11,000 net) . . . and with almost no assist from
the CLAGS board: "too busy."

NOVEMBER 23, 1989

I went reluctantly to see [*Virgil Thomson's and Gertrude Stein's*]
"Four Saints in Three Acts" . . . figuring it would probably be yet another overpraised "masterpiece." But I loved it. For a piece 50 years
old, it has a startlingly contemporary camp tone. Indeed, it prefig-
ures a sensibility said to have been invented at Stonewall. In our
seemingly endless (and repetitive) debates these days about "what
constitutes 'gay culture'?" it will do well to remember "Four Saints."
Its attitude of mocking irreverence, its refusal of the familiar—even
of the standard juxtapositions of language and narrative structure—
comes close to the heart of "gay sensibility." It is subversion disguised
as inconsequence.

NOVEMBER 28, 1989

In classical Athens (according to David Halperin) sex was performed
by one person on another: sex was not *with* someone, was not done
with their cooperation nor for their benefit—let alone enveloped in
an ideology of emotional mutuality. Sex is asymmetrical and polariz-
ing, not shared and unifying. I think this comes closer, even today, to
describing how most people would *prefer* (if moral ideology had not

dulled their instincts) to have sex. Thus the penchant of many gay men, those less bound by social convention, for the anonymity of bath-houses, piers and orgy rooms. Here as elsewhere gay men *have* done basic reclamation work, have, in their sexual explorations, led the way for everyone out of the claustrophobic chambers of bourgeois ro-mance—and for their efforts earned enmity and fear.

DECEMBER 7, 1989

Panel at CLAGS on "butch/femme." Eli and I were practically the only men in a sea of 500 women, standing room only. Yet the women in our immediate environs were friendly; none of that "why are you invading our space?" stuff of only a few years back. Another notable shift in sensibility was the wholly *un*controversial nature of the subject matter; no matter what any of the panelists said, she was greeted with a tidal wave of supportive applause. . . . Almost all the hard questions—"To what extent does butch/femme ape and parody patriarchal models?" "Can a sexuality not based on mutual pleasur-ing be considered egalitarian?" etc.—the ones that until recently used to turn such symposia into cauldrons of contentiousness, were evaded or dealt with simplistically. The celebratory note seems to have wholly displaced controversy. . . .

DECEMBER 12, 1989

A fascinating evening last night listening to Dick Isay's talk at the New York Psychoanalytic Society. The talk fascinating, and also the response. Isay is smart *and* self-aware. He's able to acknowledge that in disclosing his homosexuality to his patients, he runs the risk of using self-revelation as a means of forming social alliances to coun-teract his professional isolation. And he sees, too, that disclosure, weighted on the side of "reality" rather than fantasy, can inhibit transference (a risk worth running in a homophobic culture, given the likely gain for the patient in self-esteem when confronted with the reality of a positive role model).

As deeply sympathetic as I felt toward Isay, and as admiring of his courage, some doubts persist. He assumes sexual orientation is a biological given, whereas there is considerable contrary evidence. . . . plus radical gay analysis that urges us to work for a breaking down of the dualistic categories of gay or straight. . . . Also *does* empathy hinge on sameness? Does sameness guarantee empathy? Isn't it possible deeply to understand another even across a divide of differentness? Probably yes—*if* the desire exists really to understand, and to put in the needed work carefully to elicit details about a life centrally different from our own rather than glibly and quickly assuming our ability to empathize.

Given the audience response to Isay, few heterosexual analysts are yet willing to commit to a serious effort to understand the differentness of gay lives and relationships. Otto Kernberg arrogantly announced from the floor that analysts are not conventional people and do transcend the narrow prejudices of the culture in which they function—thereby conveniently ignoring the history of psychoanalysis in America, a record of slavish devotion to mainstream mores.

*B*y 1990, *gay activism surrounding AIDS had galvanized the community, heightened visibility, and produced some measurable political progress that would have been unimaginable a decade earlier. As late as 1986, President Reagan had refused even to utter the word AIDS, let alone allotted any resources to combat it, and his attorney general, Edwin Meese, had sanctioned firing anyone who co-workers merely perceived as having AIDS and causing them to fear contamination. That same year William F. Buckley published a piece advocating that gay men with AIDS be tattooed on the rear end (and drug users on the arm). Three months after that pitiless prescription, the Supreme Court, in its notorious decision* Bowers v. Hardwick, *ruled that the state could legally arrest gay people having sex in the privacy of their own homes.*

By early 1990 more than fifty thousand people had died of AIDS, with double that number known to be affected with the virus. No successful treatment had yet emerged, and every effort to spread "safe sex"

information had been blocked by a frothing batch of conservatives insistent that any allocation of resources for prevention was the equivalent of actively promoting a vile, diseased sexuality. Before the
Stonewall riots in 1969 and the formation of the modern gay movement that immediately followed, gay people would probably have hidden away from such public scorn (just as they had surrendered to
forcible electric shock treatments, lockups in psychiatric hospitals, and
even prescribed lobotomies).

But the earlier attitude of pardon-me-for-existing had given way to
a fierce assertion, led by the vanguard activists of ACT-UP, of the right
to be alive, and stay alive. These activists not only demanded that the
federal government release significant sums for research but also that
full access to experimental drugs and treatments be open to everyone;
with a new disease, they militantly argued, the afflicted were entitled
to take their chances rather than simply wait around while new drugs
wended their slow way through the pipelines of traditional research.

Many of these activists were privileged white men who had grown
up in the more permissive post-Stonewall climate and had felt entitled
not only to their sexuality, but to all else. Passivity and helplessness
weren't part of their makeup or vocabulary. Instead of collapsing, they
became angry and resistant when confronted by obstacles. They
formed buyers clubs to import promising drugs from abroad, they
marched at home against drug companies that kept their prices high,
and they pressured the Food and Drug Administration to release AZT
before completing the usual three-phase efficacy trials (until 1991, it
remained the only FDA-approved treatment for AIDS).

In 1988 thousands of ACT-UP demonstrators from across the country gathered at FDA headquarters in Rockville, Maryland, where their
representatives met with agency officials and, remarkably, succeeded
in getting the FDA's drug approval process foreshortened. ACT-UP
had confronted the federal government's indifference head-on and,
through persistent protest, had made notable dents in its defensive ar-
mor. The ACT-UP confrontations also produced considerable media
coverage, and the images many Americans saw on television or in their
newspapers contradicted the long-standing stereotypes of frightened

sissies and their roughnecked sisters. By 1990 there were fifty openly gay elected officials around the country (compared with half a dozen in 1980), and the Human Rights Campaign Fund, a gay lobbying group, ranked twenty-fifth on the list of the country's most powerful fund raisers. In 1987 only 33 percent of adults believed that homosexual relations between consenting adults should be legal. By 1989, a Gallup poll revealed that the figure had jumped to 47 percent.

There were several downsides to this seeming success story. Many gay people, especially minorities, lacked health insurance to pay for the emergent drug therapies, and lacked, too, a place at the table with government officials that ACT-UP's all-white, all-male Treatment and Data Committee had gradually won. The members of that committee, having increasingly mastered the arcana of current viral science, had become insiders, and were sharply accused by other members of the gay community with advocating primarily for people like themselves; antagonism and fractiousness became so intense by 1992, that the Data Committee broke away entirely from ACT-UP and set up as the Treatment Action Group (TAG). In the meantime, the death toll from AIDS continued its relentless rise, even as one briefly touted medication after another—AL-721, dextran sulfate, Compound Q, DDI, AZT—failed to live up to its initial promise.

On other fronts as well, matters had pretty much stalemated. In 1990, Reagan's Supreme Court twice refused to consider constitutional challenges to the military's refusal to allow openly gay people to serve. Draconian sodomy laws still remained on the books in twenty-four states, and the legislatures of only two states—Wisconsin and Massachusetts—had passed laws barring discrimination against gay people (and only seven U.S. cities had as yet put "domestic partnership," which granted gay people some of the same rights as married couples, on the books). At the same time, violence against gays and lesbians had become an increasingly popular after-hours sport: in 1990 gay people were seven times more likely to become victims of violent assault than other Americans. It was only with the brutal murder of Matthew Shepard in 1998 that the American Psychoanalytic Association would hold its very first forum on homophobia (there had been

countless ones through the years on the "causes" and "cures" of homosexuality).

Closer to my own bailiwick, academia, the 1990 report card
showed slow but discernible progress. Thanks to David Clarke's
$20,000 bequest, the $11,000 netted from Eli's benefit, and our first
foundation grant (a $10,000 matching gift from the gay-funded Paul
Rapoport Foundation, which continued to help support us for years
to come), CLAGS had finally, after five years of trying, raised the required $50,000 to start us through the certification process that in
April 1991 would finally lead to our establishment as a formal research center of the CUNY Graduate School. As a result of articles in
the Chronicle of Higher Education and the Advocate, word had earlier spread that we were about to open our doors and I began to get a
steady stream of letters from would-be graduate students eager to pursue a doctorate in lesbian and gay studies.

Alas, we were a long way from being able to offer such a program
(even today, nearly twenty years later, no PhD in LGBT studies exists
anywhere in the country). As I tried to explain to the many people who
wrote to me, we had barely gotten a leg over the barricades and the
only way CLAGS could have gotten formal accreditation at all was as
a research center, not as a department that could hire faculty and offer courses or degrees. One undergraduate major in lesbian and gay
studies did exist at the City College of San Francisco; and San Francisco State, in 1990, soon hoped to offer a minor in the field. That
was it.

At the same time, the prior advent of women's studies had helped
to sensitize academia to the importance of issues relating to gender
and sexuality—just as the Stonewall riots of 1969 had spawned a
modern gay liberation movement that had in turn quickly led to the
search for historical "roots." Long-buried and uncataloged archival
sources began to surface, providing research materials for an emerging
generation of lesbian and gay scholars—and the 1990s would see a
proliferation of books and articles, as well as new academic journals
(Genders; Journal of the History of Sexuality; Out/Look; GLQ).

There had, of course, been a few precedents: as long ago as 1897, Magnus Hirschfeld and associates had established the Scientific-Humanitarian Committee in Berlin; and in this country, the late 1950s had seen the creation in California of ONE, Inc., which had developed a research facility. More recently the Canadian Gay Archives had been established, and in this country gay activists and academics in a growing number of localities had begun to explore available source materials.

In addition, more and more gay faculty (most of them protected by tenure) had begun to offer single courses at a number of universities under the auspices of the traditional departments (English, history, etc.) to which they belonged. At the CUNY Graduate School, the existence of CLAGS encouraged a proliferation of course offerings, and a critical mass of openly lesbian and gay students were soon arriving to take them. A considerable number of those, on reaching the dissertation level, would opt for writing their doctoral theses on gay-themed subjects—even while being fully aware that they were limiting their employability. To this day, some of those who do manage to find full- or part-time academic jobs do so under general rubrics like "cultural studies" or "gender studies."

The presence on many campuses of a significant number of liberals ("Of course gay people are entitled to the full rights of citizenship") proved critical in allowing lesbian and gay studies to gain a toehold. But as I kept discovering, unpleasantly, a willingness to grant us basic rights wasn't remotely the equivalent of actually wanting to know about our lives—let alone of believing that our distinctive perspectives might have anything of importance to say to them. Even as these liberals fell in love with, and broadly announced, their own tolerance, they seemed clueless about the patronization that so often characterized their actual tone when dealing with us ("What you people need to understand is that . . .).

This was far truer of straight white male scholars than female or minority ones. The latter, after all, knew a great deal about being kept outside the centers of power—and how being on the margins often *gave them greater insight into the psyches and behavior of the Big Boys than those self-reverential smarty-pants had about themselves. Women also know—having themselves long been relegated to the private realm—the inherent falsity of such commonplace statements as "what gay people do in the privacy of their own homes is of no concern of ours."*

The liberal adoption of "the privacy principle" is an effective shield against letting too much subversive information get through, the equivalent of building a wall between gay and straight that not only perpetuates the fallacious het/homo binary but conveniently protects straight male academia from learning more about the actual complexity of gay lives and the challenging findings of gay scholarship. Even male scholars further to the left than merely "liberal" (Eric Hobsbawm, say, or Bogdan Denitch) seal themselves off from the realities of gay experience—or as Todd Gitlin scornfully put it, being "overly concerned with protecting and purifying what they imagine to be their identities."

Many left-wingers, on campus and off, position themselves as radicals on economic and class issues but are utterly traditional in regard to feminist and gay concerns. Zealous in challenging the economic status quo, they are no less zealous in defending the status quo in regard to cultural issues. Michael Tomasky, to give one example, has cavalierly dismissed "supposedly oppositional" gay culture with its "superficially transgressive ideas." Supposedly? Superficially? None of these left-wing traditionalists could conceivably express such views if they'd read a word of Eve Sedgwick or Judith Butler. If they had, they'd have to take seriously some of the basic insights of queer history and theory: the performative aspects of gender, the viable parameters of friendship, the shifting shape across time and culture of such purported universals as the nuclear family, monogamy, lifelong pair-bonding, and the uncertain linkage between love and sex—as well as the omnipresence in all of us of a wildly anarchic, unorthodox range of erotic fantasy and desire.

1990s

At the end of the "Whose History?" panel last night at the New-York Historical Society (NYHS), a young man with a large ACT-UP button on his label came up to me and said he wanted me to know how I ended up (belatedly) on the panel: "When I got the NYHS mailing," he said, "and saw that gay/lesbian history had been omitted, I wrote in protest to the director of public programs. She wrote back that NYHS simply couldn't afford another fee (a big $250). To which he responded, "That simply isn't good enough. *One way or the other* we will be represented at that event." The director got the message — and out went the call to me. Good old ACT-UP!

The "young man," I soon learned, was in fact forty-five and his name was Bob Rafsky. He'd been a public relations executive until 1989, when he quit to devote his time entirely to ACT-UP. Arrested several times in civil disobedience demonstrations, he became ACT-UP's media coordinator in New York and a well-known figure in the struggle against AIDS. Soon after the NYHS panel, Rafsky sent me the pertinent correspondence. I reprint excerpts below to demonstrate the kind of liberal double-speak I just wrote about — to say nothing of illuminating Rafsky's organizing skills and eloquent prose.

RAFSKY TO NYHS, FEBRUARY 2, 1990

"Here we are, in New York, in 1990, in the midst of an epidemic beyond imagining. One of the few consolations of these plague years — if the very idea of consolation is not obscene — is that it has forced us all to focus on the presence of gays and lesbians everywhere, and the implications of that presence — social, political, historical. . . ." NYHS's advance announcement of the "Whose History?" panel had noted that it would examine "the role of race, nationality and gender in contemporary historical thinking," and that the panelists would speak from the vantage points of women, Puerto Ricans, blacks and Asian Americans.

Rafsky continued: "But is something missing from this panel? Is something missing? I doubt you can appreciate how angry it makes me to have to take time from dealing with my life and the epidemic to write a letter that, in effect, forces me to justify my existence to you. And who are you?

"The only thing that makes me angrier is the prospect of having to deal with your reply and whatever rationalizations and excuses it trails with it. What are my obligations here? Do I have to tell you what you should do by March 29 [*the evening of the panel*]? Do I have to make clear what I think our community will do if you don't do what you should?"

NYHS'S FEBRUARY 7, 1990, REPLY, NEARLY IN ITS ENTIRETY

". . . Because of limited funding, we were not able to address the concerns of the gay and lesbian community at this time. But we do plan in the near future to have a series entitled 'New York City in Crisis,' and at that time will address the issue of the AIDS epidemic and health care policy. I will keep your letter on file, and contact you at the time of the event so that you can be in attendance. . . . I hope that what I have written brings some clarity to the issues raised."

RAFSKY TO NYHS, FEBRUARY 23, 1990, IN ITS ENTIRETY

"'Limited funding' prevented you from adding a panelist to a panel that already had four members and a moderator? And the omission just happened to be the gay and lesbian community? Aren't you ashamed, at some level, to write this sort of thing?

"No, we're not going to wait for some ghettoized panel on AIDS to be recognized by the New York Historical Society, which uses our tax money to insult us.

"We're going to stand tall with our black, Latino and Asian-American brothers and sisters. And we're going to do it on March 29, with or without your cooperation."

A few days later, Rafsky sent near-duplicate letters to both NYHS's president and chairperson, to the commissioner of New York City's Department of Cultural Affairs, and to state senators Manfred Ohrenstein and Roy Goodman (who had gotten state funds allocated to help cover the costs of the panel). To all, Rafsky sent approximately the same message:

"I assume you're not aware of the slap in the face the New York Historical Society plans to give the gay and lesbian community on March 29—with money from the Department of Cultural Affairs.

"I also assume that, once made aware, you'll take steps to prevent it. . . ."

What happened next—who stepped on whose toes, and how hard—is unrecorded. But on March 8, Bob Rafsky got another letter from NYHS, quite different in tone, acknowledging that the society had been "remiss" in not having included a gay or lesbian historian in the first place, informing him that I would now be on the panel, and thanking him for his "interest in The New-York Historical Society."

As I later wrote Rafsky, "You're a snazzy letter writer; most 'persuasive.' . . . You did a great job! One more confirmation of the respectful awe I feel for the ACT-UP generation."

Three years later, Bob Rafsky was dead of AIDS.

MAY 16, 1990

Now that we've finally raised the needed $50,000, I've started the rounds of calls and meetings requisite to getting CLAGS put before the CUNY Board of Trustees this fall. Today was Dean H. He . . .

cautions that even after we get Board approval, finding us office space—a desk!—is going to be "difficult."

W*as it ever! When CLAGS was finally approved by the board of trustees in April 1991, it wasn't until some ten months later (in the interim, my own graduate school office had to double as the CLAGS office) that a "space" was found for us. An unusable space. It contained one desk and chair, no lighting in the ceiling, paint peeling off the walls, a single window so covered with filth that one could just about make out the brick wall it faced, ancient (and limited) file cabinets, loose wires scattered all over the floor, no typewriter or computer, no working phones—and not even a key to the bathroom.*

When my complaints went unheeded, I finally did a one-man sit-in outside the office of the vice president of the graduate school. After an hour's wait in the corridor, he finally agreed to see me in his elegantly appointed office, swiveling luxuriously in his Eames chair, puffing cigar smoke in my direction. I should have laughed, I suppose, but my anger won out: "We don't, of course, expect fancy chairs—like yours—but it'd be nice to have two beat-up old ones, and—perhaps you'll think this excessive—one 40-watt bulb so that when a visiting scholar comes to call, one of us wouldn't have to stand throughout and we could at least make out the contours of each other's faces." The vice president showed no sign of chagrin, though slowly, a wire or cabinet at a time, CLAGS's physical space did become more habitable.

MAY 22, 1990

John H. has advanced lymphoma. The most vibrant and energetic of all the people at PWA [*People With Aids Coalition*]—and the one I'm fondest of—I thought of him as an encouraging example of how one can be HIV positive and yet uncompromised in health. He turns out instead to be an example of how suddenly and unexpectedly the virus can impinge . . . the "breakthrough" drugs so long anticipated are still stalled in the pipeline, thanks to the government's continuing indifference to the fate of queers and druggies.

JUNE 28, 1990

Put in my usual Tuesday from 2–6 answering the phones at PWA. Dennis was back after a bout with meningitis, back with full-throated campy hilarity, insisting he's just waiting for his welfare check before retiring to Atlanta—"the only place you can get a good haircut." What great spirit they all have. . . . It was the same when I visited John in the hospital on Saturday. There he is with lymphoma and an untreated "blood clot on the brain"—smiling and planning away. Vito [Russo], too, is a bundle of positive energy, talking about "feeling a little better every day." Is this merely denial? I don't think so.

JULY 24, 1990

At PWA today we stuffed envelopes with a grim letter describing the organization's desperate financial situation. . . . Meantime, the gloom thickens on other counts, too: Vito [Russo] is in the hospital getting chemo; John felt so bad he had to leave PWA today and go home to bed; and Ken [*Dawson*], who was here for dinner last night, looked drawn and ill, and spoke in a low, energy-less voice light years from his vibrant self—though he bravely stayed the full evening.

AUGUST 14, 1990

. . . a benefit for Barney Frank at Adam Rose's house on Fire Island . . . Barney radiates warmth and intelligence, though for my tastes, he studded his remarks with too many ritualistic apologies for his past "mistakes" [*hiring male hustlers*]. "Mistakes-schmakes," I told him privately—"big deal." He looked amused and startled, as if no one had ever before suggested that wanting to sleep with gorgeous men, and being willing to pay them, was less than a cardinal sin.

NOVEMBER 7, 1990

Vito died this morning. With no hope of recovery, and with assorted medical interventions of the last two weeks doing little more than heightening his suffering, I suppose it's a blessing. . . . Getting to know him better than ever before over these past four months [*I was part of his "team"*], I came to admire his resilient will, the resolutely positive way he faced every crisis. Yesterday, when I entered his hospital room, he was shivering under a pile of blankets—yet insisting to the doctor that he felt decidedly improved. . . .

DECEMBER 21, 1990

Vito's memorial yesterday upset me more than I anticipated. Some of it was the poignancy of the large turnout, the hugging and kissing, the sense of a genuine community, the unexpected reunions. Some of it was Vito's own omnipresence on film clips and posters—the vitality of his image in such sad contrast to the purpose of the day. Some of it was the bravery of so many—Ken [Dawson], Damien Martin, etc.—themselves weakened and endangered, in attending what must have felt, devastatingly, like a rehearsal for their own services.

JANUARY 15, 1991

We devoted the colloquium tonight to a discussion among ourselves of the mission of gay/lesbian studies. . . . W. gave one of his marbly & meandering defenses of "pure scholarship," aloof from the "transient claims of the everyday world." To which I and others reminded him that the "pure" data sometimes best reveals itself to the researcher who brings to it the richest experience—including that of "the everyday world." I don't believe CLAGS should focus or tailor its work to the current needs of a political community, but I do believe that an individual's involvement in the community will quicken & enrich whatever scholarship he or she pursues apart from it. Our scholarly agenda should not be tied to political needs, but our scholars—for the sake of their scholarship alone, to say nothing of pay-back to the community that spawned it—need to be as humanly broad as possible.

As we were talking, we could hear a peace march in progress on the street below. Possibly we should have adjourned & joined it, though there will be ample such opportunities in the weeks ahead as [*President George H. W.*] Bush attempts to push *his* manhood by cutting off the lives of thousands of others. As brutal & stubborn as Saddam is, Bush seems only marginally less so—intransigently refusing a general conference on the Middle East which *might* (no more than that) lead to an Iraqi pullout from Kuwait. As the momentum builds toward war, no sights are more gruesome than the nightly TV interviews with gung-ho American twenty-year-olds seemingly eager to "bring things to a head" & "do the job we're here for." No one seems to remember the Vietnam bodybags—or seems ever to have seen the mangled wards of a VA hospital.

JANUARY 17, 1991

We're twelve hours into war. Bush came on TV last night with his usual obfuscating patriotism; the real message is his presence—the affectless voice, the thin, cruel smile curled around his mouth ("The war toys work! We *are* the biggest bully on the block!"). Briefings from [*defense secretary*] Cheney & [*General Colin*] Powell, neither of whom are exactly heroes of mine, were far more presidential, their tone conveying some appropriate sense of the possible toll in lives. As of now, the toll is low, but when and if the Iraqis counterattack, and ground forces are engaged, that will change gruesomely. The one hope now is for a quick end.

JANUARY 22, 1991

The country is crowing over the "technological precision" of our marvelous new weapons of death. That is, when it isn't self-righteously wringing its hands over the three civilian casualties in Israel from Saddam's missile attack. We, of course, our commentators tell us,

are fighting a *clean* war against military targets only (as if the death
of Iraqi soldiers, some of them terrified 16-year-olds, is less than
nothing). But that claim is crap anyway. Our carpet bombings are
killing thousands of Iraqi civilians, though no mention of it gets on
TV (is it solely managed news, or also managed brains?) Yes, Saddam is despicable, but the Beast of Baghdad is not the only one with
blood on his hands.

JANUARY 24, 1991

Meeting in Bob [*Robert Jay*] Lifton's office to discuss an organized response to the war. About 20 people. Some old hands from REDRESS
[*a protest group I was part of during the Vietnam War*] — Florence
Falk, Karen Malpede, Peter Weiss . . . But mostly people I didn't know;
a few of whom I quickly grew to dislike — especially N., a smug, glam-
orous 30-year-old with volubly firm opinions on *everything*.

The point wasn't to make new friends. Not that the political talk
was particularly inspiring either — mostly the noisy trading of the
minimal information we all already have. And suggestions for how to
proceed were the usual compound of sense and nonsense: Open a
"citizen's dialogue" with the Iraqis! Have a citywide teach-in! *Demand* a cease fire and a Middle East peace conference! . . . The upshot of two hours of talk was the usual feeble result: a committee to
draft a newspaper ad. Well, at least that will offer something to respond to, and a possible rallying point for more potent efforts in the
future. It doesn't do to be too cynical about *any* effort to put a dent
in Bush's 80% approval rate.

*F*rom a piece I wrote for the Village Voice *on the war:*

> *Remember Anita Bryant and her campaign to "Save the Chil-
> dren"? Gay people knew that what she was really trying to save
> was her own narrow traditionalism, that if she cared about
> children she would have been campaigning against heterosex-*

ual males who do 98% of the molesting, and would have been
working to create educational and job opportunities to rescue
the young from despair.

Well, strong women and gentle men, get ready. The fake
sloganeers are back in force, Saving the Peace with carpet
bombing, Bolstering Democracy by censoring the news, Liberating Iraq and Kuwait by destroying them. And in the process,
once again, making our own land safe for macho militarism.

The notion of strong women may fare better in the war climate than that of gentle men. Women are being allowed to
drive jeeps, run supply depots, service aircraft and—to the horror
of our patriarchal Saudi allies—appear in full uniform on the
nightly news making appropriate gung ho noises, their subterranean grief and doubt either erased by TV censors or by the
felt responsibility during their ten-second bite to Say the Right
Thing—the thing that will make the folks back home Proud.

The young men in uniform, interestingly, are being allowed
this time around to express fear (though not doubt). Repeatedly on the TV screen, a sweet-faced, earnest 20-year-old will
confide to a reporter that, "yes, I'm scared." The jaw will be set,
of course, and the confession will be quickly followed with a reassuring "we'll get the job done we've been sent here to do."
But it is now apparently okay for men to acknowledge that killing is not something they do with spontaneous, fearless relish.
One might even be tempted to claim this new male expressiveness as a victory for feminism—possibly the last victory in some
time.

For differentness of all kinds is about to take a beating.
The United States has never been able to go to war while at
the same time preserving (not to mention extending) free
speech and dissent. During the Civil War Lincoln suspended
the right of habeas corpus. During World War I President
Woodrow Wilson—he, too, wanted to make the world "safe for
democracy"—had radicals like Emma Goldman rounded up

and deported (to Russia, of course, and on a leaky vessel that had been condemned as "not seaworthy"). And during World War II, as even Hollywood has gotten around to showing, Japanese-Americans were confined to prison camps—just in case they might be tempted to dissent.

Even before the war in the Gulf, the government had shown its impatience with bleeding hearts and bleating losers. As the gap between rich and poor widened during the eighties, as cities decayed and the environment deteriorated, as millions of Americans went without decent health care, satisfying work or work at all, blacks were told they already had all the civil rights they needed, women that they were neglecting their children, people with AIDS that they were making "unreasonable" demands for speeded up research. The sum of compassion in the eighties was "God helps those who help themselves." The unspoken motto was "I'm all right, Jack."

It can only get worse now. George Bush and the mirror-image boy/men who surround him—like the boss cold, shallow and vindictive—feel wonderfully vindicated by the triumph of traditional "virtues": by our ability once again quickly to mobilize resources for war, to outperform everybody else in the technological wonder of our killing machines, to reassert our claim to be the toughest kid on the block, to matter. Everything worth doing, in the Bush hierarchy of values, we have proven we can still do superlatively well. That excludes, of course, waging war against poverty, discrimination and disease.

None of which is to say that Saddam Hussein is not a bloody tyrant and, probably, a psychopath. But he is not as direct a threat to our well-being as are undernourished children, despairing teenagers, AIDS-infected young people and homeless multitudes (Oh, what a single day's war costs—a billion dollars—would do to ease the suffering of these outcast Americans!). Nor is Saddam a threat of Hitler-like proportions to the globe—not when all he could manage after an eight-year war was a stalemate with neighboring Iran.

Besides, why have we been so selective in our opposition to dictatorship? Why did we not move against the brutality of Idi Amin? Why did we not come to the aid of the massacred people of East Timor? Why, indeed, were we indifferent to Saddam's own previous slaughter of the Kurds? Why is it only now that we have decided he is a monster who must at all costs be stopped?

Is it just possible the decision has something to do with matters other than a selfless defense of democracy (the "democracy," mind you, of Kuwait, where no women and only 8% of the male population is allowed to vote)? Like wanting to protect our oil supply, say. Like making it necessary for Germany and Japan to deal directly through us, as the next century's resident power in the Middle East, for its energy sources. Like, perhaps most basic of all, allowing the élite of white men who control our country once again to believe that they cannot be bypassed or supplanted. Neither patiently waiting for sanctions to work, nor joining a general Middle East peace conference would serve those ends nearly as well as a screeching, terrifying display of brute power.

And to reassert this macho meanness of spirit, many must die—including multitudes of Iraqis no less innocent than the many American soldiers forced to an impossible choice between an understandable wish to win certification at home and their own humane instincts. Abroad we will become hated conquerors, a hate that will pursue us for generations. At home we will see the suppression of all impulses to non-conformity, all dissent from the heterosexist white male model.

The body bags and V.A. hospitals will soon be filling. And Anita Bryant is singing in the wings.

When I accepted an offer to join the CUNY system back in 1972, I was asked to teach at the Graduate Center as well as on one of the undergraduate campuses. For the time being I declined, preferring for a while just to teach undergraduates. I'd grown tired in recent *years of the dutiful way graduate students wrote down everything I said as if it was Truth. But I did offer to sit on PhD exams and read PhD theses until the urge to produce scholarly offspring returned.*

By the mid-seventies, I'd become increasingly involved in the brand-new field of the history of sexuality and at that point I went back to the Graduate Center and said that I'd be willing, after all, to offer a course on that subject—that I needed older students with more information and experience to bounce ideas off. The reaction was immediate: no. Gertrude Himmelfarb, chair of the Graduate Center History Department at the time, acerbically told me that the department felt that sexual history wasn't "real" history at all; it had been spawned by political polemics, not scholarly necessity. As if activism hasn't always ignited scholarship—the feminist movement and feminist studies, the black movement and black studies. As if a scholar's political and social views don't always, consciously or not, color their narratives (Himmelfarb herself, a right-wing conservative, being among the more notorious current examples). My standing as a legitimate scholar, she told me, might well be at stake.

I wasn't entirely surprised. Back in 1974, Dennis Rubini, an openly gay historian at Temple University, and I had submitted a proposal for a panel on "the history of sexuality" (not the more inflammatory "lesbian and gay history") for the American Historical Association's annual convention; not getting any response, we'd inquired and been told that the proposal "seems to have gotten unaccountably lost." We resubmitted the following year, and this time were formally rejected.

While prepared for the Graduate Center's turndown, it nonetheless angered me and I reached for the only card in my deck. If my scholarship was now regarded as tainted, I told the history faculty, then surely it wouldn't want me contaminating its innocent students: surely it would be best if I no longer sat on PhD exams or read PhD theses. Should the faculty decide at some future point that the history of sexual behavior was a legitimate subject, I'd be glad, once more, to serve as a PhD examiner and mentor.

*And there the stalemate held for some fifteen years, as the national—
and Graduate Center—climate slowly changed. Finally, in 1991, my
graduate seminar on gay and lesbian history was formally approved.*

FEBRUARY 7, 1991

Thirty seven students showed up last night for the seminar ("Reclaiming Gay/Lesbian History, Politics and Culture") at the Graduate Center—including two faculty members, students from NYU,
Rutgers & the Univ. of Rochester, & representing nearly every con-
ceivable field (yes, even Japanese literature!) *except* history (Joe W.
says the history students are afraid to sign up because the dept. is no-
toriously conservative). The official registration list had only sixteen
names & the actual turnout stunned—and thrilled—me. It confirms
the wish/need for gay/lesbian studies & sends a clear message to the
university's powers-that-be.

Since my whole point in giving the course is to excite interest in
the field, I'm not going to turn anyone away (tho I had originally cut
off enrollment at 20, wanting to preserve an intimate, informal atmosphere). But I told them last night that they were all welcome &
to keep the size manageable I would break the group into two parts
& give a second seminar on another evening. We'll put that decision
off until next week, to see if the same number turns up. Anyway, I'm
hugely excited, & gratified. . . .

FEBRUARY 14, 1991

Not only did the seminar number hold last night, but it went *up* to
40! I've divided them into two separate groups, Mon. & Wed. nights.
It's going to complicate my life—I was feeling over-extended without
the additional seminar—but I couldn't in conscience do otherwise.
The actual session was an eye-opener. This *is* a different gay generation! At times during the discussion, I felt as if I was scrambling to
keep up; the new deconstruction terminology, of which Amanda

and Liz seem especially adept, indeed dazzling, had me recharging every remaining synapse. I was so excited when I got home that I didn't fall asleep until 3:00. . . .

FEBRUARY 21, 1991

My first talk of two [on "Gay and Lesbian Studies"] at the Museum of Natural History went well—about 400 people showed up. It had the excited feel of an historic occasion—the first time one of NYC's major cultural institutions opened its doors fully to gay/lesbian subject matter. It became clear why in the dressing room prior to my going on. Malcolm Arth, head of programming at the Museum, came by to get some info for the introduction and came out to me directly (though he says he's in the closet still at the Museum). From what I could gather, he dislikes the new administration, has chosen to retire at the end of this year & saw this two part series as a kind of nose-thumbing at the powers-that-be. He also said that the Museum is honeycombed with gay curators, none of whom are out, all of whom would be in avid attendance at the lecture.

FEBRUARY 26, 1991

. . . That trio of whiz kids, Amanda, Liz, and Joan, had at me with stilettos for my presumptuous privileging (oh, that newest catch-word) of the ability to tolerate contradictory impulses (and therefore to play a variety of sexual roles) over the unvarying, fixed desire of, say, a stone butch or a sadistic top. Their scorn for my "knee-jerk humanism" had me grinding my teeth . . . like all good students, they have to test whether I'm smart enough, progressive enough, tough enough, to warrant their trust and respect. Whether I passed the test is problematic . . . they certainly had me on the ropes for a bit trying to define "intimacy" (or even "prove" its existence, other than as a stale bourgeoisie invention), trying to argue that its presence in a relationship was something to be especially valued. . . .

MARCH 5, 1991

The Monday class was a pisser again. I opened it by saying how much I'd been thinking about what happened last time and that I needed to share some of my feelings. I reiterated my view that each person has the right to do what he/she wants to with their body, and said I regretted if some of my remarks had suggested otherwise, apparently making several of them feel that their S/M lifestyle was under attack. But I didn't want simply to make nice. I reiterated, too, that I thought we were all inescapable judgment machines, and that I'd hoped in the safety of the seminar we could give those private judgments expression, deeply using ourselves (my old sixties shtick!) in conjunction with the reading material—that in regard to today's topic, transsexualism, for example, we could freely explore whether we felt it was pioneering gender transformation or was intrinsically pathological (displaced homophobia). Several of them immediately insisted instead that we use *texts* (their nineties shtick!) as our channels and intermediaries for discussion. So we had what in fact was a quite traditional, impersonal two-hour seminar in which we skillfully dissected the "ideological paradigms" of the reading. At the end of it, I expressed some discontent with the even-keeled, even tedious impersonality of the discussion, and this time Matt jumped in to say we were "copping out" in our refusal to accept and express our value judgments. But he quickly succumbed to the three-way female counterblast. It all left me deeply unsettled, feeling simultaneously angry at their intransigence, incompetent in struggling with their new vocabulary and perspectives, chagrined at the prospect that the fierce three viewed me as an "old" gay . . . one more old fogey in power. Anyway, if I can stay open, can continue to voice my uncertainties and try to listen to their objections, this could well turn into the most important learning experience for me in the twenty years since I've been at Lehman [*the undergraduate CUNY campus*], teaching well, but on automatic pilot, to adoring fans.

MARCH 7, 1991

The Wednesday seminar, unlike the Monday, is proceeding in the warm, excited, harmonious way I had fantasized—which may mean I'll learn less from it, but it'll be a helluva lot more pleasant in the short run. Actually the two should be a good balance: I'll get solace in one, opposition and challenge in the other. . . .

MARCH 12, 1991

Monday seminar: So there I am, primed to be bighearted and dazzling—and the three scorchy talkers are absent! . . . All that impassioned dialogue in my head during the week stayed bottled up, so let's dump it here: Been thinking about why we're unable or unwilling to talk about our lives; why we choose to deflect contact through high-tech abstraction; why the rhetoric of "nonjudgmental acceptance" should sound so denunciatory; why we've chosen to view safety and honesty as opposing forces, and why we've privatized safety; why the possession of values and the wish to express them should be viewed as some sort of moral failure. Been wondering whatever happened to love, why and how a fixation on pleasuring bodies came so wholly to supplant any interest in the connection of souls.

MARCH 26, 1991

The Wed. group gets even more trusting & lively: the last session, taped by Stacey D'Erasmo for an article in *Rolling Stone*, & the tricky subject of "extreme" sex seemed to me an impressive blend of personal narratives & distanced analysis—but let's see what Stacey makes of it.

*H*ere, in part, is what Stacey made of it (Rolling Stone, *October 3, 1991):*

> *"The subject is fist-fucking. Martin Duberman . . . wants to make sure everyone in his Wednesday-night seminar, "Reclaim-*

ing Gay/Lesbian History, Politics and Culture," is comfortable
with the overall topic—what he terms "extreme sex" (fist-fucking,
man-boy love, and sadomasochism). "It's dangerous, volatile
territory," Duberman says. "Does anyone have any anxieties or
expectations?" Everyone around the seminar table is com-
posed, pencils ready, all with the astute, weary look of graduate students. . . . But for the first half-hour or so . . . the class
members seem somewhat at sea, if not the teeniest bit bored.
Duberman is attempting to be a provocateur, to raise questions about how these students (and by extension the culture)
decide what is or is not acceptable, but so far they remain unprovoked. A guarded sophistication reigns. . . .

When Duberman, still looking for an edge, suggests that
the class conduct an anonymous poll to find out where each
person actually draws the line sexually, there is at first a silent,
collective groan (How touchy-feely! How retro!) and a prolonged debate over methodology. Betsy Andrews, after object-
ing several times to the whole concept of marking some
behaviors "extreme," hits enthusiastically on the truth-or-dare
approach: "Let's concretize it to what we've done." Everyone
laughs. Duberman comments offhandedly, "I don't think many
people would have a long list of what they wouldn't do," but
English major Christopher Varga says: "I was raised Catholic.
I'd have a long list of what I think I shouldn't do, starting with
kissing." Masha Gessen offers that she "went from vanilla sex
to S&M to boredom," while Ira Elliott asks simply, "Should
we annotate the list?" . . .

Andrews unfolds the replies and reads them aloud. Some
are funny ("No animals, except maybe a nice llama or vi-
cuna"; "Necrophilia only if it's a serious relationship"), some
open-minded ("I would not personally do pain, but the thing
is, I really like my tits chewed on, so what can this mean?")
and some sad ("I draw the line at sexual acts to which at least
one of the partners cannot consent, and I say this as someone
who thought I began consenting to sex at the age of twelve")—

but bit by bit these individual acts add up to a larger cultural complexity.

The room begins to fill with ambivalence. In fact, fisting comes in third on the list of things that people find personally repugnant (sex with children and bestiality are the first two; anonymous and unsafe sex come in close behind). The discussion turns to how sex is regulated, to questions of power and cultural coercion. As feminism has long maintained, the personal is political, and Duberman is able to push even this canny group of students into an understanding of how their private lives are more determined by forces outside themselves than they might have thought. Finally, Ira asks somewhat plaintively, "Is sex sex or is sex something else?" . . .

MARCH 27, 1991

Harriet [*one of the graduate students in my course*] stopped by the office to say she has never seen a class (the Wednesday group!) run more according to feminist principles—everyone's name quickly learned, facilitators shifted, attention to process, etc. The imprimatur! Amanda does not have my number!

APRIL 17, 1991

I attended the student strike demonstration at the Graduate School. [*It was against Governor Mario Cuomo's proposal to cut $80 million from CUNY's budget, including financial aid grants; since 40 percent of CUNY's students came from families that earned less than $16,000 a year, higher tuition and decreased financial aid meant the abandonment of CUNY's 150-year-old mission of providing access to higher education for everyone seeking it. After several weeks of demonstrations on eighteen of CUNY's twenty-one campuses—some broken up by the police—Cuomo somewhat scaled back his demands.*] I was glad to see so many of the gay/lesbian students present and active. . . . And they eloquently articulated the issues, emphasizing the class/race aspects of the proposed cuts. It's good to see this generation of gay activists getting beyond the single issue politics that for so long has kept our movement marginal and isolated.

When asked by some of the lesbian and gay students involved in the protest to lead an alternative forum, a sort of "open class" on the history of radical protest movements and related topics, I readily agreed. But I ran into trouble with the CLAGS board. There were only two or three politically centrist board members, but when they caught wind of the planned forum, they argued vehemently against my participation: the CUNY board of trustees was about to take up our formal accreditation as a research center and after such a protracted struggle to legitimize gay/lesbian studies as an academic discipline, it was "a matter of self-preservation" to remain neutral in the strike.

I argued just as vehemently that I had the right, as an individual, to do as I pleased in the matter. They denied that: the board, they insisted, was the governing body of CLAGS and the executive director (me) its creature. To my surprise, a slim majority of the board sided with the centrists and voted against my participation in the forum. I felt torn by conflicting loyalties: I was bound by the board's collective decision, but I strongly agreed with the strike and wanted to lend it my support. The unsatisfying compromise I came up with was to sit in the audience during the forum, but not lead it; and to "visit" the strikers but not to urge that they take over the building. The lesbian and gay strikers knew I was in a bind and exempted me from criticism. But they did—in print—denounce the CLAGS board; as one of them wrote in Outweek, then the leading gay publication in New York, "While CLAGS can study activist movements, it cannot take an activist stance." Touché, I guiltily thought—"guiltily" because the board's stance contradicted the spirit in which I'd founded CLAGS: as a research institute that would be a haven for scholar-activists.

The board membership soon shifted, and CLAGS's original spirit was reclaimed, but in the interim I had pangs of doubt as to whether the institutionalization of lesbian/gay studies wasn't, after all—as some of the community-based scholars had earlier warned—fully com-

patible with the sort of activism that directly confronted the powers-that-be. Which didn't mean that scholarship couldn't be a form of activism. Nearly a year later, I had some reassuring confirmation from an unexpected source:

> [April 22, 1992]: *A nice call from a Gene Barfield in Vermont to tell me that* Hidden From History *[a collection of original essays on LGBT history I'd coedited with George Chauncey and Martha Vicinus] swung a key conservative vote (Megan Price) in the state legislature in favor a gay rights bill. Apparently a friend of Price's came out to her and then gave her a pile of books to read, all of which she found to be "junk," until she came to* HFH, *which genuinely changed her mind. A good example to use against those quick to denounce gay scholarship as "ivy-towered élitism" unrelated to frontline activism.*

APRIL 17, 1991

The Monday group continues to limp along in an atmosphere of simmering tension. I don't absolve myself, with my too-ready eagerness in the early sessions for no-holds-barred discussion of touchy subjects, which may have helped to establish a climate of alarm; but the continuing & relentless theoretical nit-picking by Amanda & Joan has gone a long way towards immobilizing the others, fearful of "not measuring up" to the lit crit abstractions, & in the bargain encouraging the wrath of A. & J. After I defended the right of NAMBLA to rent space at the Graduate Center & march in the Gay Pride Parade, Amanda wheeled on me & said with a smirk, "But of course you wouldn't extend those rights to S/M." She staggers me with her insistent misrepresentation of my views.

APRIL 22, 1991

The Geraldo Show called. Would I appear tomorrow with a man who "has documentary proof that he can cure homosexuals?" No, I would not. "What?!—you mean you'd let his views go unanswered!" Listen, I bellowed, his views wouldn't *have* to be answered if you would stop giving him publicity. "Why in the hell do you keep featuring these right-wing nuts, giving currency to their crackpot notions? Why don't you do a show about how mainstream 'experts' have abused people who are different?!" "Oh . . . er . . . that's an idea . . ."

APRIL 30, 1991

The CUNY Board of Trustees, without apparent dissent, formally approved CLAGS last night. At last! It's been a long struggle. . . .

MAY 5, 1991

We devoted a special meeting of the CLAGS board yesterday to the problem of how to make the center more inclusive. . . . W. said he felt no need "to apologize for being an intellectual," and insisted abstract work *can* be socially transformative. . . . L., shaking with self-righteousness, announced that he's "delighted" these days (thanks to his recent tenure) to be on the "inside," that nobody can any longer "touch" him, and that he will "never again be mau-maued for not being radical enough . . ." Cheryl [*Clarke*] asked L. to think more about his "unfortunate" use of the term "mau-maued," but L.'s jaw clamped down still tighter.

Cheryl herself made what to me were the most subtle & impressive comments. She asked us to acknowledge that there are "many ways of knowing" and to stretch our definition of what scholarship can & does consist of. Yet she also sounded W.'s theme: "We shouldn't be guilt-tripped" for not being in the streets (though the streets made us possible); even though our movement *is* in an activist phase, we need people to do other things too. Alisa [*Solomon*] wisely added that to become more inclusive doesn't necessarily mean to move in the direction of anti-intellectualism. . . .

MAY 14, 1991

The final meeting of the Monday seminar last night ended in a kin-
dling (as opposed to blaze) of concord. All hands gave serious attention to the assorted tensions that had arisen in the group, & though
the Rashomon version of what had gone on continued to suggest
separate realities, all hands vigorously united to assure (& re-assure)
me that tales that several of them had early on dismissed me as an
unregenerate sexist/racist had been grossly distorted by some evil elf
up to no good. In any case, there was more mutual affection & respect evident last night than at any time preceding, and that seemed
a good note to end on, however wobblingly sounded. But even last
night, I picked up some disquieting overtones. Amanda (who I *am*
growing fonder of) reiterated her claim that it is *right* to silence those
who mouth "immoral" sentiments. And Jeff added, that he *never*
wanted to speak, as a privileged white man, in a less than "responsible" (politically correct) way. A praiseworthy goal, of course, but also
a little suspect; it seems, in Jeff's case, a way of never letting himself
be known, never letting anyone close enough to see the messy
undersoil beneath the scrupulously correct rhetoric. And as for
Amanda, the notion of snottily "silencing" someone struggling to express, sometimes in an inchoate way, feelings and views which (if
understood & acknowledged) could evolve into progressive forms, is
tantamount to negating the gay movement's rhetorical goal of inclu-
siveness. In theory, Amanda advocates diversity; in practice, she
moves quickly to stomp on any manifestation of it not consonant
with her own (narrow) values.

MAY 16, 1991

At the final meeting of the Wed. group last night, we had an invaluable discussion of the course pros and cons. Some of it, inevitably,
came down to damned-if-you-do-damned-if-you-don't contradictory
advices (directly ask/don't ask the quiet students to participate more).
But most of the critiques were thoughtful & helpful — impressing

me all over again with the level of commitment & intelligence. . . .
I need to remember, too, that it was a rough assignment from the
start: the students arrived with vastly different discourses & levels of
information in their heads, and with (it turns out) the unattainable
expectation that a mere academic seminar would magically integrate their lives. The seminar *was* a start, however rocky, and the appreciation they expressed last night was just as palpable as their
complaints.

MAY 27, 1991

I've had to deal with W.'s bullying tactics on the CLAGS board (be-
ware the lordly interiors of the outwardly obsequious!). He's written
me that I *must* rein E. in. . . . Lord, I loathe these petty tyrants — and
loathe, too, having, as director, to deal with them. I would prefer for
W. to stay on the board — his conservative views help the rest of us
sharpen our arguments — but only if he can somehow learn to yield
when outvoted, instead of bolting or browbeating.

LETTER FROM ME TO W., MAY 26, 1991

". . . I don't think that E. speaks 'only pure nonsense.' Like most of
us, she is sometimes a little prolix. But that's okay: none of us speaks
in perfect sentences, or always makes total sense. Besides, it's mostly
due to E.'s tenacity, to her refusal to let us off the hook on the issue
of board diversity, that has finally produced a genuinely multicultural group. (Just in case you haven't heard, all six of our invitations
have been accepted and we've added to our board one Hispanic,
three African-Americans and two Asian-Americans). We *are* a genuinely diverse bunch, and must learn, I think, to be more respectful
of each other's perspectives. . . ."

The publication in 1991 of my memoir Cures: A Gay Man's
Odyssey, *centered on my strenuous efforts from the mid-1960s to
the early '70s to change my sexual orientation through psychoanaly-*

sis. I hadn't expected the book to receive much attention and was surprised at the large and mostly laudatory number of reviews. It even became the first gay-themed title to be chosen by the Book of the Month Club, and for a time was the leading seller among its "Alternative" selections.

I was surprised, too, that there were so few homophobic reviews. Kirkus weighed in with "weep-o-rama" and the New York Times headlined the boxed excerpt that accompanied its review SLOW TO JOIN THE CAUSE (I'd in fact come out in my plays in the pre-Stonewall sixties and again in my 1972 post-Stonewall book, Black Mountain). My personal favorite (first I winced, then I laughed) of this less-than-welcoming batch was in the Washington Post. It was written by the well-known historian William S. McFeely, and expressed his heartfelt regret that now that I'd embraced a gay sexual orientation, I "may come to miss the multiplicities of life, the subtle, delicious torments with which other less unambiguous mortals contend." Huh? What "multiplicities of life" did McFeely have in mind? Bisexuality? Promiscuity? Rearing children? Raising dogs? Arguing with one's spouse? So far as I knew, all such options remained available to me, even if I might choose not to exercise them.

And what could McFeeley mean that a by-product of accepting my homosexuality would be the bypassing of life's "subtle, delicious torments"? Not even the most zealous gay chauvinist had ever before made such a claim. Was McFeeley right? Would adopting a homosexual lifestyle guarantee freedom from life's miseries and distress? If so, conversion therapists would be well advised to bolt their doors. Hordes of frenzied heterosexuals will soon descend, demanding a change in orientation.

Yet what's most curious, and significant, about McFeely's review is that he also refers to Cures as "a book of admirable affirmation." This is a puzzling, and of course contradictory reaction, and typical, I'd suggest, of liberal academia's attitude toward homosexuality—indeed of "liberalism" in general. By 1991 most liberals had learned to adopt (publicly) an attitude of "acceptance" (or its kissing cousin, studied indifference) toward gay people; many even seemed convinced that their acceptance was unambiguous and unqualified. But in reality most liberals remained riddled with ambivalence about homosexuality.

For the older generation, this is understandable. Like me, they'd grown up in a cultural climate dominated by the combined fury of religion and psychiatry (sin/pathology) against gay people. I may have come further than McFeeley by 1991 in freeing myself from that unholy duo of experts, but I still had plenty of scar tissue to show from all the years of breathing in toxic fumes about the inherent disorder of homosexuality. I couldn't pretend that I myself in 1991—or 2008, for that matter—was so free of self-hate that I could overtly mock a straight man who was at least ambivalent about homosexuality.

I received more letters from readers of Cures than from any other book of mine, before or since. Many of them were from gay men of roughly my own age who identified with what was at base a generational story and who wanted to share their own comparable experiences. But a number of letters were special:

From a forty-year-old black inmate in the state prison in Angola, Louisiana: "I've been incarcerated 16 yrs., serving a 33 yrs. Sentence for a Jewelry store robbery. . . . I've been on permanent lockdown for the past three years. . . . Being autodidact, I often had to stop reading [Cures] and consult my dictionary to make sure I fully understood where you was coming from, but took away none of my pleasure. . . ."

From Bonn, Germany: ". . . At the beginning of '43 I have been denounced to the police, I and a friend, because of something we said, I suppose, at midnight of the New Year's Eve of '42/'43, when some neighbors came into the apartment where we were celebrating. So this was for the moment the end of my career. . . . I was condemned to 8 months of jail. . . . At the end the director of the jail said to me: 'because you are so young—that is your chance—we are not sending you to a concentration camp.' I was 17."

From one of my college roommates: "I have searched my memory . . .

for data, scenes, and symbols. After 40 years they fail me . . . how terribly little I knew you. I blame myself for that. . . . I suspect Cures *will be read by more gays than straights—and that's too bad. . . ."*

From Clovendale, Oregon: ". . . *I'm a dairy farmer, gay at that. . . . It sure would be nice to read something describing yourself as gay and happy with that fact. Your partner must be a saint to put up with some of your opinions. It seems to me that you people in the Arts love to be fatalists . . . don't you feel that you should take notice that life is getting pretty short and begin enjoying? . . ."*

From "Anonymous," who described himself as "homosexual until 1956": ". . . *after a great effort of thought and study have been exclusively heterosexual ever since. I do not agree with your book that you cannot do the same. I think you must expend about 100 times as much effort to accomplish this or else you just do not want to convert badly enough. You can do it."*

From Falls Church, Virginia: "*The way you people have anal sex is also the cause of AIDS because when a diseased penis is inserted into the rectum it is only inches away from the adrenal gland and when the adrenal gland is destroyed with its all health giving cortisone one becomes vulnerable to all the diseases of the world and dies."*

From a Jesuit priest at Canisius College: "*I just finished reading your book* Cures. . . . *As a gay man who—at the age of 35—has only just recently begun the journey of self-acceptance, openness and liberation . . . your book will be very helpful to me—and I'm sure to many others—as we journey away from our closeted lives into the light and openness of healing and life."*

An exchange of letters with Gore Vidal, whom I knew slightly:

Gore to me: "*. . . I did not dream that anyone was still worrying about being straight or gay in the '70s. In my era ('40s) nervous folk who had to make a living in a hostile world did not (always) try to change so much as to learn the art of disguise which fags know from birth in a crazed culture like that of the US. I went once to a shrink at the behest of that dreaded chicken hawk A. [Anaïs] Nin who wanted ever more perfect unions, and I can still recall the look of shock on the* rabbi's face when I said there was no reason on earth to confine oneself to either sex. I had of course been in business since the age of twelve at St. Albans . . . as long as society says that fags are a definite category and undesirable because sick, etc., then resistance is in order. But, this is the hard part, simultaneously, one must aver that there is no such thing as the two categories—and that's where the victory—or true battle, at least—lies. I am perfectly willing to join a death squad and kill Jesse Helms pour encourager/decourager les autres—I believe in violence when necessary but, attached to the corpse, should be a note to the effect that he was killed by a category that did not—does not—exist, and until this nonexistent category can serve in the army, etc., more phantom reprisals will occur."

Me to Gore: ". . . The fact that categories of sexual behavior are socially constructed does not make them less imprinted than if they'd been biologically derived. Nature, I'd agree, never intended anyone to be exclusively gay or straight. But most people in our culture do operate out of those exclusive categories and cannot cease to simply for the wanting. I, for example, have long pined for that bisexual indiscriminacy which you seem to exemplify, but the blessed state has nonetheless evaded me—and not for want of prayers and exhortation. . . ."

Gore to me: "I just bought yr. memoir in Cambridge (Mass)—I am not ideal—or even PC—for this sort of thing. First, I don't believe in "gay sensibility." . . . I don't believe in American-made categories like queer or straight: the reflection of that mono-theism which wrecked the Western world (I tactfully avert my eyes from the middle east). But the categories have been inflicted upon us by the state, invoking monotheistic superstitions. Since I am quite willing to nourish the tree of liberty to protect myself or any despised minority, I have a problem. I am not gay. I am not straight. I do this or that or, alas, nothing. To allow the state to assign me a category with all sorts of rules is to accept a kind of totalitarianism without protest. Contradiction does not begin to describe this mess & explains why I don't live in a country that manages to get everything wrong. I'd consider a public trial & execution of Helms. Irritably, Gore."

From "Albert Igen," as he's called in Cures, *the Yale professor of psychiatry whom I saw as my therapist in the late 1950s and early '60s; I stopped treatment with him only when I took a job in another city. Igen had been the one undogmatic, compassionate human being I'd met during my far-too-extended passage through the world of psychotherapy. Igen: "You rightly raise the question of what is 'normal' in human behaviour. Of course there is no such thing. . . . As far as I can see everybody has homosexual feelings . . . The question is why do people develop a specific sexual orientation? . . . No one really knows, but many therapists think they know. Theories abound, but as far as I am concerned are unsatisfactory. The binding mother/absent father theory is one such useless oversimplification. . . . I really don't blame you for being angry with therapists and psychiatrists. I am sure many have not worked out their own psychological problems . . . psychoanalysis was given far too much glamour in the '50s and '60s I am afraid, and psychiatrists were often looked at as the 'final experts' and were mostly not deserving of that status. . . ."*

From Judd Marmor, past president of the American Psychiatric Association and a pioneering figure in getting homosexuality removed from the "disease" category in the Diagnostic and Statistical Manual of Mental Disorders *(the DSM): "Unhappily, I have known too many psychoanalysts over the years similar to those whom you described, with the same sense of righteous conviction that their approach both in theory and in practice was the* only *path to mental health in general, and the 'cure' of homosexuality in particular . . . the shoddy falsity . . . of the vast majority (if not all!) who claimed 'cures.' . . ."*

Given the understanding nature of the preceding two letters, a warning may be in order. Over the past several decades there has unquestionably been a more accepting shift in how both the public and psychoanalysis regard homosexuality. But—sadly and remarkably— touted cures for the "illness" not only still exist but to some extent have

thrived of late. The emergence in the nineties of the National Associa-
tion for Research and Therapy of Homosexuality (NARTH) is cause
for particular unease, though the younger generation of openly gay
therapists doesn't seem to regard it as much of a threat.

To give an example: After the publication of Cures, *I was (ironi-*
cally) invited to give a speech at the annual convention of the Ameri-
can Psychiatric Association. During my remarks I alluded to the APA's
1973 vote deleting homosexuality from the category of "illness," and
expressed concern that if the vote was taken today, the outcome might
be different. Several members of the audience assured me that such
apprehension was unwarranted, the progress made was irrevocable. At
that point my introducer, Dr. Richard Isay, an openly gay senior psy-
chiatrist, took the microphone to express agreement with me and to
caution against blind optimism. He reminded us that it was only that
very year, 1991, that the APA had finally prohibited its training insti-
tutes from denying admission based on sexual orientation.

NARTH's presence continues to be felt. Alternately known as "the
reparative therapy" movement, it is largely funded by right-wing reli-
gious organizations. In essence NARTH is a throwback to the central
psychiatric doctrine of the 1950s: homosexuality results from some-
thing "going wrong" during an individual's developmental process.
I'm not suggesting that we're on the verge of anything like a sharp re-
versal; indeed, in December 1998, the board of trustees of the APA it-
self voted unanimously that reparative therapy was a dangerously
misguided modality that could do serious harm to patients, reinforc-
ing the self-hatred already present. It's well to remember that Manhat-
tan isn't Oshkosh, that the comparatively liberated big cities aren't
synonymous with the country as a whole. Homophobia has declined,
but has far from disappeared. And the amount of suffering it induces
remains significant.

AUGUST 18, 1991

Three more deaths, one after the other: Craig Davidson, Allan Bar-
nett, Damien Martin. On it goes . . .

SEPTEMBER 14, 1991

A talk to the Gay/Lesbian Columbia group, preceded by lunch with
five of the students. They booked a room that seats forty, but it over-
flowed to some sixty. The interest in gay/lesbian studies has become
extraordinary—& exhilarating. *All* of the students I had lunch with
are writing their doctoral theses in the field, & the topics are wonderfully exciting—e.g. "The Search for Amazons"; "The Effect of Gay
Male Literary Critics pre-1950 on the Canon." I suppose it's wise to
be cautious—this, like Reconstruction, or the '60s counterculture—
could go into reverse. But the proliferation—not a day goes by without an inquiry or two, and, literally, from around the world, about
how to enlist in the field—is certainly heady stuff.

SEPTEMBER 25, 1991

Alerted by Donna [*Jensen*], we ran up to the NYU Emergency Room.
Todd [*his partner*] had found Ken [*Dawson*] semi-conscious on the
floor; all last night he convulsed and vomited. They wouldn't let Eli
and me in to see him, but Donna reports that he's now more stabi-
lized, whatever that means. Poor, dear Ken. Why does it seem to be
mostly the decent ones . . . ?

OCTOBER 6, 1991

. . . It's two days since CLAGS's inaugural event. On one level it was
a flat-out triumph. 450–500 people attended, $26,000 grossed, the
speeches brief and effective, the food superb, Alice Walker [*who
cochaired the event with Adrienne Rich*] gracious and focused, the
mood throughout buoyant. *And* I was able to announce Dave's
$110,000 gift *with* Dave present [*David Kessler, an old friend of mine,
had endowed an annual lecture/celebration of a noted lesbian or gay
scholar; over time, "the Kessler" became a significant community event
and the first ten years of lectures were published as a book*]. As several
people said, "I can't believe a fledgling organization put this together."

And how did it? Eli, plain & simple. Yet . . . not a word of congratulations and thanks from the Board . . . Instead, what did Eli hear from various members?

—"the contribution boxes on the brochure don't match those on the fund-raising envelope."

—"for next year's event, the fund-raising committee will want to oversee all decisions more closely" (i.e., Eli somehow transgressed his authority. By raising too much money?).

And what was the sum of what I heard?

—"You forgot to acknowledge so-and-so—you should call and apologize."

Are we really so damaged that we can't afford to thank somebody for work well done? Are we so routinized to negativism that we're unable to be pleased at such a triumphant outcome against such high odds? I thought we—our group of oh-so-politically-hip people—had at least learned from the feminist movement that *everybody* needs acknowledgement for work well done. . . .

OCTOBER 10, 1991

We celebrated Ken's 45th birthday last night in his hospital room. Jed [*Mattes, the literary agent*] brought a cake, Eli & I party favors, & 7–8 people lifted their seltzer water. As Ken was about to blow out the candles, Jed said, "We're all wishing just what you are." We threw silly putty on the walls & ceilings, laughed at the hospital food, admired the pink amaryllis, & had something that actually approximated a good time. Ken's spirits *are* good. He reports that all of his tests have improved & that he hopes to be home by next week. What does he allow himself to know—that is, consistently? Does he hold out real hope of recovery? If terrors *are* gnawing at his innards, his smiling face belies it. This is more than WASP training, more even than a saintly disposition. . . . He had a tough battle with depression, but now jokes about naming each of his remaining dozen t-cells "after a strong woman friend." And the homophobes dare tell us we have a "character disorder"!

OCTOBER 13, 1991

Ken started to tell us about the visit of a Boston friend who's raising a child, and couldn't hold back the tears—strangulated words about being glad that life goes on. . . . He's lost control over his sphincter. Plus a lung has collapsed. Yet on he struggles . . .

NOVEMBER 3, 1991

The Gay/Lesbian Studies Conference at Rutgers yesterday was a sore disappointment. Too many cute titles, too little content. . . . And there was much too much on popular culture (did we need *two* panels on Madonna?), not nearly enough on the social sciences. The plenary session on race/gender/sexuality was borderline retrograde, as led by Cherrie Moraga (a genuine hero in several other contexts) patronizingly telling two HIV+ male questioners, who wanted to know how to build bridges, how to concentrate our forces in the fight against AIDS, that "people work where they feel comfortable, that is, with their own—that's the reality." Not good enough, not nearly. If we can't reach out & support each other's issues, then ethnicity becomes a trap. Besides, are there no cases of AIDS in the Chicano/a community?

One mustn't be too negative about these gatherings, I suppose. Even if nothing substantial of an intellectual nature gets transacted, the chief—if unintended—advantage is simply *gathering*, seeing each other in force, knowing the gay/lesbian studies enterprise *is* feasible & necessary.

NOVEMBER 10, 1991

The proliferating CLAGS work gets me down because it keeps me from writing; especially frustrated now because I'm in the home stretch [*of the book that became* Stonewall] and I'm afraid I'll lose the momentum. Yet ordinarily CLAGS meetings, lunches, phone and mail is now manageable. That is, unless one of our prima donnas throws a fit and I have to put in additional hours soothing and negotiating. . . . Last night, for example, H. did a no-show, leaving me to get out yet another (my third this week) mailing. I hope to God I won't be saddled with the director's job too much longer.

NOVEMBER 13, 1991

Ken's suffering goes on unabated. . . . [He's] back in the hospital, lung again collapsed. They were due to operate this morning at 7:00 a.m., but now (2:00 p.m.) he still hasn't gone up—no explanation offered. The routine brutality of our medical system is appalling; and Ken is a middle-class white man!

NOVEMBER 14, 1991

Ken is in agony. They had to take out more of his lung than hoped; apparently the pneumonia has severely damaged it. He just lies there, lips parched, each cough a knife through his body. . . . A little tea and a partial massage was all I could offer; makes me feel inadequate, awkward; such a dear man, so little anyone can do . . .

NOVEMBER 20, 1991

Last night's CLAGS event, "The Nation and the Closet: Latin America" was to my mind a mixed bag. Given that whites don't turn out for any topic other than their "own" (narrowly perceived), an audience of 75–90 was pretty good. All three papers were smart, but narrowly literary and filled with deconstructionist jargon and tight textual analysis that at times bordered on parody. In short, super-academic . . . $137 collected in donations at the door; pitiful, given the precarious state of our treasury. About half our own board didn't bother to show, which to me is simple disrespect for colleagues.

DECEMBER 2, 1991

Spoke yesterday at the Museum of the City of New York on gay/
lesbian history . . . the audience small but enthusiastic. Except for
one motor-mouth during the question period who, shaking with self-
righteousness, denounced the inclusion of the Cuba essay in *HFH*
[Hidden From History, *a book I'd coedited*] as an affront to Latino
gays. He was certain he knew *why* it had been included: because I
was an apologist for socialism. No, I said, I considered myself closer
to anarchism than socialism, & my hero was Emma Goldman not
Karl Marx. His jaw fell open. He seemed more not less aghast—
probably because he'd never heard of Emma Goldman.

DECEMBER 3, 1991

A.W., *Daily News* reporter and a self-declared gay man, calls me up.
Ah-ha, thinks I, he wants to write about CLAGS, or specifically
about our "Gay Brain" conference on Monday. Not at all. He wants
to write—yet again—about the "resurgence of promiscuity" among
(read "those irresponsible") gay men. Turns out he's never heard of
CLAGS. Doesn't he think the Monday conference is newsworthy?
"Naw—it's *scholarly*." But so was Simon LeVay's original article and
that landed on page one of the *New York Times*. "Uh—I guess
so. What name was that?" Listen, A., here's why it landed on page
one: because the mainstream wants to believe that homosexuality is
biological in origin. That way, they can remove the impulse from
everybody and assign it to a despised few. "Uh-huh," says A., clearly
dying to hang up. With gay reporters like A., who needs straight
enemies?

DECEMBER 13, 1991

CLAGS board meeting last night. At my invitation, David Kahn of
Brooklyn Historical, Holly Hotchner of New York Historical Society,
Rick Beard of the Museum of the City of New York, plus two other

staff members, came to tell us about incipient plans for a joint celebration of Stonewall's 25th in 1994. Their presentation was open,
warm and politically hip, yet in response our board sat mostly mute
and I had to dig deep to present ourselves as *the* essential academic/
political touchstone for any such celebration. Then, as soon as the
museum representatives left, some of the mute came to life—to nit-
pick of course: "Can we be sure that *our* agenda will match theirs?"
"What if they want us to work too hard?" (this from several people,
none of whom have done anything since arriving on the board),
etc. . . . I reminded them that a citywide celebration of our history
and culture would be an enormous boost to gay people everywhere.
And to CLAGS: to affiliate on an equal basis, and without having to
raise any of the money, would hugely help in putting us on the map.
I finally got a reluctant sub-committee of five to agree to first-level
discussions with the museums.

DECEMBER 20, 1991

At last night's benefit for GCN [Gay Community News, *the most politically progressive gay publication*], a pathetic dozen people showed
up—and that's including the three hosts (me, Jewelle Gomez, David
Feinberg [*the novelist, who subsequently died of AIDS*]). True, it's the
busy week before Xmas, and it was a bitter 15 degrees outside. But
it turns out that GCN only has 200 subscribers in the New York
area. That, I suppose, constitutes the left-wing of the movement. Ah
well . . .

JANUARY 4, 1992

Lunch today with Dick Isay. We got on the biological component to
homosexuality. On limited evidence (which he sees as "overwhelming"), he holds stoutly to the pre-determination view. And I resist it
just as stoutly ("How do you account for bisexuals?") Today I saw
my position in a larger context. I argue against *all* purportedly fixed
differences—including those of race or gender. "Do you include tal-

ent?" Dick wanted to know, "do you think everyone is born with equal gifts?" I suppose I do. Or at the least, I believe most talent is a gift of privilege not genes—the needed attitudes ("I am special") and skills (with paint, words, whatever) inculcated at an early enough moment, and with enough success and satisfaction following quickly enough to imprint a lifetime pattern. I don't think there's much mystery to achievement. Everybody wants to understand and express his/her experience—but only a few are given the opportunity. And why does the expression come in words, say, and not in math? Just an accident of which tools were provided when? I don't know. And does my environmentalist view account for genius as well as talent? I doubt it (many besides Picasso were "given the right tools"). Is my sort of egalitarianism based on real evidence? I'm unsure—which the Isays, in attacking egalitarianism, aren't.

FEBRUARY 1, 1992

An exciting first meeting of the "Stonewall 25" planners last night. *If* it all comes off (which hinges on the Rockefeller Foundation coming in), and in conjunction with the Gay Games, June '94 should be an astonishing celebration of gay/lesbian life. We started last night with a clarification of CLAGS's role. I got everything I asked for: equal billing with the cultural institutions as a co-sponsor, and no financial or staff contributions. I presented us—fairly—as the "think tank" for the event; we *are* well-equipped to pinpoint the participating scholars—*and* the potential political hurdles. . . .

FEBRUARY 22, 1992

. . . I spoke to the gay/lesbian Master of Social Work organization last night. Seemed a likely pool of people to be interested in CLAGS. Ha! The most hostile reception I've ever gotten. And I had a reality check: Michael, who came up afterwards to apologize for the nitpicking nastiness. It ranged from a challenge to my assertion that lesbians have less money than gay men to the declaration that CLAGS sounds like just another men's club (this was *after* I'd reported our board's 9–9 gender split and our firm commitment to gender parity). Go figure. I think a fair amount of the hostility that I get relates not to what I say but how I look. No matter how much I dress down I manage to look prosperous; no matter how old I get I apparently come across as vigorous; and of course I *am* a white male. All of which invites automatic anger based on past experience of being humiliated by people who, judged by outer looks, I seem to represent. But couldn't we at least learn the basic non-racist lesson?—do not judge the individual on his/her *apparent* (looks) membership in a particular group. A disheartening night.

MARCH 3, 1992

I asked Esther [*Katz*] and Cheryl [*Clarke*] [*cochairs of the CLAGS board*] to tell me what *I'm* contributing to the non-stop brushfires on the board. They don't think anything, but *are* puzzled and will let me know if they come up with a bit (or bits) of behaviors on my part that seem contributory. I have some ideas of my own: I expect (unrealistically) the same level of high performance from others that I turn in. In an age of non-performance, this is labeled "perfectionism," and the "performance freak" gets resented for getting more done, with less hysteria, than others. The resentment wears me down and works itself out in weird ways. If I don't go to every CLAGS committee meeting, someone will imply that I'm neglecting my duties as director. If I do go to every committee meeting, someone will imply that I'm trying to control all aspects of the organization. These accusations usually come from people who *occasionally* show up for a board meeting, never return phone messages and never show up for committee meetings.

MARCH 16, 1992

CLAGS's "Homosexuality and Hollywood" event proved a mixed bag. On the plus side was a large turnout—standing-room (over 250) for much of it; on the minus side was the self-importance of some of the panelists. . . . Since we only took in $120 in donations at the door, I decided to pass the basket row by row, which netted us another $275. I hate compromising the notion of free events, but we do need to survive, and I made it clear that those on a tight budget need not/should not contribute. But really, was any of that crowd too poor to spare a dollar?—rush as they do twice a week to $7.50 movies.

MARCH 17, 1992

Ken is drifting further away. At the hospital yesterday we ran into his doctor and got a full report. PML has been definitely diagnosed in the brain, which accounts for the in-and-out-again lucidity. Even when lucid, he now responds tersely. . . . He's showing remarkable tenacity in staying alive. . . . [*Ken died on April 10*].

MARCH 25, 1992

Why do lesbian couples often seem so hell-bent on introducing a MAN into their infant son's life? Having found a way to successfully avoid male culture, with all its adolescent posturing and violence, they now voluntarily re-introduce it. A function of two things, I think: some women's residual kneejerk deference to the "superior" gender; and the inherent conservatism ("he needs a man in his life": the binary notion of gender) within the purportedly outsider lesbian/gay culture.

MARCH 27, 1992

Insufferable meeting of the graduate school's history dept. exec. comm. A letter from Rickie Solinger protesting her rude, discouraging treatment as a graduate student ("I was consistently accorded a shocking level of disrespect . . . [Is it] possible to write a dissertation in women's history at CUNY?"), was passed around, and it produced not soul-searching but snickers. Just in case their patriarchal smugness was in doubt, they proceeded to vote *down* [*the distinguished feminist scholar*] Renate Bridenthal's application to teach at the graduate school; only Barbara Welter (the sole woman on the exec. committee) & I were in favor. Plus they were on the verge of turning down Pres. [*Frances*] Horowitz's request in regard to voting in a black scholar from the Staten Island campus until I successfully used a strategic argument on them: soon after the flap over the lack of a Latin American history course, wouldn't a negative vote on the black scholar, I asked, be taken as a sign of entrenched conservatism? That carried the day with these self-protective smugies — but oh, what a bunch! And they can hold me up — "we let Duberman offer a gay course!" — as proof of their open-mindedness.

MARCH 30, 1992

The Rockefeller Foundation's scholarly panel has recommended CLAGS for funding — 250,000 bucks worth! Only one hurdle remains: an April 3 on-site inspection to make sure facilities are available for the two scholars that CLAGS will choose each year (for three years) for $35,000 residency grants, plus an extra $2,000 for travel expenses. The on-site visit is no mean hurdle, given the shabby pit into which the Graduate School has dumped us. G.C., who sat on Rockefeller's panel, told me the committee's sole doubt concerns the degree of institutional support for CLAGS. The Graduate School has given us no money, though it did give us some in-kind help (access to the print shop, etc.) and a free office — even if it is a dingy hole with minimal equipment and no circulating air. I'm trying to raise a little hell between now and Friday to get Pres. Horowitz to lend her office and provide a catered lunch [*she most graciously agreed, and throughout her tenure was a staunch supporter of CLAGS*].

Imagine — $250,000 . . . If the grant comes through, it will make CLAGS eminently more fundable with other foundations, and put gay/lesbian studies irreversibly on the map. And what a boon the $35,000 grants will be to low-income, unaffiliated scholars.

With CLAGS now formally established, we steadily expanded our public offerings, even as we continued to search for the funds to support them—the Graduate Center still not providing a dime in direct financial support. Ironically, the more frequent and elaborate our offerings became, the more the impression grew that we were rolling in money—what else could explain our productivity? Similarly, it was widely assumed that CLAGS was the recipient rather than the channel for the $250,000 Rockefeller Humanities Fellowships; in fact, we got to use a mere $15,000 for operating expenses.

By 1992, CLAGS was increasingly producing a number of major (one- to three-day) conferences, and maintained a monthly colloquia series as well, an informal gathering at which scholars presented work-in-progress. A scholarly directory—the first of its kind—of university faculty offering courses or doing research on lesbian and gay subjects was, after two years of gathering and checking listings, about to go to press. Also, through specially earmarked gifts, we were now able to offer an increasing number of grants and awards that ranged from $500 grants-in-aid for CUNY graduate students to two $5,000 research grants in lesbian and gay history to the broad-gauged yearly Rockefeller Fellowships of $35,000.

Yet, perhaps predictably, criticism of CLAGS continued from various quarters, and included a range of grievances. One prominent lesbian psychologist, for example, wrote to me early in 1992 to complain that our public programming inadequately reflected lesbian perspectives. This, I thought, was patently unfair, though I adopted a gentle tone in response. Our governing board, I pointed out, had absolute gender parity, and both its cochairs were women; the first Kessler Awardee had also been a woman (Joan Nestle). In regard to our public programs, our most recent conference, "The Brain and Homosexuality," had four female and four male panelists. Our upcoming two-day conference on "AIDS and Public Policy" would devote one full day to "Women and AIDS." Seven of the nine speakers at our planned fall '92 panel, "Feminism and Lesbianism," organized by Judith Butler, were women. "In this male-haunted world," I wrote the psychologist, "I think we're doing pretty well. I hope you will eventually come to agree.

*In any case, don't stop telling us what you think." I never heard from
her again.*

In the spring of 1992, CLAGS *held a panel at the Graduate Center
on "the future of gay/lesbian studies." As I wrote in my diary (May 1,
1992), it proved "unexpectedly contentious." Two of the women panelists, J. and S., both writers and nonacademics whom I like and respect, started off with surprisingly negative comments. S. challenged
academics to surrender their "place of safety" and make their work
"relevant"—define, please—to the community's needs. Do unaffiliated
scholars or adjunct faculty occupy any safer places than do writers? And
is the demand constantly made on writers to leave their desks and do
"relevant" work? J. called for a "coherent political framework" for gay/
lesbian studies—whatever that means, other than a PC framework, itself ever-shifting. They both assumed a false dichotomy between activism
and scholarship; I told the story about* Hidden from History *changing
votes in the Vermont legislature, but it shifted no one's position. Besides, they actually implied that scholarship was barely worth doing,
invoking the ancient equation (once true) of scholarship with élitism.*

Maybe I'm tired of friends attacking each other—while the common enemy escapes scot-free. Maybe I'm gun-shy after all the battles
in and around CLAGS. But I apparently rebutted them both with
more fervor than I intended—leading them to deny the positions I ascribed to them, me to apologize (I'm tired of that, too) for possibly
overreacting, and J. and I having an onstage hug. Still, I have a bad-
dish aftertaste. How we love to employ the rhetoric of diversity, yet how
slow we are to allow it in practice; in this case, to allow each to make
his/her contribution in their own (not somebody else's) way. And—
recapitulating yet again the movement's history of factionalism—how
quick we are to hold each other to perfectionist standards and lam-
baste every minor inadequacy.

That same theme, with some high decibel variations, was again
sounded—this time by Larry Kramer—in the fall of 1992. In a long
interview with Gore Vidal for* QW [at that point the leading gay publication in New York], *Larry repeated some charm-laden remarks sim-*

*ilar to those he'd earlier made about me in another publication: Du-
berman "was one of our so-called leaders who were most silent when
the* community *most needed leadership. What role has Duberman
played in helping our community respond to the greatest crisis* [AIDS]
it has ever known?"

As Larry admitted to me many years later, after we'd reconciled,
his comments were in part fueled by long-standing anger at me for the
scorching review I'd earlier written, before we knew each other, of his
novel, Faggots. *He also seems not to have known or cared that I continued to do the low-profile volunteer work of answering the phones
one afternoon a week at the People With AIDS Coalition; not a "leadership" position, to be sure, but some "role" in the crisis nonetheless
(and not the only one—of the rest I choose not to write, to preserve the
privacy of others).*

*Due perhaps to oversensitivity and defensiveness, or perhaps to
having felt like a dart-board of late, I decided, this time around, to let
Larry have it:*

"*. . . In the seventies," I wrote to* QW,

> *my movement work included the kind of frequent participation
> in organizational meetings and marches that apparently would
> qualify me for Larry's approval as an "activist"—though by his
> own admission, he himself was nowhere on the scene in those
> years. . . . I don't need him as my commissar. My activism has
> taken different forms in the eighties and nineties from those of
> the seventies, but activism is what it remains.* [I then cited my
> various current commitments, from teaching lesbian and gay
> history, to running CLAGS, to helping organize a citywide
> set of programs to commemorate Stonewall's twenty-fifth
> anniversary.] . . .
>
> *Apparently, Larry thinks none of these activities qualify me
> as an "activist," or, put another way: if one is not doing Larry's
> particular work, one is, by definition, not working at all. Leav-
> ing aside the implied grandiosity, this hostility to research and
> writing exemplifies the endemic anti-intellectualism of main-*

stream America—the same mainstream Larry otherwise enjoys lambasting. . . . Will the day ever come when we all start thanking each other for our contributions to the well-being of our community instead of trashing and refusing to validate as genuine any contribution not duplicative of our own efforts? Until we do learn to acknowledge and praise the different ways people make their contributions, we will continue to do the divisive work of the oppressor.

Indubitably true—even if I myself sometimes (often?) fail to make sufficient acknowledgment . . .

Larry—as I should've guessed, as I probably would have done myself—came right back at me. He even upped the ante. In an interview with the national gay publication the Advocate, *in its November 1992 issue, he lashed out hard:*

> *. . . I get very disturbed when I see . . . essays the likes of which people like Marty Duberman now write extolling the virtues of gay promiscuity* [I'd written no such essay], *as if the plague had never happened. I get worried about organizations like the one Marty Duberman founded at City University of New York, the Center for Lesbian and Gay Studies. Second-rate academics affiliated with third-rate educational institutions studying our history, telling me that there was no such thing as homosexuality before 1890. Fuck them! That is one of the most destructive, damaging things—our own historians refuse to acknowledge that homosexuality has existed since the beginning of time. . . . So fucking what! You can't tell me that dicks weren't being sucked by male mouths since shortly after the Garden of Eden. So what if it didn't have a* name *then! So what! Does that mean my entire history and heritage is invalid and not worthy of acknowledgment?*

Last-word Marty wasn't going to let it drop there. Off went a response to the Advocate *(which printed about a third of it):*

*... Larry Kramer simply misrepresents what gay and lesbian
historians are saying. The basic distinction drawn by the new
scholarship ... is that homosexual acts can be documented
through time and across cultures, but a homosexual identity
seems to be a phenomenon of the last several hundred years.
What is it with Larry Kramer these days? His fame and his
meanness of spirit seem to accelerate in tandem, which suggests
that on some level the acclaim is providing scant balm. ...
There's a sweet side to Larry Kramer; I've seen it. There's a warm
and decent human being buried beneath the rhetoric of indiscriminate rage. ...*

*And with that, the guns finally went quiet on the Western Front.
More than a decade later, a few tentative e-mails led to a cordial dinner and since then a friendly though distant rapprochement.*

MAY 16, 1992

A desolating thought: by emphasizing gay "identity," are we letting
the rest of the world off the hook (of acknowledging their own multiple impulses) and putting ourselves on it (by insisting that our
erotic impulses are singularly confined to us)? Isn't the "gay" role essentially (in both senses) invented by *them* as a way of stilling their
own fears of same gender intimacy? In accepting it, we may deceive
ourselves into thinking that an affirmation of our separate "identity"
will do more than win our *own* respect. It may bind us as firmly into
the (despised) category of "other" as "sinner" or "pervert" once did—
& will do the same work of social stigmatization & control. A somewhat less desolating rebuttal: affirming a separate identity may not
currently be avoidable since it fits with a deeply felt "truth" (deep
enough to feel as confirmatory as biology) so many have now seized
upon in order to feel better about themselves; a gay "identity" is now
as urgently embraced as it was once fervently avoided—and for the
same reason: to approximate legitimacy.

JUNE 1, 1992

Lunch at Chelsea House publishers. They want me to serve as general editor for an ambitious "young adult" gay/lesbian series. Certainly the project would be, if done well, invaluable. . . . But doing a fullscale hands-on job would entail gobs of time and energy. What do I owe to "the community" and what to myself—to say nothing of Eli?

JUNE 5, 1992

Ken's Memorial Service yesterday had a powerful effect on me. . . . Several speakers found just the right loving words and phrases— "decent, dignified, cautious, gentle, lonely"—that encapsulate the man. John D'Emilio was especially effective, though everyone did well. What Ken stood for in the movement, beyond anyone else, was the insistence that we stop trashing each other and look for the *good* within our fellow activists. That is what "decent" means, and Ken was supremely decent—despite what Torie [*Osborn*] smartly called "the curmudgeon within."

JUNE 12, 1992

Yesterday's New School panel, which I chaired, was a cut above the usual. . . . I find almost everything that Eve [*Kosofsky Sedgwick*] and Diana [*Fuss*] have to say interesting. . . . Diana spoke eloquently about teaching as a way to *do* politics, and Eve trenchantly about the "queerness" of writing and the importance of giving straight students the opportunity to speak out of the queer spaces within them. I threw in an occasional remark only—how queer theory, in rejecting the binary, speaks more cogently to non-Anglo cultures than does the previous assumption of either/or categories. But I mostly played moderator.

In light of my sympathy for breaking open the standard categories of "gay" or "straight," it was bizarre—my clumsy attempt at a chuckle—that I made some mention, in introducing Eve, of her not, as a heterosexual, really belonging on a panel devoted to the topic of "how being gay or lesbian has affected our writing." Afterwards, she rightly chastised me, telling me sternly that she's not comfortable with being described as non-lesbian (though it's widely known that her partner is a man). How stupid of me. In employing such a dumb description of Eve I must have sounded ignorant of, or hostile to, one of queer theory's central tenets.

JUNE 13, 1992

John and Gilda [*our next-door neighbors*] all weepy across the terrace on getting the news that a (heterosexual) woman friend is HIV positive. Their pain is real, and I made all the right sympathetic noises. But I couldn't help feel anger as well. AIDS is only real to straights when it affects one of their own. John treats AIDS patients, yet his empathy up to now (by his own account) has been *pro forma*. Why shouldn't mine be towards him?

JULY 29, 1992

CLAGS executive committee meeting. . . . At one point I characterized our board as trying to be 3 boards in one: representative of our diverse communities; representative of gay/lesbian scholarship; and—which we're least good at—finding fund-raising sources. C. transposed the latter into, "See that's just what I mean—Marty has monied values and that may be part of the trouble with CLAGS." Others then tried to press C.—Shouldn't we try to raise money? Should we try to raise it from non-traditional (no foundations or wealthy individuals) sources? Could we raise enough to stay afloat? Cornered, C. . . . shifted to a new line of attack . . . one bottomline problem, I think—and Shepherd [*Raimi*] said as much during the meeting—is that a white man created CLAGS, and made a runaway success of it. I've made it clear from the beginning that I want to step down just as soon as I can (Oh, how I'd love to step down!), and have also tried hard to live up to the principles of gender parity and multiculturalism that the organization was founded on. But C. has been conditioned far too long and deeply—rightly conditioned, as a survival mechanism—not to trust whites, not to believe that I mean what I say. . . . I understand the rage but won't excuse the refusal to level it at those most responsible for producing it—instead of at coworkers doing their best to acknowledge their racism and to make amends for it. . . . After C. left the meeting, Vivien [Ng] came up to me and said, "I think you need a hug." Oh did I—and I thanked her for it. "You deserved it," she said, "not the cruelty, but the hug."

AUGUST 2, 1992

[*Susan*] Sontag speaks grandiloquently in today's *Times* of the too-thin membrane that has always separated her from the sufferings of others. Miss Compassion. Yet she has never responded to my appeals that she lend her name if not her presence to the gay struggle. And in the *Times* interview, as everywhere else, she continues to be silent about her own lesbianism. Miss Compassion upstaged by Madame Careerist.

SEPTEMBER 1, 1992

CLAGS has been keeping me going at a furious clip. Multiple meetings are the least of it. The calls and letters are reaching flood tide, and I have to be corresponding secretary along with stamp licker and room renter. This is the kind of success I hoped for, but the 10-hour-day reality leaves little room for much else. ("And isn't that," whispers the wise little voice, "what you *really* hoped for?")

SEPTEMBER 6, 1992

Today I began teaching for the term at Vassar as the Visiting Randolph Professor of History. I enjoyed the first class. Paul Russell [*the novelist*] carried me from mailbox to copy center to lunch to class,

kindly minimizing the unfamiliarity of the place. . . . I had closed
the class at 20 to ensure an informal, non-lecture format. But 30
showed up and were so enthusiastic that I finally decided to let them
all in; it felt like a pre-established community and I didn't want to
break it up.

SEPTEMBER 13, 1992

Yesterday saw the completion of the two-day conference CLAGS organized to prepare for the planned celebration of the 25th anniversary of Stonewall in 1994. We invited some three dozen scholars of
LGBT history to gather together and sort out needs and agendas before discussions begin with the consortium of major cultural institutions that's been forming under the leadership of David Kahn, head
of the Brooklyn Historical Society. Everybody had his/her say; various political positions and personal anxieties got vented and—an all
but unique result—ended not in disruption or division but in resolu-
tion, with all present committing to the project. . . . All week long reports had been coming in about Herstory's [*the community-based
Lesbian Herstory Archives*] hostility to CLAGS: we're "rich, elitest,
and dominated by white men." All this in response to our honoring
Joan [*Nestle, cofounder of Herstory*] with the Kessler award, and offering to do a benefit dance for Herstory. As I said to Joan, it's a no-win
situation: people prefer to hold on to their stereotypes rather than
look at what CLAGS has actually done in regard to board composition and public programming—because if they *did* look they'd
have to acknowledge our commitment to feminist and multicultural
values. . . .

I can well understand why community-based scholars, scarred
deeply by their struggles to do their work without any of the supports
and perks of academia, are understandably frightened at having
"their" baby (which is how they see it, somewhat inaccurately) taken
away, and brought up by better-off, uncomprehending neighbors . . .
a troop of people came to the mike to verbalize assorted grievances
and fears . . . Kendall Thomas [*Columbia University law professor*]

eloquently referred to the perceived struggle over "popular memory." Esther Newton [*SUNY anthropologist*] spoke of the vital need to *link* community-based and academic history. Jonathan [*Ned Katz, the pioneering gay historian*] worried aloud about the possibility of the museum world turning in a banal version of our history. Vivien Ng [*SUNY historian*] spoke movingly of her fear that mainstream celebration would not guarantee our survival or success. . . .

The next morning, the people of color at the conference met together and produced a set of recommendations; and when we broke into small groups, a real effort was made to see that those recommendations were concretely addressed . . . a lot of rich discussion followed. . . .

SEPTEMBER 15, 1992

I'm enjoying my Lehman class more than the one at Vassar. At Lehman the class is (apparently) all straight—& any information astonishes. At Vassar, the class is all gay, or nearly so; some seem to have heard it all, others seem afraid to admit they haven't; the dominant attitude is, "We dare you to tell us something we don't already know—& don't have a generationally superior insight into." The Vassar experience thus far reminds me mostly of the dreary graduate school seminar.

SEPTEMBER 20, 1992

. . . the continuing draining weirdness of board chemistry. At Saturday's meeting, W.—who sounds much worse than he is—managed pompously & fuzzily to assert that "the demands of multicultural representation necessarily dilute the intellectual content of an enterprise" [*i.e.,* CLAGS]. I think he meant that the need to recruit outside of academia for minority groups underrepresented within it means offering board invitations to people not expert, & in some cases not notably interested, in gay & lesbian studies. S. didn't help matters by announcing that "of course we would never consider taking a *white* graduate student on the board," thus making B. [*African-American*], & by implication the newly elected L. [*also African-American*], both graduate students, appear to have been chosen as a desperation measure only.

W. next proceeded to shout down A., who abruptly left in tears. Many phone calls of reassurance & rehashing followed, but people need to speak out to W.'s face at the time instead of later complaining about him behind his back & expecting me to "punish" him.

For our second annual benefit (October 2, 1992), which Eli again orchestrated and organized, Chip Kidd designed, free of charge, a ravishing invitation and Kate Millett, Paul Monette, and Gore Vidal agreed to serve as cochairs. Gore accepted in an inimitable note: "Against my better judgment, OK for October 2—You realize, of course, there will be a whispering campaign against me & I will end like Liberace, infamously." I wrote back reassuringly: ". . . not to worry. . . . Everyone knows your view that no such creatures as A Gay or A Lesbian exist; your appearance will be taken as a compassionate gesture toward the deluded. Isn't it interesting, by the way, that Queer Theory, now all the rage, never credits you with having spoken out decades ago against artificially firm boundaries in regard to sexual orientation? Ah well, we know you said it first. . . ."

Even with that trio of cochairs as a draw, the benefit couldn't match the excitement of the inaugural event the previous year: we drew some 250 people (rather than 450–500), and netted $9,500 (versus $15,000). For us, that was still a ton of money; yet CLAGS was still far from having a "staff," let alone even a part-time graduate student assistant for me.

OCTOBER 5, 1992

. . . dear Gore arrived at the benefit in a fearful grump, barely civil, demanding a drink, announcing he was far too jet-lagged to speak to the gathering [*as had been planned*]. On the advice of Sharon de Lano, who accompanied Gore, I quickly surrounded him with the academic version of "handsome young men"—[*the novelists*] David Feinberg and John Weir—and he was buttered up enough by all hands to turn in a witty performance at the end. . . . Kate [*Millett*] was thirty pounds lighter than when I last saw her, and temperately clear-eyed . . . she was touchingly flustered and shy—obviously moved at being made so much of. Poor Paul Monette was too ill to attend. [*He died of AIDS in February 1995.*]

NOVEMBER 9, 1992

First, second and tenth—Thank God it was Clinton!

Next, a good meeting with PEN. I went in with an idea for a single panel (on "Lesbian Literature"), thinking one would be all they would consider—never having done anything on gay or lesbian writers. But the chemistry was good and the discussion extended, and as of now CLAGS and PEN are co-sponsoring 2 days (and 4 panels) in February and April. . . .

Went next to a disastrous meeting of the Stonewall group. Disastrous on 2 counts: except for the Brooklyn Historical Society and the New York Public Library, which has recently joined the consortium, the other museums continue to drag their feet in committing either money or time. . . . The second count was the arrival at the meeting of Delores R., representing the lesbian/gay Center . . . it was only a matter of minutes before she was demanding guarantees, hurling charges and maligning intentions. I tried to say that without a certain level of trust, the enterprise was doomed, and that everything I had experienced over the past six months with the museum personnel involved had convinced me of their good intentions. But Delores would have none of it, and yielded not one accusatory inch; so it was the 2-day scholarly conference all over again—after the issues raised there had been so successfully resolved—only this time with someone implacably certain that she alone knew what the multicultural issues were & could be counted on to defend them. By the time I left I was so angry at her wanton attack on everybody's integrity that it took me hours to calm down (David says it took him the whole weekend). The entire project may well collapse; we'll know more by early December. Not only are the self-righteous out in force, but the foundations seemed sealed against the project. In the meantime, just as Delores is inveighing against our "élitism," in weighs dear old Wayne Dynes & friends with a huffy letter accusing me, among much else, of being an unregenerate Marxist. This is too much. Over the past year I'd assured him that CLAGS wasn't exclusionary and didn't peddle one intellectual line, and I'd invited him to join our monthly scholarly colloquium and to give us a paper. But he took me up on neither. Ah, the peaceful ivory tower . . .

NOVEMBER 10, 1992

Spoke to the Revson fellows at Columbia about gay/lesbian studies. What an animated group! (It helped that four of the 12 were gay). Stephanie Grant [*one of the fellows and later a novelist*] impresses me more each time I see her; she's as charming as she is bright, & I was glad to hear she's at work on her own writing at last. Impressed, too, at how non-adversarial, though searching, the discussion was (in contrast to the adversarial, non-searching Stonewall discussions). Much well-meaning talk of the need (à la 1970) for a coalition of "outs," though stymied in part by uncertainty about how deep the commonalties *are* (e.g., black homophobia: gay-bashing higher at Morehouse Univ. than anywhere in the country). Through most of the evening Eli Ginzberg sounded like a benign, sometimes bossy patriarch, but he surprised me at the end with a cogent summary. I have to watch my own tendency to view the older white man as the automatic enemy—to do to others what the Deloreses do to me. At one point, in discussing *Cures*, someone asked me how I had been able to come out on the other side of so much abuse. "Mother love," I answered, surprising myself. "My mother really did love me, and thereby built in an irreducible self-regard."

At Randy Trumbach's "tea," I got into an exchange with the novelist Dominique Fernandez. I found myself bristling at his simultaneous suggestion that the olden times were in some ways preferable, more "fun," and his insistence that Europe is "way ahead" of the U.S. in accepting homosexuality. The French *always* think they're ahead of everyone else, and I asked whether the lack of an organized gay political movement in France connoted "acceptance" or the willingness of French gays to present themselves as "just folks." He didn't seem to get the point, but most of the others rushed in to assure me—patronizing laughter all around—that I didn't understand that in France they "truly" had no need for a political struggle.

DECEMBER 12, 1992

The outpouring of applause & warmth at my final Vassar class surprised me. I'd decided the class hadn't worked well, and had been puzzling over why not. Lumping the Vassar class in with my grad. seminar of two years ago, I'd decided that *my* greater anxiety at teaching gays rather than straights had set off theirs. Tighter than usual, I was to that degree less approachable, wanting to receive validation myself—*needing* it from a younger generation of gays & lesbians—I was hardly in a position to give it (uncomplicatedly). And my residual role—the trained scholar who stands back from and critically analyzes the subject matter—set up an impossible duality of expectations with the need subjectively to plunder the material under review for vital information on how to shape and lead our lives.

But with the Vassar group, anyway, it seems I've once again judged both them & myself too harshly, assumed too soon & too completely that nothing worthwhile was getting transacted. That's a function more of my than their expectation that *everything* has to happen—and anything short of that marks a failure.

DECEMBER 13, 1992

. . . the group of "outs" at the graduate school met again today . . . to explore the formation of a new PhD program on "subaltern cultures." Ed Gordon of the City College of New York (CCNY), backed to some extent by Juan Flores, initially pushed hard for a curriculum fo-

cused on African-American, Afro-Carib & Latin-American ethnicities. He was entirely upfront about pushing his own political agenda,
and his manner was charmingly courtly. Yet the position he took was
nonetheless implicitly adversarial and, leaping as always to the bait,
I asked Ed (in a charming, courtly way of course) why he had ex-
cluded gays & lesbians, many of whom *do* identify as an ethnic
group, seeing in that legitimizing designation their only possible entry into the rights of first class citizenship. . . . I was amused (& appalled) at the several references to gay & lesbian studies having,
through the establishment of CLAGS, already been privileged at the
Graduate Center, & had to point out that we had one small room,
no staff & only limited in-kind support from the university. After I
saw the large suite of rooms & sizeable staff at Centro [*the CUNY
Puerto Rican Center*], which is 20 years old, I became still more certain that the assumption of CLAGS's entrenched prosperity is part &
parcel of the mainstream cultural view that gays are people with
endless supplies of discretionary money. . . . Still, it does my heart
good to hear gays & lesbians discussed (with a little shove now &
then) as potential allies in any coalition of marginalized, oppressed—
and resistant—peoples.

DECEMBER 19, 1992

Some revealing contrasts in reading the two sets of papers from my
Vassar & Lehman classes. Most of the Vassar students wrote about
their own lives; none of the Lehman students did—a function of
how unimportant they think their lives are. Though the Vassar students *sounded* much smarter during classroom discussions, their papers were pretty much on a par with the Lehman ones. It's a class
difference: the Vassar students have been bred to be articulate, to
sound confident—but as the papers reveal, they neither think nor
feel more deeply than their working class counterparts at Lehman.
And finally, the Lehman students enclose stamps to send back their
papers. The Vassar students don't—don't consider such small change

to be real money; don't try to please authority with gestures of courtesy; don't imagine any need to placate.

DECEMBER 21, 1992

At this morning's Stonewall meeting, the consortium dissolved in all but name. A combination, primarily, of the gay community's backbiting and (as a partial result of that) no funding. NYPL will definitely go ahead with an exhibit of its own. And the Museum of the City of NY will mount an exhibit on the history of gay pride parades. What a bitter irony that only David Kahn's institution [*Brooklyn Historical Society*] is likely to be unrepresented, since he contributed the original impetus and almost all of the work. The combined weight of all four institutions simultaneously doing exhibits & programs would have made for a powerful political statement. That gay & lesbian community groups should themselves have contributed so much to the demise of the project is a sad fact. I can understand the mistrust of mainstream institutions, but in the face of so much transparent goodwill, the distrust became pathological.

A whole new arena for frustration and contention opened up in 1993: the Chelsea House gay-themed series of young adult books for which I'd reluctantly agreed to be "general editor." My initial response had been to say no when Philip Cohen, the owner of Chelsea House, invited me to take on the job. I admired his bravery in being willing to sponsor such a series and in bucking the marketing odds. But I simply had too much on my plate, knew the series would entail a lot of work—and wasn't someone who could delegate authority on a project that carried my name.

But I gave Philip a soft no: the offer did have missionary appeal for me. There was almost nothing available at the time about gay/lesbian lives and culture that gay teens could turn to for reliable information—or that could help straight teens understand the struggles some of their peers were going through. Sensing my ambivalence,

Philip urged me to "come to lunch, we can talk in more detail." Oh well, I thought, the missionary kernel stirring under the soil, why not fully hear what the man has to say.

Philip brought along his wife, Marcia; she was, I'd later learn, an active (though behind-the-scenes) participant in all Chelsea House decisions. I liked them both immediately—they seemed hamisch, *like newly discovered relatives from my own middle-class Jewish family. But there were glimmers of quirkiness. Behind Philip's teddy-bear warmth, his eyes were unmistakably etched with pain and his bushy eyebrows arched with wariness. He later told me—he was public about all this—that he had a serious bipolar disorder.*

"No previous Chelsea House project has ever excited me this much," Philip said that first day over lunch. "Up to now, I've stayed strictly on the business side of publishing, but with this series I'm going to involve myself personally in every editorial decision." I didn't know enough at the time to feel alarmed, but Philip's enthusiasm would prove both a blessing and a curse. "But," Philip went on, "we can't do these books without you. *Harold Bloom—he's edited one of our most successful series, you know—thinks you're an inspired choice as general editor." Bloom, of course, knew nothing about gay and lesbian studies; nor, for that matter, did Philip, as would become apparent soon enough. Anyway, flattery alone, even when hyperbolic, wasn't enough to change my mind.*

But over the course of the next few weeks, Philip kept thickening the pot. Though the young adult market, he told me, was strictly a flat fee/no royalty arrangement (not entirely true then, even less true now), he declared himself willing to double *the usual fee, which he claimed—erroneously, I later learned—was $2,000–2,500 for short books of roughly 110–50 pages in length. He also agreed to let me bypass the usual pool of young adult authors and go instead to leading lesbian and gay scholars, writers, and activists; when I myself worried aloud that they might write above the heads of fifteen-year-olds, Philip dismissed my concern: "Just tell the authors to write as if they were doing a piece for* New York *magazine or the* New Yorker—any fifteen-year-old can read those." They can?—well, he ought to know.*

As our explorations continued, Philip agreed to my suggestion that two series were really needed: "Lives of Notable Gay Men and Lesbians," and "Issues in Lesbian and Gay Life" (homophobia; coming out; AIDS; spirituality, sports, literature; marriage and parenting; race and class, etc.)—for a combined total, Philip grandiloquently announced, of "no less than fifty volumes!" Further, I'd serve both series in the double capacity of acquisitions editor and line editor; I'd be responsible for matching up subjects and authors, as well as editing each manuscript. I would? I could? But did I want to? It sounded like gobs of work. Was I that crazy a workaholic, given the platterful of commitments that already had me doing a circus balancing act?

Yes, I was. What pushed me over the line, I think, was the wild enthusiasm of everyone I sounded out about the series: "What wonderful work these books would do in the world!" "What a blessing they'd be for young lesbian and gay adults!" Okay, I told Philip, let's do it.

While my agent, Frances, began negotiating the specific terms of my contract with Chelsea House, I started to put together the combinations: the writer Randall Kenan on James Baldwin, the literary scholar Sharon O'Brien on Willa Cather, the novelist Jaime Manrique on García Lorca. Philip wasn't thrilled. Who ever heard of these people? He wanted stars—famous authors writing about superfamous subjects. How about k.d. lang on Elton John? Madonna writing on Janis Joplin? I placated him somewhat by getting Terrence McNally, whom I'd known casually for many years, to agree to take on Tennessee Williams (though in the upshot Terrence would never turn in a manuscript).

That was more like it! And to get more such combinations, Philip promptly took to vetoing (though I supposedly had "total control" over choosing subjects and authors) most of the ones I was the most eager to commission: Dennis Cooper on Cavafy, Dale Peck on Carson McCullers, Jewelle Gomez on Audre Lorde, Sarah Schulman on Allen Ginsberg, Bertha Harris on Gertrude Stein (Philip had heard of Ginsberg and Stein, but not Schulman—"forgetaboutit!"). For the "Issues" series, I had still more trouble. I did get Philip to agree to what would become several of my favorites (Jan Clausen's Beyond Gay or Straight:

Understanding Sexual Orientation *and Ruthann Robson's* Gay Men, Lesbians, and the Law*) but Philip's personal vetting machine nixed any number of other titles I thought necessary: "Transvestites and Transsexuals," "Race and Class in the Gay World," "Gays and Lesbians in Other Cultures," etc.*

Somehow, by late summer 1993, twenty contracts had actually been signed, fourteen in the "Lives" series and 6 in the "Issues" series. By that point, the progressive educator Herbert Kohl, who'd read our first published volume, James Baldwin, *warned us that the book was "way above the heads of most high school kids. You don't understand* how *low reading skills are these days." An understandably nervous Philip called an abrupt halt, refusing to issue any more contracts until he could see how well the initial batch sold and was received.*

Meanwhile, problems arose with some of the authors. I understood why they might regard the assignment as a side project, one they'd turn to when some free time opened up on their calendars. Still, a few of them did behave almost as badly as Philip and his staff; they dithered for months, missed promised deadlines, and then either turned in short, mediocre manuscripts or dropped out entirely. But the behavior of a few hardly warranted the abuse almost all suffered at the hands of Chelsea House: contracts delayed, calls unreturned, agents avoided. I felt terrible about this. The writers—often as a result of my missionary pitch—had accepted assignments that provided little money or prestige; they at least expected decent treatment, if not a classy operation—and had trusted me to ensure it.

I was determined to do just that. By the summer of 1994 I was so fed up with the continuing negligent, even dismissive attitude toward the writers that I told Philip flat out that I'd walk unless I could get some guarantees of improved author relations. I didn't want to walk: by then I'd invested two years of hard work and still had high hopes for the potential impact of the series.

Philip swore the writers were exaggerating their plight, but I began to get more than a sniff of homophobia (what do these second-rate folks expect, fer chrissakes!), however unconscious and unintended. Philip was a warm and decent—if high-handed—man. And he had,

*after all, undertaken to produce a set of young adult books sympa-
thetic to lesbians and gay men, which no one else had dared to. But
like racism, homophobia can lurk unacknowledged in even the most
broad-minded breasts (including within gay people themselves).*

Philip did issue some pro forma apologies to some of the worst-
treated authors, but no real changes were made in policy. Nor did he
cease to complain bitterly at the way some of the writers kept making
promises they failed to keep, thus jeopardizing production and publicity schedules. One of his editors, on the side, told me that Philip was
also furious at me—at my ongoing insistence on gender parity in the
biography series, and my immovable refusal to sanction the likes of
Judy Garland, Janis Joplin, or Leontyne Price as possible subjects; if
he was willing, I said, to add "Bisexual" to "Gay and Lesbian" in the
series's title then I might consider such names.

His attitude wasn't improved when two of the first five manuscripts
turned in by my touted authors were so poor in quality that I had to
completely rewrite one and a Chelsea House editor the other. Those
two authors were talented, even heralded writers (no names please),
and their shoddy performance deeply puzzled me. I would have thought
them incapable of such lousy work and even wondered if they'd farmed
out their assignments to some low-paid hack. But then why would they
allow their names to be attached to substandard fare? Had they
thrown themselves a curve by holding in their minds (despite my
telling them not to) the image of a fifteen-to-sixteen-year-old reader capable of understanding only short, declarative sentences?

Most of the manuscripts that would be turned in over the next two
years would be of good quality and some would be superb—the classicist Jane McIntosh Snyder's Sappho, writer Daniel Wolfe's T. E.
Lawrence, literary scholar Jeff Nunokawa's Oscar Wilde, and (in the
"Issues" series) novelist Jan Clausen's Beyond Gay or Straight. But it
was clear early on that the Chelsea House project was going to be difficult all the way—with no guarantee, despite the homily's claim, that
the end result would be all the better for it.

An additional problem from the beginning was the instant, and
negative, reaction of assorted school officials. No sooner was the Chelsea

House 1993–94 catalog published, with a splashy double-page an-
nouncement of the two series, than Philip began to receive outraged
letters. From the principal of the French Academy in Illinois: "I will
not allow these types of materials to be placed in the library. . . . Homo-
sexuality is an aberration. . . ." From the media director of the Trinity
Presbyterian School in Alabama: "I was shocked and appalled by the
new series. . . ." From the librarian of the Culpeper County Middle
School in Virginia: "I doubt many school libraries will purchase these
books. I certainly consider this series inappropriate. . . . After all, you
wouldn't publish 'Great Alcoholics' or 'Famous Fat People' would you?
Please rethink this venture. . . ."

To Philip's credit, the letters—and they would continue to arrive—
made him angry rather than dampening his resolve. But he did start to
shift his marketing strategy away from a strictly young adult pitch to
"these are books for everyone." He was bolstered in that decision by the
considerable amount of national publicity and mostly favorable reviews
that the first published books attracted. But he remained anxious and
continued to hold the line against commissioning additional titles. In
the meantime, complaints from authors continued to arrive ("I haven't
heard anything"; "I have received neither a written or a telephonic re-
sponse"; "I have never had anything approaching such a farcical rela-
tionship with a publisher"; "Is the series in fact going forward?"). I felt
deeply embarrassed, and increasingly angry at Chelsea House.

On all counts—the hate mail, the favorable press, the mounting
tension between Philip, a straight publisher, and his gay authors—the
Chelsea House morass reflected, in miniature, some of the broader
currents of the day. Philip's alternating beneficence and contempt mir-
rored the increasingly conflicted attitude of the general public toward
gay people in general.

Back in 1986, William F. Buckley, not a religious crazy (though a
decided anti-Semite), had published an article insouciantly calling for
gay men with AIDS to be tattooed on the rear end (and drug users on
the arm). That kind of unpitying scorn would—excepting, of course,

among far-right nut cases—have been much less likely in 1993. In the intervening seven years, there had been mounting awareness of the agonies suffered by people with AIDS—and awareness, too, that heterosexuals would not be exempt. Moreover, ACT-UP's angry, macho legions, and their daredevil protests—raining down money, for example, on the Wall Street trading floor to protest against the exorbitant price of AZT—had upended the public's stereotypes of limpwristed sissy boys.

The new imagery of homosexuals looking and acting like "real" men—as culturally defined by our quaint stereotypes—was further enhanced by sympathetic television and film portrayals of "normal"-looking gay men (And the Band Played On and Philadelphia, both released in 1993). By then, too, the gold-medal diving champion, Greg Louganis, had come out as both gay and HIV-positive, and the heterosexual athlete-heroes Magic Johnson and Arthur Ashe had publicly confirmed that they had AIDS.

While all of this somewhat softened the public's attitude toward gay people, it did nothing to stop the epidemic. A dozen years into the AIDS crisis, viable treatment was still illusory; it was in 1993 that the so-called Concorde study, a large-scale European trial, found that AZT, currently the most popular drug for treating HIV, was essentially useless in prolonging life.

The softening of homophobia was real. In a culture with a profoundly contradictory heritage of conformity and permissiveness, the way forward would necessarily be gradual (though only if the demands were for full and instant change; you ask for the whole pie in order to get a portion of it) and would periodically be marked by retreats—yet the fact would remain that nowhere else in the world was there a comparably vibrant and effective gay rights movement. In the 1970s, when the first gay civil rights measures were submitted to public referendum, only 29 percent of the voters reacted favorably; by the early nineties, the percentage had risen to 39 percent—and would continue to climb. In 1993 a Newsweek article wrote us up as "the new power brokers" (a weird exaggeration) and the cover of an issue of New York magazine read "The Bold, Brave New World of Gay Women."

Yet the early nineties also saw a 30 percent increase in assaults and hate crimes against gay people. The dragon of homophobia had hardly been slain. The slow increase in respect and acceptance amounted to no more than a fragile inclusion, and the inclusion was pretty much confined to those gay people who looked and behaved like "normal" folks—meaning primarily middle-class white men who put their faith in polite lobbying, eschewed confrontational tactics, and shied away (as the seventies gay movement had not) from left-wing issues relating to racism, sexism, and economic inequality. The April 25, 1993, March on Washington, which I took part in, exemplified the turn away from "extremist" ACT-UP zaps; to me it seemed a bland, juiceless event—more parade than protest—especially when contrasted with the earlier marches in 1979 and 1987.

The effect of AIDS on public opinion had by then become a double-edged sword: heightened fear of dreaded gay "carriers" counterbalanced by increased sympathy for their suffering. President Clinton's new administration in 1992 exemplified the contradiction: when his initial impulse to lift the ban on gays and lesbians serving openly in the military met with a barrage of opposition, he scurried for cover, settling with relief on a "compromise" solution of "Don't Ask, Don't Tell" that all at once fully exploited the military service of gay people while pretending they didn't exist as human beings.

At the core of homophobia, it has always seemed to me, lies the central fear of "differentness." Why the full, splendid spectrum of humanity should inspire terror in some people rather than joyful wonder is a puzzler. What can be learned from a neighbor whose expressions, habits and values are a duplicate of one's own? "Nothing!" exults the crowd, "and that's exactly the way we like it. It was hard enough learning the dominant social codes; having finally mastered them, and feeling accepted and comfortable, let us alone!"

During 1992–93, a battle over school curriculum erupted in New York City that exemplified such fear and anger. A new curriculum called "Children of the Rainbow" emerged from the desire in some quarters (I sat in on a few planning sessions) to foster awareness and respect for various races, countries, and ethnicities. It suggested teaching music to youngsters through the Mexican hat dance, folklore through Chinese classical stories, etc. That was enough to create uneasiness. What created an explosion was the suggestion that when teaching about families, it was important to remind everyone that some students came from gay or lesbian households.

Half the city's thirty-two local boards balked at the idea of introducing the Rainbow Curriculum earlier than the fifth or sixth grade. After liberal school chancellor Joseph Fernandez made that concession, the board of District 24, largely blue-collar, still held out; its president, Mary Cummins, fiercely denounced the gay/lesbian portions (a small fraction of the whole) of the new curriculum as "dangerously misleading propaganda." When District 24's board members refused even to meet with Fernandez, he suspended them and appointed trustees to work with parent groups on a compromise curriculum.

New York City was far in the lead in trying to introduce the subject of gay life in the early grades, but many schools across the country were beginning gingerly to deal with AIDS awareness for teenagers, and then with the questions AIDS generated about being gay in general. The trend was quickened after a 1989 federal study showed that one-third of adolescents who committed suicide were struggling, usually alone, with defining their sexual orientation.

The bitter fight in New York City over when and how to teach younger children about homosexuality—at a young enough age, I would argue, when it might actually matter, when the children are still genuinely open and malleable—continues to cause sharp dissent around the country. Nonetheless our schools are somewhat safer environments than they used to be for LGBT students—and especially in locations where a proliferating number of gay-straight alliances now exist in high schools. Most parents, however, remain reluctant to have the subject taught even on the high school level for fear it might legitimize homosexuality or "entice" their children into its ranks. Irrational though these fears might be, for many people they easily take precedence over any concern for the bigotry, rejection, and violence that so many minority youngsters still experience in our schools.

By 1993 acceptance was more advanced on many college campuses and wasn't restricted to liberal hotbeds on the two coasts. On the campus of the University of Kansas in Lawrence, surrounded by sod farms and wheat fields, a full week of Gay and Lesbian Awareness in 1993 included a parade, lectures, a dance—and a "kiss-in." Emory University's Coming Out Ball in 1993 was billed as "The Queer Prom You Never Had." Still, the millennium had hardly arrived: of the 30 percent rise in violent hate crimes against gay people in the early nineties, two-thirds of the attacks took place on college campuses. At Cal State, Northridge, fliers appeared offering free baseball bats for gay bashing, and at Syracuse University some students sported T-shirts that read HOMOPHOBIC AND PROUD OF IT.

Nonetheless, single courses relating to LGBT studies were appearing on a growing number of campuses: "Homosexuality in American Culture" at SUNY, Albany; "Queer Fictions" at Amherst; "The History of the Lesbian Movement" at the University of Oregon. At San Francisco State an undergraduate minor was successfully established in the fall of 1993, and at Brown University all incoming freshmen were required to attend an educational session on homophobia. At CLAGS, I was receiving an increasing volume of letters, some from around the world (Spain, Germany, China, Brazil), asking about everything from syllabi to our (nonexistent) PhD program to finding housing in New York while researching a gay-themed article.

Thanks to finally having a part-time graduate assistant, Matt Rottnek, in the office, I had time personally to answer every query that came in. For those about to pack their bags for New York to enroll in "CLAGS's PhD program," I had to explain that we'd been established as a research center, not as a department able to appoint faculty and offer courses. There was no university in the country, I pointed out, that offered even a master's degree in lesbian and gay studies (and in 2009 there still isn't).

I tried to be scrupulous in pointing out to correspondents that *there were any number of campuses where one or more faculty members offered gay-themed courses, and that at a few places—in 1993, Duke, preeminently; both Eve Kosofsky Sedgwick and Michael Moon taught there—something like a real enclave had emerged. As for CLAGS, our mailing list now surpassed five thousand, and nearly five hundred scholars had returned the forms we'd mailed to them for the first Scholarly Directory in Gay and Lesbian Studies—which was published in September 1993. We'd also been having somewhat more success financially. For our third annual fund-raising event that year we were able to enlist a remarkable group of people (Terrence McNally, Gloria Naylor, Grace Paley, Stephen Sondheim, and Danitra Vance) to do a set of readings for us that brought down the house—and loosened the purse strings.*

It was also true that CLAGS's presence at the CUNY Graduate Center, and its growing visibility—we continued to produce packed one-to-three-day conferences ("Queer Theater," "Crossing Identifications," etc.), as well as monthly colloquia, had also led to the presence of an increasing number of openly gay graduate students determined on writing gay-themed doctoral dissertations with one of the faculty's sympathetic members as their mentor. The students were a hardy bunch: they entered a new field where fellowships and grants were all but nonexistent and where future academic job prospects were extremely limited. Thanks in no small measure to their bravery, a critical mass of faculty and students involved in gay and lesbian studies had finally coalesced at the Graduate Center.

When success rears its head, one can count on a heightened response from detractors. As an increasing number of remarkable works—Eve Kosofsky Sedgwick's Epistemology of the Closet, *Judith Butler's* Gender Trouble, *etc.—had emerged from the presses challenging the naturalness of traditional binary thought on gender (male/female) and sexuality (heterosexual/homosexual), the full radical potential of the new scholarship began to make itself felt, and to seriously rattle conservative critics, both straight and gay. In* Illiberal Education, *Dinesh D'Souza denounced the "sham communities"* and "victim studies" that had begun to proliferate on campuses as "a combination of sloganeering, accusation, and intimidation"—and decidedly not serious scholarship.

The gay world, as CLAGS had long since learned, had its own conservatives. Perhaps the best known was Bruce Bawer, who argued in his book A Place at the Table that university-level gay studies programs were presenting a dogmatic view of a separate gay sensibility and identity that reinforced the notion of gay people as Other— thereby holding back the desired goal of assimilation. Within CLAGS itself, that same bunch of conservative white gay male scholars, most of them CUNY faculty members, who'd initially tried to prevent our founding, continued to hiss in the grass around our feet.

The leader of the pack was that old familiar Wayne Dynes, professor of art history at Hunter. The attack this time around came as a considerable surprise. Wayne and I had pieced together at least a partial reconciliation over the preceding year. Also, the occasion for his latest denunciation was the two-day conference of some three dozen lesbian and gay scholars that CLAGS had held many months before (September 1992) to help plan the museum displays that we hoped would be part of the upcoming citywide celebration of "Stonewall 25."

In a letter to David Kahn (which David passed on to me), Dynes, joined by fellow conservatives Warren Johansson, a freelance scholar, and Hunter College professor of history Jim Levin, demanded to know why they hadn't been invited to the conference (given their public hostility to CLAGS, the question seemed disingenuous). They had their own explanation, a fairly breathtaking one. They'd been kept from participating because "Duberman and the others in his inner circle . . . want only a collective monologue with those who parrot the 'politically correct' slogans and clichés. . . . Their stance perfectly mirrors the historical failure of the left in the United States . . . in the writings of Marx, Engels, Lenin, Trotsky, Stalin and Mao Tse-tung there is not one sentence on the subject of homosexuality that is ever so slightly positive. . . . Duberman and his followers are guilty of a monstrous act of self-deception if they look to this tradition. . . ."

We never had. But pointing out the obvious would hardly have *persuaded the Dynes clique that CLAGS wasn't some sort of semisecret cell of the Communist Party. The signatories' further claim that they (unlike us)* "all have a commitment to the canons of academic integrity that would not allow us to compromise the truth for any advantage" *proved downright laughable. Dynes headed up the Proudly Noncommunist group of scholars who turned out the* Encyclopedia of Homosexuality, *a text that had exactly one female contributor, a woman named "Evelyn Gettone," who no one in our "self-perpetuating" group of scholars had ever heard of. With good reason, it turned out. "Evelyn Gettone" didn't exist. Dynes and Johannson had written a number of articles for the* Encyclopedia *under her name in order to claim at least one female contributor. Even had "Gettone" been real, her inclusion would hardly have been the equivalent of gender parity to which CLAGS and most progressive organizations subscribed.*

When that bit of misogynist outrage was publicly exposed and the Encyclopedia *eventually turned over to other hands, no more was heard from Dynes & Company for some time. But then, at the end of 1994, Wayne sent me a letter more bizarre than anything preceding: ". . . no one in the United States knows as much about homosexuality and its scholarship as I do . . . any sensible research institute would be eager to take advantage of the services of someone of my caliber. . . . The time is now overdue for massive corrective action. Here are two essential remedial steps. As soon as possible I must be permanently appointed to your Board . . . [and] for next year I will take charge of an all-day CLAGS Conference, the topic and personnel to be chosen by me. . . ."*

I gave up and turned over his letter to the executive committee of the CLAGS board for response. It was (perhaps too) scoffingly brief: ". . . After carefully considering all your points, the Committee decided that CLAGS cannot agree to your requests. However, we appreciate your interest in CLAGS and its work." Thus endeth—again— the Hundred Years War.

Well, almost. Yet one more footnote awaited. In its fall 1995 issue, the conservative journal Academic Questions *published an article by Dynes ("Queer Studies: In Search of a Discipline") attacking the creeping blight of "political correctness" on campus, turning sturdy green ivy into leafless stalks. Apparently CLAGS, with its "resolute, even defiantly" correctness, exemplified the trend. Why CLAGS even insisted, Dynes indignantly wrote, on gender parity, which, "euphemistically camouflaged," was the obvious equivalent of "quotas."*

"As much a part of CLAGS," Dynes went on, "as its ideological commitments is a certain cronyism based on the personal penchants of its 'maximum leader,' Professor Duberman," as well as the commitment of CLAGS's inner circle to "the socialist-feminist faith. . . . CLAGS's aim is . . . to effect social change by an Orwellian program of thought control." We were, in short, a "cabal," one tied to the waning fortunes of the academic Left and multiculturalism.

There seemed a lack of verve in Wayne's attack this time around; it was as if his heart was no longer in it. Ours certainly wasn't. I think I must somehow have expected, way back in the eighties, that getting gay/lesbian studies established on the university level would be characterized by a serene concord of shared beliefs and mutual affection. This proved naïve in the extreme. That kind of unruffled communal harmony certainly hadn't been true of the process surrounding the formation of women's studies or African-American studies. Both had been rent by ideological warfare, wounded egos and lasting anger. In all those ways, CLAGS broke no new ground.

JANUARY 20, 1993

Clinton's inauguration. His words were effective, not extraordinary. But . . . he *did* mention AIDS on the first day of his presidency; Bush never managed it in four years.

FEBRUARY 5, 1993

Discussions continue at the Rockefeller Foundation—with Tomas's [*Tomas Ibarra-Frausto, the Rockefeller program officer who'd done so much to help CLAGS win the $250,000 Humanities Fellowship Award*] active participation—about the possibility of the five humanities grantees joining forces. . . . In my view there was too much focus on institutional comparisons (the size & duties of our support staffs, etc.) & not enough precise discussion about our political & intellectual agendas—about how much we *actually* shared in common. For example, I said, what about the pronounced homophobia within Latin, African-American & Asian communities—& the reverse discrimination in the gay world toward our own Latin, African-American & Asian minorities. Once I'd raised those questions, the others did prove willing to discuss them, but a certain embarrassed reluctance continued.

FEBRUARY 15, 1993

Lunch today with some half dozen wealthy members of the gay community, as arranged by one of our board members. . . . I emphasized how CLAGS, in serving as a clearing house for campus courses, was helping to build safe havens & self-esteem around the country. . . . I can't help but feel distaste for trying to appeal to the often undeserving, accidentally rich to give money to a cause for which they feel little respect or commitment (but which can, one is required to add, inflate their own reputations for beneficence).

At the meeting for the incipient multicultural PhD, Ed Gordon (saying he spoke for the Chancellor) unexpectedly returned to his earlier insistence that the focus be on African-American and Latin-American studies, and several others signified their agreement. Stanley Aronowitz leaned over to me and whispered, "I don't believe the homophobia that's going around." I challenged Ed on several grounds. We cannot focus, I argued, on what seemed "safe" to the Chancellor and what "can be moved through the Trustees with the greatest ease" without sacrificing our principles. Or what I thought we'd agreed *were* our collective principles. Gordon got huffy and snapped back that he was merely concerned that African-American studies not be forced yet again to take a backseat (this, right after we'd heard from Stanley that the Graduate School had offered Manning Marable a Center, $100,000 a year toward its budget and 3 work/study graduate students—ooh for gay studies to be "left behind" in such fashion!). It would be a disaster, though, to pull apart as allies just at the moment when our combined strength seems likely to make a difference, and conciliatory noises were made all around. Still, when Gordon proposed a resolution "to include all minority identities," I had to add, "as equal partners." He scowled, but assented.

I went from there to doing last minute details—from seltzer to programs—for the PEN/CLAGS "lesbian literature" event. . . . The evening was an unqualified success—a packed auditorium, two vivid panels, and an enthusiastic response all around. Jill [*Johnston*] had threatened to bolt up to the last minute, with Bertha [*Harris*] threatening to "shoot her in both legs" if she didn't show up, but in the upshot Jill was benign. Bertha herself turned on Irene Fornes, demanding to know what her sexual orientation *was*. "Uh-oh," I thought, "this is going to get nasty." To my surprise the audience seemed to favor Fornes (conflating, I think, her closetry through the years with sexual "fluidity"—*their* current emblem), and Eileen Myles denounced Bertha's infringement on Fornes's "freedom." On the second panel, I thought Blanche [*Wiesen Cook*]—elegant and underplayed—and Dorothy [*Allison*]—eloquently raucous—were a perfect team, though I could have done without some of NB's 22-year-old pontifications. . . .

MARCH 28, 1993

Two days at Tarrytown House for reps from the 5 Rockefeller grant centers to discuss an agenda. People pleasant, the site gorgeous, but the tedium of a 2-day talkathon has left me groggy. We did come up with a set of proposals relating to the Rainbow Curriculum & a budget to present to Rockefeller, so the two days were well spent.

MARCH 30, 1993

The doctors have given Craig [*Rodwell, an early hero of gay libera-tion; among much else, his Oscar Wilde Memorial Bookshop in Greenwich Village was the first in the country devoted solely to gay ti-tles*] only a few months [*though only in his fifties, Craig had liver can-cer*]. When I visited today, he said he felt "lucky" to have such news in advance so he could settle his affairs. When I hinted that several efforts were in the works—and pre-eminently through the Publish-ing Triangle [*an organization of LGBT people in publishing*]—to do him honor, he smiled shyly, flushed with pleasure, & told me to "squash" them. I told him I would do no such thing.

APRIL 5, 1993

First copies of *Stonewall* have arrived. I've been feeling no anticipa-tion at all, too preoccupied elsewhere. But in the taxi on my way to Dutton to pick up some copies, I felt a surge of excitement. . . .

APRIL 23, 1993

The April 20th CLAGS/PEN event, "Gay Male Literature," was cu-rious, and taken as a whole dispiriting. Instead of utilizing the talent present, most of the questioners from the audience seemed con-cerned only with mouthing off about their own tired agendas ("How dare you put an Asian character in your book when you're not Asian?!", etc.). And although the auditorium was as packed as for the February 19th event on "Lesbian Literature," the feel of the crowd was much different. Where the women were mostly joyous, warm & supportive, the men were sharp-edged & hostile (so what else is new about women & men?). And dispiriting, too, in that both events were almost entirely self-segregated by gender, with perhaps a few more men at the women's event than vice versa. With so little interest in each other's literatures/lives, how consolidated can a gay/lesbian movement be/become?

On the first panel, I thought Ed [*White*] was best—clear & strong, and especially when cautioning that the politics of identity can lead to a loss of kinship with other oppressed groups. On the 2nd panel, the surprising standout was 25-year-old Dale Peck. Looking like a wild Tatar boy &, speaking in a rapid-fire staccato, he was never less than intelligent and, in his defense of David Leavitt, eloquent. . . .

MAY 5, 1993

The book party for *Stonewall* last night came off well. The bar [*the Stonewall Inn*] was spruced up, flowers & food first-rate, about 150 people showed up, including Ruth Messinger & Quentin Crisp (not invited so far as I know; I guess he has to fill up his *Native* column), and an excited, happy feeling in the air. Five of the six whose stories are told in the book were there, but not, alas, Craig [*Rodwell*], who hoped to come until the last minute but is in terrible shape. [*He died soon after.*]

Maua, [*Yvonne Flowers*], also not well, came by late. Foster [*Gunnison*], shaved pate & girth growing, stayed the course, as did Sylvia [*Rivera*]—in drag ("I wanted to come as a whore"), voluble but not drunk, forlorn around the eyes at the final goodbyes. Karla [*Jay*] seemed happy (a new girlfriend), but Jim [*Fouratt*], in a brief cameo appearance, looked vaguely accusatory, as if, once again, his true stature had failed to be acknowledged. I was glad so many people snapped photos of the five and asked them to sign copies of their books—a most deserved, if belated due . . .

The only bad moments at the party came when someone bore down on me, book open for signing, a cheery, "Hi, Marty" on their lips. With two seconds to figure out a) who they were, and b) what the hell to write in their book, I sometimes resorted to "now I want to get this right: exactly how do you spell your name?", praying the answer would not be B-I-L-L. In a fit of euphoria, I wrote in someone's book, "For one of our heroes," and thereafter, when absolutely stymied, I found myself scribbling the same phrase—leaving a half dozen wholly apolitical types forever after puzzled at the accolade (with doubtless at least one angrily deciding that that bitch Duberman was being ironic, the line meant to read in full, "For one of our heroes of apathy").

MAY 2, 1993

I met with Mark Thompson to discuss my writing the introduction to the *Advocate Reader* (I readily agreed). As for the *Advocate* itself, Mark reports that Niles Merton made a string of disastrous financial decisions & a group of wealthy gay lawyer types were called in and stopped the hemorrhaging through huge cut-backs. Among the casualties, Mark reports, was a 1,000 word rave review by Bob Sumner of *Stonewall* & a 2-page spread with photos—all reduced to a disjointed single paragraph. Ye olde crap shoot.

MAY 28, 1993

I arrived today at PWA [*People With Aids Coalition*] to hear the awful news that 7 of the staff had already been laid off, with the entire office likely to close shortly. I heard various versions & finger-pointings during the day, but most pointed to mismanagement. After 4½ years there, I felt sad at the pending separation, plus a little queasy at the overarching "decay of our family" feeling. . . .

JUNE 22, 1993

The jinx holds: the Sunday *Times* review is in and its mixed-to-negative. As with *Cures*, it's a negative in a sea of raves; and as with *Cures*, it'll stop the book's momentum in its tracks. It makes me crazy. The reviewer, Sara Evans, is heterosexual and writes about women's history—which is either a case of the *Times* conflating women & gay men, or of its once again deliberately reaching for an inappropriate reviewer. There's no way to *guarantee* a negative review but by going consistently to inappropriate or uninformed reviewers, they do the next best thing. Evans complains about the book's lack of contextualization—and I prided myself on success-fully embedding gay history in a general sixties cultural frame—and the street language (should I have converted Sylvia's expletives into wooden academic prose?) What shitty luck—*again*. And there's not a damn thing I can do about it.

The Times *received a raft of letters protesting the review—I know because people sent me copies—but printed not one. The August 9, 1993, entry in my diary spelled out the* Times's *position:*

> *In response to Frances's inquiry, Rebecca Sinkler of the* Book Review *called her to say "the* Times *does not print letters that rewrite the review—unless they're by prominent people. We only print letters that correct factual errors." Bottom line: they will* not *be running any of the letters protesting the Evans review—though by several definitions those letters cor-rected "factual" errors & were, from several professional van-tage points, written by "prominent" people. Is it any wonder I continue to think the* Book Review *has a built-in animus against my work?*

> *I should have written, more accurately, "against left-wing/gay work." In recent years, the* Times *has simply ignored most gay-themed books, while continuing, time and again, to give left-wing ones to reviewers known to be antagonistic—a fate not shared by conservative books. I didn't feel in 1993, and I still don't today, that I was being paranoid in seeing a pattern, because a member of the* Times Sunday Book Review *had privately told me that my biography of Paul Robeson had, in 1989, been intentionally given for review to a neoconservative in the conscious hope that he'd denounce both Robeson and the book; in the upshot he'd denounced only Robeson, and in hoary cold-war terms that outraged many.*

JULY 29, 1993

Last night was Craig's memorial service. I was afraid no one would
show up; I saw no announcement of it & I figured the old timers
were too scattered & the young too oblivious to history to produce
much of an audience. But the small space (the Alexander room at
the Center) was packed with about 100 people. The room was airtight & sweatsoaked, and a dozen people spoke — each of us officially
confined to 3 to 5 minutes, though Randy Wicker did go on. . . . But
over all the evening was a moving tribute to a modest (but not mild)
man who would have disparaged it, tho he deserved far more.

I *wrote an obituary of Craig for the* Village Voice:

"Telling the truth," Craig Rodwell insisted, was invariably the
best policy. In his 52 years he told it consistently, told it to the
police, the politicos, the honchos of the homophile movement,
the press, everyone who ever had authority over him, his own
family, his friends and his lovers. As a boy in the Chicago
Junior School, Craig immediately stepped forward when the
principal demanded to know if the rumor that had reached
him was true that "boys were inserting their penises into other
boys' mouths"; yes, it was true, Craig said, he had himself par-
ticipated often, and what was wrong with it anyway?

And in the final two years of his life, when I interviewed
him over many months for my book, Stonewall, *he went over*
every transcript, searching for errors of fact, scrupulously cor-
recting any possible exaggeration (and especially — hating
cant and immodesty — any embellishment of the extraordinary
role he had himself played in the pre-Stonewall homophile
movement).

Craig Rodwell moved to New York in the summer of 1958,
at 18. Among the first things he did was to go to the office of
the New York Mattachine Society, the fledgling gay political
organization, and try to join up. Told that he would have to

*wait until he was 21, he promptly volunteered to help out in
the office and before long was editing the newsletter—and denouncing Mattachine's lack of activism and visibility, its frightened reliance on "expert" opinion, its refusal unequivocally to
denounce the consensus psychiatric view that homosexuality
was an illness.*

*Advised to adopt a pseudonym to avoid FBI investigation—
as did almost all the members of Mattachine (and those in the
lesbian organization, Daughters of Bilitis as well)—Craig angrily dismissed the suggestion as "paranoia." He then further
scandalized the many conservatives in Mattachine by organizing a half dozen other brave souls to picket the draft board on
Whitehall Street in protest against its policy of releasing information on sexual orientation to employers.*

*Craig's daring caught up with him one day in 1961 at Riis
Park, the beach in Queens then popular with gays. A local or-
dinance banned "suggestive" bathing suits, but the police en-
forced it only against gay men. Some made a camp production
out of covering their bikinis with towels when needing to go on
the boardwalk where the cops were stationed. But Craig
scorned camp indirection in favor of straight-out protest. He
marched past the cops without a towel over his bikini and
when they confronted him, angrily berated them for antigay
harassment. The cops dragged him into their station, knocked
him around, and then hauled him off in handcuffs for arraign-
ment. He landed in the Brooklyn House of Detention where he
was beaten up again for "insolence."*

*The experience hardly made Craig contrite. Nobody, he
insisted, had the right to put him down. And he said as much
to the conservative young actuary—a man named Harvey
Milk—who was his lover at the time. Harvey was horrified over
Craig's Riis Park arrest, fearful it might get in the papers and
somehow implicate him. Harvey eventually cut out for California, where Craig's tutelage in self-assertion stood him in
good stead.*

Craig went on to become a participant in the first efforts at organizing regional and national homophile alliances; to start Mattachine Young Adults (he got in a running battle with the Village Voice—*which he eventually won—over its objections to using the words "homophile" or "homosexual" in the ads Craig placed); to helping wrest control of New York Mattachine from the conservatives; to joining the small band of militants who held a series of demonstrations in the mid-Sixties in front of the Pentagon, the Civil Service Commission, the State Department and the White House in protest against the exclusion of homosexuals from federal employment and the armed forces; to creating the Annual Reminder, a yearly demonstration in front of Independence Hall in Philadelphia that from 1965–69 served to remind the country "that a group of Americans still didn't have their basic rights to life, liberty and the pursuit of happiness"; to opening in 1967 the world's first bookstore devoted solely to gay and lesbian titles—the Oscar Wilde Memorial Bookshop.*

When the Stonewall riots erupted in the summer of 1969, Craig immediately realized—as many did not—that a historic turning point had been reached. He dashed to a nearby phone booth on the first night of the riots to notify the dailies that "a major news story was breaking." He got to sleep that first night at six a.m., and was up again within a few hours to write and distribute a flyer (GET THE MAFIA AND THE COPS OUT OF GAY BARS) analyzing the event and announcing a set of demands for the future.

In losing Craig Rodwell, we have lost one of the true pioneers of the gay and lesbian liberation struggle. But he has left us an abiding legacy: "Be proud of who you are, and always tell the truth."

AUGUST 4, 1993

No, the Community of Mindfulness isn't it. Eight of us gathered last night in an upper westside apartment for three 20-minute sits and two walks, with no more introduction than that. I got thru it—itself a surprise, since I doubted I could meditate that long (or whatever it was I was doing, between squirms & eyeopenings). But I need more articulation, some semblance of a philosophical framework—requirements that I suppose automatically slot me as a hopelessly rationalistic Westerner, incapable of becoming a daffodil, or of smiling like one. Too bad; I do need, or will soon need, some way of "emptying myself" or distancing myself from (too much) feelings; or of fearful, despairing feelings. *Can* one empty out selectively, getting rid of anguish, holding on to gladness? Not this inbred, ancient son of Manhattan.

SEPTEMBER 18, 1993

A marathon of CLAGS meetings. I don't resent it the way I did several years back. Many of the people are enjoyable and you get to see them far more clearly when focused on a particular task than when donned in chatty social guise. What I guess I'm saying is that I'd rather spend time in a CLAGS meeting than at a dinner or a cocktail party. CLAGS *is* my social life, and possibly the best I've ever had.

OCTOBER 10, 1993

Neither Wilde nor Whitman, our most cited 19th-century progenitors, in their own day joined hands with the small band then actively defending homosexuality. Along with being a gauge of the nascient nature of that defense, Oscar & Walt's reticence can also be seen as typical of the way in which the *largest* natures ever refuse to be contained—"dishonesty" or "cowardice" don't get to the heart of it—within the confines of a single label.

OCTOBER 17, 1993

The benefit Friday night (October 15) came off in spectacular style. Not only will we clear nearly $20,000, but the readers were, each in their distinctive way, superb. Sondheim, who came last, broke down twice while reading his lyrics—which endeared him to everyone. Triumph though the evening was, there hasn't been a single call from a Board member over the weekend congratulating Eli [*who organized the event*] for his superb work. Lord, what an ungenerous time, and city, we live in!

. . . The morning after the benefit (yesterday), I flew up to Harvard for my panel on the "Life Likenesses" conference. Ragged from the benefit and from being on antibiotics all week for bronchitis, I "did a Sondheim" while talking about Robeson at his last 1949 concert in Moscow—when he spoke emotionally of Itzik Feffer, and sang as his sole encore the Warsaw Ghetto song, "Zog Nit Kaynmal." The tears took me completely by surprise, but although the moment felt authentic, I wouldn't put it past my competitive unconscious to have plotted the whole thing: "I, too, am a super-sensitive man, deserving of the same acclaim Sondheim got." Well, it's like me to distrust myself even when I'm at my most spontaneous. Anyway, I of course *got* the acclaim. People swarmed around me afterwards, pumping my hand, saying how moved they were at my being moved; the simple display of emotion in our society by a man becomes an event! Or rather, a man *crying*. Michael Eric Dyson, also on the panel, certainly displayed a gallon jug of emotion—of excited passion. I was hugely taken with him.

NOVEMBER 7, 1993

Yesterday's day long retreat of the organizing committee for CLAGS's planned event, "Queer Nations/Black Nations" was a delight. There are now some 15 of us, several of whom I'd never met (Cheryl Dunye [*the filmmaker*] is especially appealing . . .), and not only did we get a lot done, but had fun doing it. . . . I'm the only white on the committee. I've repeatedly suggested that at this point in the planning I should stop attending, but my offer hasn't been taken up. I . . . was surprised at how much general hostility was directed at what I had taken to be universally admired black intellectuals. bell hooks came in for a particular drubbing as a self-absorbed careerist, and Cornel West got his lumps for failing to speak out more firmly against black homophobia — and particularly in the church.

NOVEMBER 9–10, 1993

At Dickinson College in Carlisle, PA . . . to inaugurate the Bud Shaw memorial lecture series; an unusually promising gay Dickinson graduate, he'd died of AIDS a few years ago. . . . I spoke on the subject of "Reclaiming the Gay & Lesbian Past" . . . at the reception I was introduced to a student who this very week has had daily death threats over the phone, and rocks thrown through his window. Outside the liberated urban zones, America continues to be America.

NOVEMBER 17, 1993

At today's meeting about the new multicultural PhD, I questioned the disparity between student ($1500) & faculty ($3000) stipends for working this summer on the core curriculum. Francesca [*Sautman*] & others took up the cry and we succeeded in getting all the available money put into one pot and divided evenly. I also pointed out that the gender balance on the steering committee was way off (many more males of course), but on that made little headway for now. . . .

NOVEMBER 18, 1993

Strange happenings tonight at the Neutral Zone, where I'd agreed to be on a Stonewall panel as a joint fund-raiser for the Zone (a liquor/drug-free place for gay teens to hang out) and for The Gay Museum's Stonewall 25 "window" project. The most vocal people in the audience of about 50 were old-timers, clawing for a little recognition. Randy Wicker & Bob Kohler got into a cat fight, each accusing the other of grabbing the limelight beyond what he deserved. Pathetic—especially in the context of a pre-Stonewall period where so few were doing anything that can be remotely described as political—which hiding and passing are not.

DECEMBER 6, 1993

At CLAGS's December 2/3 conference [*"At the Frontier: Homosexuality and the Social Sciences"*] Mark Blasius came barreling up to me to announce that Ken Sherrill and "other" political scientists (including Mark, I presume) were so "furious" at political science not being represented in the conference that they were boycotting it. "Too bad," I replied, "they'll miss a good conference." Then I added something tart about sociology, American history & Asian studies also being absent, and how *adults* understood that all subjects can't be discussed simultaneously. I was not at my most diplomatic, but I really resented being brought down (yet again) from feeling good about what CLAGS was accomplishing.

DECEMBER 8, 1993

In my role as a gay Grover Whalen, I met today with Kathleen Martindale from Canada and, later, Sally Munt from England. Kathleen came by for a general, enjoyable chat; I was especially buoyed by her view that the field of gay/lesbian studies is, like women's studies & black studies earlier, rent with generational tension & the massacre of innocents; I felt less the lonely victim.

Sally Munt came by looking for nuts & bolts financial support. I steered her in as many directions as I could think of (gay foundations, etc.), but she seemed startled to find CLAGS itself living so marginally. As Kathleen also confirmed, the general feeling is that CLAGS is loaded with money & staff—how else could we be doing so much so stylishly?

JANUARY 3, 1994

Foster [*Gunnison, one of the six people I'd portrayed in my recent book*, Stonewall], is dead—suddenly, of an apparent heart attack. He left the world as he resided within it: unconnected, leaving neither a will nor a close relative. Through his friend, Joe Terzo, I'm trying to salvage Foster's huge and invaluable archive of the pre-Stonewall gay movement, which might otherwise land in an incinerator, and have alerted Mimi [*Bowling, chief archivist of the New York Public Library*] and Fred [*Wasserman, who was working on NYPL's "Stonewall 25" exhibit, "Becoming Visible"*] to the need for intervention— if at all possible. Poor Foster! His archive was his raison d'être. And yet he left it unsecured.

JANUARY 23, 1994

Another all-day meeting of the steering committee for "Black Nations/ Queer Nations." . . . An impressive determination—thus the many meetings—to ensure the conference represents and attracts a *variety* of African-American communities, rather than just an academic one. Impressive, too, is the group's refusal to regard the medium of print as the exclusive conduit of wisdom & truth, or to automatically assume (as scholars are wont) that it is the only way to reach people . . . the warmth, high spirits, political sensitivities—*and* sensitivities to one another—make these gatherings thoroughly wonderful for me. . . .

JANUARY 31, 1994

After 2½ months without meeting—though in November we'd decided on every two weeks—the committee for the new PhD ("Studies in Multiculturalism") finally convened again. It started a ½ hour late & Ed Gordon exited 45 minutes early. . . . Stanley [*Aronowitz*] later confided that the long delay resulted from Frank Bonilla/ Ed Gordon maneuvers to situate direction firmly in their own hands. More power-playing over little power. It does worry me—put together with earlier hints at homophobia—that gay/lesbian studies could yet be shunted to the sidelines.

FEBRUARY 3, 1994

Lunch with Constance Jordan, the beginning, I thought, of the usual lengthy campaign to woo someone as a CLAGS donor. But after the briefest pleasantries, she said she had decided to commit to a 3–4 year, $4,000 per year fellowship for a graduate student working on a dissertation in literary studies "with historic content." I almost leapt the table to embrace her. As Eli said, "maybe you're really getting into it."

FEBRUARY 5, 1994

At the CLAGS board meeting, E. came at me like a shrew for having requested her vita for our next Rockefeller application without asking for her input on the application (yeah sure, like we would have gotten any, since she rarely shows for committee work or anything else). But the details are beside the point. She & J. are always at me for one egregious crime or other. If there was any iota of sympathy or camaraderie in their litany of complaints, that would be one thing. But the spirit is unflaggingly adversarial—& venomous. . . .

F.'s speechifying about "Black Nations/Queer Nations" triumphing despite the indifference of CLAGS's development committee was finally too much for me. . . . F. had done nothing but make grandiose promises about his "connections"—and had then disappeared for the summer. He ultimately did do some fundraising work, but only after Sheila Biddle [*the Ford Foundation's program officer*] made it clear that she would not write the $50,000 grant to document the conference until the organizers had shown that they'd be able to raise the money to put it on. I pointed out to F. that I, too, was a member of the development committee and that it had been my tenacity—along with a major assist from Alison Bernstein, a Ford vice-president—in pursuing Ford that finally got us through the door (Ford had never before given a gay-themed grant); and I was the one who set up contact with the Funding Exchange—hardly examples of "indifference." F. tossed his velour scarf grandly around his shoulder, and proceeded to scold Esther [*cochair of the board*] for having written to inquire if he wished to remain on the board, after he'd missed 3 meetings in a row & the by-laws called for a member being automatically dropped after missing *two*.

"Why wasn't I reminded of the board meetings?" F. demanded imperiously. But you were, repeatedly. The full list of the year's meetings was given out in advance and an additional reminder sent before every meeting to every board member.

F: "You should have called as well. I don't 'do' mail."

Try topping that one! I used to worry that the angry threesome might resign; now I hope for it. I'm no innocent about racial politics & the need these days to swallow a lot. But I won't swallow accusations without foundation, outright falsifications. I'm always quick to like people & still *do* like F., L. (& at least admire) J. I'm too quick in many cases—before I know someone well, thus opening myself to subsequent surprise and disappointment.

FEBRUARY 21, 1994

. . . My egocentrism was previously mediated and expressed, at least in part, through political channels ranging, sequentially, from antiwar protest to educational reform to anarcho-socialist theory. These days, with socialism (purportedly) discredited and values being deconstructed as sophisticated variations of self-delusion and self-defense, only the gay movement retains any compelling hold over me. Though a gay movement without any links to radical energy and alliances—as is mostly the case today—is necessarily diluted in importance and impact.

MARCH 7, 1994

... All day Sat. another planning meeting for BNON. It started alarmingly, with both J. & F. expressing doubt that enough time remained to pull the conference off & suggesting a postponement. I argued against, on the grounds that we *could* pull it off—& in style—& that all the work already done warranted some payoff. In the end, we scaled back enough—really very little—to soothe their nerves.

Just back from two days at Allegheny College. I actually enjoyed most of it. Having Eli along made all the difference. Plus, the people on the Committee pushing for a gay/lesbian undergraduate minor are an awfully nice bunch—I took to Sonya Jones especially. Plus, I barely referred to my notes during the evening lecture—& the spirit did speak. Several surprises: word of CLAGS has still not spread as widely, even to gay/lesbian faculty, as our 7,300 person mailing list would imply; and, far from finding the predictable entrenched homophobia (Meadville, PA!) of a small, rural campus, the president of Allegheny has come out in cordial support of the proposed minor. It will almost certainly be in place by fall—making Allegheny the second campus (along with S.F. State) to introduce such a concentration (C.C.S.F. [*Community College of San Francisco*] has a 2 yr. major). *Allegheny!*—go figure!

MARCH 29, 1994

The CLAGS Rockefeller jury met yesterday and out of 88 applications [*for the two $37,000 awards CLAGS offers*] chose Alan Berube and Janice Irvine. I'm delighted with the results (though those of us from the board were sworn to absolute silence during the deliberations, confining our role to serving lunch and to tabulating the jurors' secret ballots).... The deliberations were as thoughtful & earnest as last year's—& entirely cordial. . . .

One of the side pleasures of the Rockefeller competition is getting to see all the wonderful work in gay/lesbian studies being inaugurated everywhere. I brought home stacks of "supporting documentation" from the applications to read at leisure—a great way of surveying work-in-progress. Would that we could fund it all!

APRIL 14, 1994

I can't get the attenuated BNQN committee to move on the various budget items Sheila Biddle requested six weeks ago. Nobody seems willing to take on the job—and they'd howl if I did. I've tried leaving gently urgent messages for F. & J., but I no longer get return calls, which means I'm already resented as a bossy white man. Meantime Shepherd repeated the remark from an unidentified black board member that the BNQN event "cannot afford to be sponsored by a white-dominated organization." That helps to explain the reluctance to credit CLAGS on the flyer—despite the fact that the idea for the conference & the first proposal were mostly my work—just as, to date, all of the fundraising for it has been. . . . This is keenly frustrating— and potentially dangerous. I'd rather lose the Ford grant and cancel the conference than have the African-American members of the board resign in a huff. They could anyway, of course, rather than agree to CLAGS's continuing sponsorship—which we *have* earned. From this point on, I'm going to keep a very low profile.

The continuing meetings on the multicultural PhD are producing more results, though the high-flown level of abstraction that has set in over discussions of curriculum has me gasping for air. "Epistemic forms of knowledge as intersected by discursive acknowledgment of how meaning is produced" isn't my notion of how to move with clarity & dispatch toward a consideration of core curricula, but I mostly hold my peace & try to imagine that irritation over vocabulary comes from my own undernourished skill in theoretical speculation.

Did a "Second Tuesday" talk at the Gay Center on the Chelsea House series. Surprisingly well-attended and *very* enthusiastic over the series' prospects. Philip [*Cohen*], meantime, is in the hospital. They're trying him on a new medication for manic-depression (the lithium having begun to effect his kidneys). Poor guy; at our last meeting I did think he was showing signs of precipitous mood swings.

MAY 1, 1994

CLAGS's Board meeting got a little heated over BNQN. Though Shepherd had promised to make inquires about CLAGS's sponsorship, etc., in only the most kindly, supportive way, he was instead peremptory & even a little patronizing. Neither F. nor J. were there, so the burden of response fell to L. on her very first board meeting & she was clearly miffed at Shepherd's approach. . . . The CLAGS executive committee has extended an invitation to meet with the BNQN committee—which we hope they'll accept so that all this can be ironed out well this side of a potentially explosive situation.

MAY 4, 1994

Last colloquium of the season. A fascinating one: Suzanne Kessler analyzing the destructive nature of "corrective" surgery on intersexed children. Eloquent plea for legitimizing intersex identity as humane in itself *and* as a potent way to destabilize the gender binary.

MAY 7, 1994

"Homo-Economics" conference yesterday. All the panels were worth hearing, but at its height no more than 75 people present. Advance inquiries were heavy, so it's something of a puzzle. At least we've learned that spending $1,500 + to open the Graduate School on a Saturday is pointless. I was most taken with Lee Badgett's modest, thoughtful paper (gays are, if anything, economically *dis*advantaged) and, personally, with Michael Piore, though his views seem sweetly naïve. He's decided other oppressed groups—blacks & labor—made the greatest progress by stressing "human dignity" rather than narrow interests. Yet simultaneously he deplores the gay movement's failure to push forward its drag queens—somehow presuming *that* would appeal to the mainstream. He wholly misses the point that civil rights are won by the (repugnant) strategy of claiming we are "'just folks," and doesn't see that *hiding* our drag queens is part & parcel of that strategy. Like Piore, I prefer to stress ways in which gays are *different*, but unlike him I don't expect that to lead to civil rights victories.

MAY 10, 1994

Reading Mab Segrest's *Memoir of a Race Traitor*. How vastly different the struggles against racism & homophobia are when fought out on a local, rural level. In a place like New York we're comparatively protected by strength of numbers and demonstrated political clout. Violence happens, but not presumptively. Segrest literally puts her own life on the line every time she marches or speaks out. It's heroism of a wholly different order. . . .

MAY 13, 1994

F. came to the CLAGS Exec. Comm. last night, clearly aggrieved and bearing peremptory messages from the BNQN committee ("we demand absolute autonomy in planning the conference and in arranging for publication of its proceedings"). He & I had talked at length the day before, so I was fully prepared & led off the discussion by characterizing BNQN's position as completely understandable—& necessary. The others agreed (happily, neither Shepherd nor David were in attendance), though Esther came perilously close a few times to asking, dangerously, for additional reassurance that CLAGS would receive appropriate billing for its investment of energy, support & money. As I said after F. left (he had declared himself "satisfied"), better that CLAGS ends up at the bottom of a list of 50 convenors— or not on the list at all—rather than risk a rupture with the African-American members of the board, & the blow that would be to our reputation for serious commitment to multiculturalism . . . discussion turned to what more we could do to meet the needs of lesbian and gay students at the Graduate Center, however difficult to define. Upshot: a new subcommittee to try to pinpoint those needs & meet them, plus a decision to devote the $4,500 I raised last winter entirely to an "emergency fund" for gay & lesbian graduate students—for travel, books, photocopying, whatever. . . .

MAY 26, 1994

Hearing that Foster's* cousin, Mrs. Henstenbury, had decided to give his papers to the Univ. of Conn. rather than NYPL [as I'd urged; the New York Public Library, under the initiative of Mimi Bowling, the chief archivist, had been actively soliciting gay-related manuscripts, amassing an exceptionally strong collection], I decided to make a last-ditch appeal to Mrs. H. The news was worse than I thought. She revealed over the course of a 45-minute phone call that (a) her husband had already destroyed the correspondence between Foster's doctor & mother ("much too personal"); (b) that she "can't seem to find" that "extensive correspondence file" I had earlier alerted her to—(though Foster sent me dozens of photocopies from it, which I will now give to NYPL as apparently the only surviving remnant of it); (c) that she does have one file of correspondence with a Robert Martin [Stephen Donaldson] which she "isn't sure what to do with," given its personal nature (I think I talked her into saving it & into consulting with Donaldson. . . . ; (d) that she's already "discarded" the huge mound of newspapers—"yes, I'm afraid even the early gay/lesbian ones"—though she did save the "valuable" sets of Opera News (Oh Lord, deliver us from our straight custodians!); (e) that the Univ. of Conn. won out because it's building a wing to house the papers of "prominent Conn. citizens"—& Foster "would have been so pleased" at their excitement over featuring his 3,000

*Foster Gunnison [see also January 3, 1994 entry] had amassed a huge archive about the early, pre-Stonewall homophile movement in which he'd been active. To protect the archive, I'd urged him to write a will leaving instructions about its deposit. But he'd waved me off, saying he was "healthy as a horse." In January 1994, Foster had died of a heart attack, intestate.

books on railroading. And what about access to the other (apparently far less valuable) gay material? "Oh, they assured me that they would take *all* his papers, and would make them available to scholars." *When?*—would they process them soon? Have they agreed to a date for the completion of processing? "Oh, I didn't think to ask for any promise of that sort."

And so Foster's life work—*not* railroading—as an archivist has been partly destroyed (the most singular parts), partly buried.

JUNE 2, 1994

All-day retreat on the 31st to discuss the core curriculum for the "Studies in Multiculturalism" PhD. Some strange cross-currents persist, especially from Frank, who tends to be self-congratulatory about his awareness of gay/lesbian issues—and then confesses they were omitted from his course on migration, where the post–WW II gay movement to the cities should have been a natural; and from Ed Gordon, who continues to express his courtly "discomforts" with any new doctorate not focused on Latino & African-American subjects ("Not every issue needs to be considered from all perspectives"). Even Dorothy, who overall *is* well-disposed, offered a descriptive example of how all of our perspectives could combine in a course on, say, political economy—and then omitted the gay/lesbian perspective entirely. I and the four other people from CLAGS I asked to attend the retreat held their feet to the fire on all these points—or rather the embers, since we *are* still hoping for collegiality. It's still something of a wonder to me that we've gotten this far in establishing an equal toehold. I think we can hold to it—and that will be a giant step toward embedding gay & lesbian studies in the university world—*if* the multicultural umbrella under which we've taken refuge isn't itself destroyed by an accelerating right-wing tide. The core curriculum strikes me as so innovative, I want to sign up for it myself. Who *will* be fit to teach it? We could all use a faculty NEH summer seminar to prepare—an idea I suggested to the committee.

Meantime, BNQN continues in a negative direction. It looks like the conference will be either pared down or postponed. I again tried arguing against the latter—enough money *is* in hand; we could be embarrassed with the Ford Foundation, etc.—but don't think I made much headway. Anything I do or say is wrong—a sign of either interference or indifference. J. has turned ice-cold mean—as if it's my fault half the committee doesn't show for meetings or do their assignments—& our promised fund-raiser, F., has again gone off to Paris for two months. This all makes me very unhappy—given the high state of promise & camaraderie when we started meeting some 6–8 months ago. But such is the state of racial politics—which is sadder still.

Even for someone who likes to keep busy, June 1994 sated all needs. The recent publication of my book Stonewall *coincided with celebrations for the twenty-fifth anniversary of the Stonewall riots that inaugurated the modern gay movement; as a result, I did a considerable amount of travel, interviews, and speeches. In New York City itself, the original coalition of institutions to create a broad set of exhibitions had disintegrated, but the Museum of the City of New York put on a minor exhibitions of photographs, some of them mislabeled, tucked away at the end of a corridor with inappropriate music seeping in from an adjoining exhibit across the hall—a sloppy, insulting effort. The New York Public Library, at its main branch on Forty-second Street, however, more than made up for it with a large-scale, brilliantly mounted pictorial history ("Becoming Visible") that proved unforgettable (I'd played a minor role during the planning stages). Finally, an enormous, international march was held that blanketed the city.*

JUNE 6, 1994

One of the wilder ones:

    11:00 *Miami Herald*
    12:00 *TIME*

2:30 *Washington Post*
5:00 "Party Talk"—TV
7:00 Fellowship Comm.
9:00 *The Australian*
10:30 WFNX Boston

And tomorrow we go to Boston for 2 more days of "Yes, Stonewall was a milestone. No, gays & lesbians are not free of oppression."

"Party Talk" was the nadir. It took the host 45 minutes to decide whether his plaid pants with tunic was better highlighted by a vinyl vest or a simple black pullover. Much filler talk about the "wonders" of MAC makeup—"Madonna says it's her favorite!" Then 4 whole (silly) minutes on camera.

JUNE 7–9, 1994, BOSTON

The official cocktail reception was *very* upscale & high-toned; a fair number of the 75 or so wealthy guests, I was told, were still closeted. I used the occasion to pitch CLAGS to the crowd; and Eli followed up by pocketing the list he saw on the sign-in table of names and addresses & how much money each had contributed to the event. What a team!

The evening event at Fanueil Hall drew a few from the cocktail party, but was overwhelmingly younger, more informal, more multicultural. The black gay mayor of Cambridge, Ken Reeves, introduced me & then—Great Scot!—presented me with a key to the city & an ornamental plate of some kind. On entering Fanueil Hall earlier in the afternoon (Eli & I spent a pleasant day touring the North End), my eye had instantly fallen on the "Compromise of 1850" painting above the stage, with Daniel Webster prominently featured. The "Divine Daniel"—critic of the antislavery movement, always ready to barter away moral principle. I knew I had the opening for my speech: "Daniel Webster was wrong. He was wrong about the antislavery struggle. He was wrong in general about how social change is achieved. Slavery was ended because the agitators *continued* to press the question. That, to be sure, brought trouble and disorder to the country. But the pursuit of justice always entails some disarray—because that pursuit antagonizes entrenched privilege, and power never voluntarily yields its sway. . . ."

JUNE 16, 1994

The opening tonight of "Becoming Visible" at the New York Public Library at 42nd Street, was spectacular. Just seeing the huge banner above the main entrance made my heart stop. . . . The superb visual mounting of the show—curators Molly McGarry and Fred Wasserman did a great job—was equal to the fascination of its contents. Not that I could concentrate on much of it: I was too excited to squint at more than a few captions. I'll digest it at leisure on future visits. Mimi's [*Bowling*] done a magnificent job, and against heavy odds. [*There had been opposition to the exhibit from members of NYPL's board of trustees*]. As I said in the note attached to the flowers I sent her this morning: "The gay community is forever in your debt." It's right to be suspicious of mainstreaming, but . . . [*the exhibit's*] sensitive attention to gender parity & multiculturalism in this case erased all doubts.

The one sour note was a sign at the entrance to the exhibition hall: "This exhibit may not be appropriate for all viewers" (or something like that). I cornered an NYPL staffer & told him if anything was inappropriate, it was the sign. He nervously said something about "concern for visitors from Peoria." "But those are precisely the people who need to see the exhibit," I replied. "Well," he conceded, "the sign is certainly inappropriate tonight," and to my surprise he went over and turned it to the wall. It may return tomorrow, but a number of people said they intended to write letters of complaint about it.

Who would have dreamed 25 years ago that we would see the pink triangle floating over one of the city's premier cultural institutions?

JUNE 19, 1994

The opening of the Gay Games last night in Wien Stadium (Columbia Univ.). Steamy, uncomfortable weather, but an exhilarating
evening. The ceremonies were an hour and a half late, the sound
system alternately mute & shrieky, the heat sweltering. But the
procession of athletes put all to rights. Thirty-six countries were represented, including Bulgaria, Ghana, Taiwan and Oman. The
cheerful, colorful throngs—in the end there were more athletes
than spectators—turned us all into enthusiasts.

True, it was based on an Olympics sporting model that rewards
stereotypic bodies, emphasizes competition and reinforces whole-
someness—but with a difference. Anyone who wants to participate in
our Games can, and a number of warriors looked charmingly out of
shape. And several of the speakers at least paid sweetly utopian lip service to avoiding rivalry & aiming only at one's personal best. True, too,
that politics (excepting references to AIDS) was notably absent . . . no
calls to organize and demonstrate, no manifestos & demands. . . . But
a gathering of this size & joyfulness certainly is political by other definitions: the thrill of mass visibility & assertiveness reinforces the commitment to coming out & staying out—and that at least provides the
potential for recruitment to organizational work.

JUNE 22, 1994

An astounding turnout last night at the CLAGS co-sponsored
"Twenty-Five Years After Stonewall" panel. Not only was the auditorium jammed, but an overflow crowd of some 100 had to be shunted
to the screening room on the 3rd floor. I thought everyone on the
panel did well, in his/her different ways—and the audience (mostly
non–New Yorkers, I'd judge) was certainly enthusiastic. I'd never met
Carmen Vazquez before & found her warm & charming. But I didn't
agree with her remarks that "our movement is *all* about sexuality"—
with not even a mention of gender non-conformity (despite her own
"butch" self-description, & tie and jacket to match).

Today, for the first time, I feel worn-out. Too many highs, too many interviews, too much talk. And still more to come: a panel tonight at the Roosevelt Hotel; CBS at 7:30 a.m. tomorrow, etc. The worst part is having to hear my own now-canned responses. It's disconcerting to have the same sentences fall out of my mouth over & over again. Not good for the "creative" self-image, but I suppose inevitable given the non-stop, repetitive nature of the interviews.

A few of the written contributions I made to the festivities were somewhat less hackneyed than the spoken ones. Richard Schneider Jr. of the Harvard Gay & Lesbian Review, *for one, did a broadgauged interview with me and subsequently provided a transcript, thereby allowing me to clarify my thoughts further about a number of issues:*

> *. . . There was nothing inevitable about the Stonewall riots. They did not have to happen in June of '69 in Greenwich Village, New York . . . by the end of the '60s conditions were ripe for a Stonewall. It could have happened in any number of large cities—but only in a large city, where a critical consciousness and mass had been achieved. On the other hand, it could not have happened in 1959. The country had to have lived through the decade of the '60s, meaning the across-the-board challenge to authority in many areas of American life— whether emanating from the struggle against the war in Vietnam, the emergence of the feminist movement at the end of the decade, or, of course, from the granddaddy of all movements, the black struggle for civil rights going back to the '50s.*
>
> *Two common messages began to resonate during the '60s: "don't trust the experts" (like those Southeast Asian "specialists" who got us into the war in Vietnam); and "it's okay to be different." (I, for one, had turned over my life during much of the '60s to those experts in psychiatry who claimed they could "cure" my sexual orientation.) Though I'd been outspoken about the Vietnam War and in defense of student radicals, it*

had taken a while before those '60s messages began to seep into my defended brain, before I could abandon the psychoanalytic insistence that I had a character disorder and that homosexuality equaled pathology.

The second '60s message about being different came essentially from the black struggle: that black is different and beautiful. And that view began to resonate for many gay people as well: We don't have to go on apologizing for who we are and trying to conform to standards outside of ourselves, to white middle-class values as to what is viable behavior or a "decent" lifestyle.

What had also preceded Stonewall was at least an incipient gay and lesbian struggle per se. I myself didn't get activated until 1971. But there were a handful of people in the '60s who stood up, who joined the Mattachine Society or the Daughters of Bilitis. These were people who in a sense had remained "unsocialized"—who hadn't (like me) dutifully internalized the social norms of the day that insisted gay is sick, disturbed, second-rate. Somehow a few hundred people didn't absorb that message and we owe them a great debt; we're all standing on their shoulders. Yet where they're acknowledged, it's usually in patronizing terms: "Yeah, there was this primitive little gay political movement before Stonewall, but these people were essentially assimilationists and apologists." And to some degree they were, but they were also subversives, and also engaged in some dangerous political actions—like picketing the State Department or White House, like demonstrating annually in Philadelphia in front of Independence Hall. Those were remarkably brave acts in the context of those years. The participants could easily have been beaten up on the street, or arrested, or lost their jobs and apartments. No media would have considered assaults against such sickos as newsworthy. No support groups existed to succor their wounds.

Another point: There tends to be a lot of East Coast provincialism surrounding the pre-Stonewall years. Few Easterners know anything about what was happening in California, and when told, tend to be disbelieving and dismissive. The largest pre-Stonewall gay organization, for example, SIR (The Society for Individual Rights) was on the West Coast and had thousands of members. Also, several riots had taken place in San Francisco and elsewhere—such as the large protest at Compton's Cafeteria—that preceded Stonewall. Compton's could easily have become the mythic symbol of the modern gay movement. Why it didn't and Stonewall did will always be something of a mystery. . . .

America has always had a genius for swallowing up its dissenters. Almost every social protest movement in this country has been inaugurated by radical passion, but has then been quickly co-opted by reformist caution, with the radical crowd displaced and never again viable. Because finally, profoundly, we're a conservative nation, and a conformist nation, and there isn't much tolerance for either equity or for difference. Reformism, paradoxically, does produce some real gains. Some would say that the New Deal did little more than stick a few band-aids on the worst wounds of the Great Depression. But band-aids can sometimes help. "Mere" reformism can provide some real solace and some real diminution of suffering. The problem is that reformism always leaves the society untransformed, suffering (perhaps) diminished, but still far too omnipresent. The New Deal did create workmen's compensation, but it helped to destroy a previously viable socialist movement that might have done away with the still currently sharp distinctions between workers and bosses.

Currently I find little sympathy within our own community for radical solutions. Remember when some protestors a few years back invaded St. Patrick's and one ACT-UP'er DARED to trample the host? Well! An awful lot of gays went through the roof in their outrage at so "sacrilegious" an act, even though the Church has promoted homophobic brutality for centuries, and down to the present day. The Church did everything it could for 15 years to defeat a gay civil rights bill in

New York City, and it finally passed in 1986 over the strenuous opposition of the Catholic hierarchy (along with orthodox
Jews and Protestant fundamentalists).

I'm not sanguine that the gay movement is ever going to
reach its full potential. The potential is there. Look at the way
some gay and lesbian people, in line with radical feminists, are
redefining gender, as well as the relationship between gender
and sexuality (women, not men, may well have the larger ap-
petites and capacities for sex). These are critical transforma-
tions in the meaning of what it is to be a woman or a man, to
be involved in a primary relationship, to realistically expect
from friendship. What, we're finally asking, is this much deplored thing we've been calling "promiscuity"? Does the answer hinge on how many different partners or how many times
a week with the same partner?

I think the central potential in the gay movement relates to
definitions of gender: Are there any intrinsic properties to
maleness or femaleness (other than the obvious anatomical
ones), any innate psychological or intellectual or emotional
differences, capacities, qualities? I, for one, have never been
persuaded that there are. Gays have long experimented with
different ways of being "male" or "female." But the whole glorification of machismo that began to typify the gay male style
in the late '70s is based on a scorn for "effeminacy." This reifi-
cation of machismo holds the potential to destroy any significant attempt to redefine gender.

The same is true of sexuality. Before AIDS, people had
stopped using the pejorative word "promiscuous" and had substituted the more affirming notion of "sexual adventuring."
That included validating back-room sex, bathhouse sex, sex in
the backs of trucks or on the piers, any and all kinds of unconventional ways of coupling and having orgasms. Trying on all
kinds of roles—sometimes in the course of a single evening—
was celebrated as a way to one's finding out where fears were
couched, where ecstasy resided—and even why.

But with AIDS we began to hear a lot of apologetics in the gay male world. The apologists weren't saying what the right-wingers were saying, that AIDS is God's punishment. But a lot of people—and I'd include Larry Kramer—were deploring the "destructive" nature of gay male promiscuity, saying it was time to "grow up," time to recognize that every human being really does long for the same thing, namely a committed, sustained, intimate relationship. That last may be true. But people are different. Even the same person at different ages seeks different satisfactions. Though at this stage in my own life I want nothing other than the comfort and dailiness of an ongoing, committed relationship, at earlier periods in my life I didn't want that at all. I wanted a lot of excitement and variety. Apologetics for what we once were is in essence a denial of our passionate, youthful truths. . . .

For the Village Voice's Stonewall issue, I took on the somewhat off-beat topic of media coverage of the 1969 riots:

We didn't even get to cover our own riot.

Which is no surprise. In a heterosexual universe, it had long been assumed that gay men and lesbians were not reliable witnesses on their lives (let alone on anything else). Our experience had to be explained to us, we were told: we lacked the "needed objectivity," and our "pathology" further compromised our ability to see straight (as it were). Surely no one would recommend that operations for cancer be performed by the afflicted patients themselves.

And so even the countercultural Village Voice—itself at the journalistic center of sixties protest—assigned two heterosexual reporters to cover the outbreak of gay rioting at the Greenwich Village bar, the Stonewall Inn. The lead sentence in Lucian Truscott IV's piece referred to the sudden "specter" of gay power having "erected its brazen head and spat out a fairy tale the likes of which the area has never seen." In his sec-

ond sentence, Truscott described "the forces of faggotry . . .
prancing high and jubilant in the street . . ."

To be fair, this was 1969. Not too many gay people were using kinder, more accurate words about themselves (certainly I
wasn't; my idea of liberation in those years was to put myself in
the hands of a therapist promising to free me from my "afflicted" orientation). Besides, Truscott also commented in his
article on the riots creating prospects for gays to assert "presence, possibility, and pride"—a potential not widely seen at
the time, though many now claim, retrospectively, to having
immediately understood the significance of the riots.

Truscott also alluded to the way the riots had been covered
in the Daily News as having been "anything but kind to the
gay cause"—and few other straight reporters of the day would
have considered the degree of kindness in an article about despised homosexuals as being a relevant gauge for evaluating its
journalistic worth (unlike, say, its ability to sell newspapers).
Jerry Lisker, the author of the Daily News article, may not
have been responsible for its headline, HOMO NEST RAIDED,
QUEEN BEES ARE STINGING MAD," but he most assuredly was
for the adjectival mockery ("lisping," "prancing," etc.) of its
prose, and its smug, derisive characterizations of "honeys
turned Madwomen of Challiot."

The New York Times was above so coarse a frontal assault.
It had its own dismissive strategy, one more appropriate to its
high-toned readership: avoid covering news about gays at all, or
do so briefly and antiseptically in a back-page throwaway story.
For its short article about the first night of the riots, the Times
chose the headline 4 POLICEMEN HURT IN 'VILLAGE' RAID—
the lives of the men in blue, not the boys in skirts, was what mat-
tered. The Times did mention that the police had "confiscated
cases of liquor from the bar," but said not a word about the way
they had wantonly smashed jukeboxes, mirrors, and cigarette
machines, ripped out phones, plugged up toilets—and pock-
eted all the money from the cash register and safe.

The Times *article reduced the rage of thousands to what it characterized as "a rampage" by "hundreds of young men." The paper further implied that the arrest during the riot of the popular folksinger (and heterosexual) Dave Van Ronk had resulted from his "having thrown a heavy object at a patrolman." In fact, the police had grabbed Van Ronk at random out of the crowd, had dragged him by the hair back into the Stonewall Inn where they had retreated from the mob, and had proceeded to give him a severe beating. When it looked as if Van Ronk was about to pass out, he'd been handcuffed and Deputy Inspector Pine, the ranking officer, had snapped, "All right, we book him for assault."*

And so the limited, distorted coverage went . . . The Voice's *second article, by Howard Smith, did mention police vandalism and overall was free of Truscott's homophobia. The* New York Post—*then a liberal paper—did do a follow-up piece headlined* THE GAY ANGER BEHIND THE RIOTS, *which responsibly discussed resentment over Mafia control of the Stonewall (and all other gay bars), over the huge profits that never went back into the gay community, and the huge payoffs that went to the police. And both* RAT *and the* East Village Other, *organs of the counterculture, also carried sympathetic accounts.*

But these were marginal voices in a coverage that overall reflected all too accurately the dominant bias of the culture. Its perfect creature, Time *magazine, summarized the majoritarian view when, some four months after the riots and in response to the publicity they had generated, it published a lengthy "analysis" of gay life. The article characterized "the homosexual subculture [as] . . . without question, shallow and unstable," and warned its possibly wavering readership yet again that "homosexuality is a serious and sometimes crippling maladjustment."*

There we have the authentic voice of mainstream America, circa 1969. And it is a voice once again sounding loudly

*through the land as the legions of the religious right methodi-
cally prepare for battle against the "gay lifestyle" . . .*

JUNE 23, 1994

How naïve I can still be. I thought at least the most prestigious organs of the mainstream press would get it right for Stonewall's
25th . . . [yet] they manage to string inaccuracy after inaccuracy. Today's *Times* piece talks about faux pearls, handbags, patent leather
pumps & beehive wigs—none of which were in view—in relation to
the first night's rioting; gets the time of the raid & the number of police wrong; has patrons of other bars joining in (in fact the most prominent of them, Julius's, turned its back & may have held rioters for the
police); maximizes the role of drag queens (& dresses them in *contemporary* drag); minimizes the role of more "ordinary" gay men; and
reduces the extensive rioting of the 2nd & 5th nights to "flare-ups,"
whereas two of the four were far more. Even Andy Kopkind, in the
Nation, manages to distort—crediting the chino crowd with far more
insight into their own effeminacy than they had, and designating
Stonewall "the purest cultural revolution of them all"—whatever
that means. It's not that the gay press has done better—the *Advocate*
refers to "men in dresses" at the riots—and indeed may have originated many of the misstatements that the straight press subsequently
picked up. I'm entitled to feel annoyed, but not surprised: Of what
else has the recording of "history" ever consisted?

JUNE 24, 1994

. . . The last few days I've been saying no to additional interviews. I
probably would have yielded to Dutton's [*the publisher of my book,*
Stonewall] entreaty that I at least accept the "Good Morning America"
show, but when I heard that it was to be me and Bruce Bawer, I refused. As I told "GMA," it was offensive and absurd to have two middle-
class white men serving as sole spokespeople on "the future of the

gay and lesbian movement." They seemed startled—and unper-
suaded. I gave them a list—Barbara Smith, Donna M. [*Minkowitz*],
Cathy Cohen—of people who could & should replace me, but
doubt if they'll choose from it.

Later: Amazing! The "GMA" producer called to *thank* me for
alerting them to the mistake/injustice of having on two white men,
and to say that they were going with Paula Ettelbrick as my replacement. A black woman would have been still better, but Paula *is* an
articulate leftie. So hooray for (semi-) miracles!

JUNE 26, 1994

. . . reading at A Different Light [*a gay bookstore*]. When I got to the
very end of the reading—the last few paragraphs of the book, I mo-
mentarily choked up. It *is* a throat-catching realization to see where
we were then, and how far we've come. To be sure, progress is re-
versible, and continuing struggle essential; but even if *some* reversals
are a-foot, I doubt we could ever be thrown back into quite so dark a
world.

Today's culmination—the March—was, curiously, something of
a letdown. The massive numbers were impressive indeed, but there
wasn't enough raucous splash to make the day thrilling. In emphasizing internationalism, the (mostly non–New York organizers) rightly
resisted the usual commercial floats & bar sponsorships, but they
threw out the baby with the bath. Not enough high-spirited, ironic,
frivolity—not enough *gayness*.

OCTOBER 18, 1994

My Lehman class this term is the most enjoyable in several years. I
ascribe it mostly to the outspoken presence of two lesbians, Riva &
Michelle, both as warm & likable as they are passionate in defense
of their own lives. It also helps that there's only one man out of 28
students—& he appears irregularly & says nothing. Several of the
women are obviously homophobic, and two of the youngest are

(loudly) dim-witted as well. But the talk is spirited and respectful, and I get revved up all over again with the extraordinary, alive diversity of CUNY students. It makes me crazy to read the current crop of negative articles in the press about the "failure" of CUNY as an institution, the "destruction of academic standards." Admittedly, our students are often not well read or well prepared. But the critics show no appreciation of the horrendous struggle they have, day in day out, to prepare at all — to sandwich in the occasional hours between full-time jobs and family obligations. No, at bottom the animus is against "those" people gaining access at all to the university world — giving those "animalistic" Others the (narrow) skills & values passed down from middle-class white fathers to middle-class white sons (& recently, to some daughters).

OCTOBER 19, 1994

Sheila Biddle called to say we *have* gotten the Ford grant—$50,000 to document (not stage) the BNQN conference. I was thrilled at the news—we've cracked open another major foundation, and hopefully other gay & lesbian enterprises will now have an easier time getting funded. But after the euphoria passed, I got in touch with some anger, too. I've worked my ass off to get this grant, hounding Biddle till I finally got a foot in the door. And for that effort have largely drawn resentment in the BNQN committee. I learned today that a new "core committee" for the conference has been formed, and I am not on it—though B. & D., neither of whom attended a single meeting over the summer, are. I think I can accurately say that I neither wanted nor expected to be singled out for special praise; but I didn't expect overt hostility either—which, given current black/white tensions, may well have been naïve of me.

OCTOBER 24, 1994

First meeting (at Alisa Solomon's) to put together the Queer Theater conference for April. Three and a half hours—but fun. A genial, smart bunch. I was especially drawn to Ellie Covan of Dixon Place and to David Román. . . . Two curious reports in regard to the Public Theater's co-sponsorship: we have carte blanche as to who gets invited—with one exception: Terrence McNally, who for some reason is persona non grata at the Public; we're inviting him anyway. Second, George Wolfe, who we had hoped would be a keynoter, refuses even to give welcoming remarks. "Squeamish" about any direct gay association, is how Alisa put it. I enjoyed all the theater talk; its been a while—& realizing just how long made me a little sad.

NOVEMBER 2, 1994

The CLAGS benefit last night came off all right—but no better than that. Decidedly *not* an Eli production. It was good of S. to take on the job at all, but his skinflinty side took over at the last minute and (without my knowing it) he cut the food order to 50 people (with some 150–200 in attendance); it (all 3 cucumber sandwiches) had entirely disappeared within a minute of the start of the reception. Of the performers, Holly Hughes was the highpoint (a powerful, moving presence) and Nicky P. the decided low. Both Tony [*Kushner*] & Terrence read well, Terrence more relaxed than last year, Tony more hurried & monochromatic. I doubt we'll do this again; the Benefit skein has played out. Henceforth, the fund-raiser route seems to be house parties, individual donor cultivation, and foundations.

NOVEMBER 4, 1994

Out to Hofstra yesterday to keynote their theater conference. Judging from the glitter of the program & the size of the staff, they spent a fortune—how dearly CLAGS could use it!— on gathering 75 or so scholars to read papers to each other that were better mailed or published. . . .

NOVEMBER 9–10, 1994

Flew to Columbus, Ohio, then drove 4 hours to Univ. of Charleston, West Virginia, to avoid more time fearfully aloft. I was warned that some of my audience had brought bibles with them, but I spotted a few smiling gay faces in the crowd, which gave me heart—oh hell, I was looking forward to a little confrontational rowdyism! But the hostility was marginal & mostly idiotic ("Just how many men do you think can get erections with other men?" All of them, silly). My "host," Prof P. was a thoroughly self-important, smarmy '50s throwback. A gay student later complained to me that P., though gay, had turned a deaf ear to all entreaties to help form a gay group on campus. There still isn't one, & the associate controller of nearby Marshall University told me that the 40 people who'd turned out for last year's gay pride march were set upon by 200 angry anti-gays, and some of the marchers injured. How lucky we New Yorkers are—and how easily we forget that much of America remains proudly, patriotically homophobic.

NOVEMBER 17, 1994

Our evening event, "Great Dykes," co-sponsored with the Publishing Triangle, seemed to me a mediocre affair. Neither Cheryl [*Clarke*] (ill) nor Sharon [*O'Brien*] (missed train connections) showed, which left the usual suspects performing their usual scenarios: Joan [*Nestle*], the femme goddess of mellifluous warmth; Kate [*Millett*], beseiged between fiction and truth; Jill [*Johnston*], the disjunctive pixie coming at everyone & everything from an angle so oblique as to seem vaguely loony (and calculatedly contentious). Jenifer [*Levin*], the new guy on the block, played the palely fierce Jeremiah, full of calamitous warnings. On top of which, the panel utterly lacked focus—and often simple coherence—and the audience (about 150 people) was lethargic. Jane De Lynn, during the question period, angrily ascribed the desuetude to the evening's academic sponsorship ("there's no lack of energy at the Clit Club or at Lesbian Avengers")—and her indictment drew applause. How simple. That same auditorium has often breathed fire & burst with electricity under the same "academic sponsorship." The difference this time is that the evening was under-planned and the panelists lazily self-indulgent. Coming on top of the mediocre Aging event, I now see clearly that we must no longer easily lend our co-sponsorship (& facilities). We need more control over the contents, need to ensure the careful, extended planning that has characterized the events we've done by ourselves.

DECEMBER 7, 1994

Randy [*Trumbach*] has persisted in asking an unpopular question or championing a line of argument out of synch with the board's sometimes knee-jerk deference to *anything* said by a non-white member. At the meeting last Saturday, for example, he insisted on some answers about the legal & financial nature of the BNQN/CLAGS relationship, and (sharply) expressed disapproval over the *lack* of credit the BNQN committee has been giving CLAGS in its promotional materials. For which daring, he was greeted with a chorus of hissing disapproval, led by H. (who never even shows up for a committee meeting) using the occasion for one of his throbbingly self-righteous defenses of multiculturalism—which nobody had attacked. Randy is admirably fearless in his insistence on stating unpopular views. He cares more about his integrity than his popularity. And he puts his energy where his mouth is, working hard for the success of CLAGS's programs. Though I, too, have felt annoyed & put-upon by Randy, my affection & admiration for him have grown greatly over the years.

DECEMBER 8, 1994

Jacqui Alexander's colloquium last night was astonishingly impressive—eloquent & intricate. My awareness was heightened yet again at how different, and how much more difficult, the path is for non-Northern European non-whites; and how difficult (& perhaps misguided) it is to encode our "liberatory" demands into repressive neo-colonial structures. How Jacqui the individual has ever survived, laboring as she has under several different, and even criminalized, identities is something of a miracle—and something more of a tribute to her fierce intelligence. She's been personally cruel to me on occasion, and at times grossly unfair to CLAGS, but my hurt & anger dissolved in the face of the overwhelming, lifelong cruelties inflicted on her.

DECEMBER 13, 1994

Paul Jr. is at it again. He's gone so far this time—in a Rutgers newspaper—to say "Duberman's ideological standpoint is that blacks can't have a culture." And more. The infuriating libel tempts me to go to court—were it not that Frances has (misguidedly) told him we do need his signature on the The New Press contract [*to reprint a new paperback edition of* Robeson]; and the fact that I can't bear the idea of having that bizarre man back in my life. But if he refuses to sign the contract—& I'm giving him till exactly December 19 to decide—I'm going to proceed with The New Press anyway (presuming they're willing) & let *Paul* sue if he doesn't like it. The notion's been growing in me anyway of late that the time has come to write up the whole nasty business of "the making of the Robeson biography." Not to respond in any fashion to his string of calumnies may well be the path of statesmanship (and sanity), but it's also to suggest that I'm unable to answer . . . at the very least I'm going to have my lawyer put him on formal notice that his continuing defamatory remarks about me are compromising my scholarly reputation and opening him to a libel suit. Whether I choose to pursue the suit, of course, will depend on how I feel after factoring in the costs, financial & psychological.

MARCH 14, 1995

In the midst of all this, came the BNQN conference March 9–11. It came off in *far* better style than any of us would have thought possible only 2 months ago. The turnout was huge—with hundreds turned away—all three plenary sessions were first-rate, and a "mobilization session" at the close of the conference produced enough enthusiasm and volunteers to suggest there may be future BNQNs. There were the usual litany of complaints when the mics were opened up to audience participation: why are we meeting in a white institution & under the sponsorship of a white-dominated organization? Where are our un-credentialed sisters and brothers on these panels?! Why was no session scheduled on youth issues or spirituality? Etc. All valid questions, and poignant as an expression of the *in*visibility and lack of access the vast majority of people of color continue to feel. Yet the statements took up so much time that precious little was left over to engage with the many provocative remarks of the panelists themselves—and especially (from where I sat) those of Urvashi [*Vaid*], Tony Appiah, Kobena Mercer and Wahneema [*Lubiano*]. Coco Fusco finally lost patience with the audience's "questions" and bluntly asked that critiques of the conference and its organizers take a rest and *some* response given to the panelists' comments. Many of the panelists had interrogated "black," "nation" and "queer" in the name of breaking down fixed positions & narrow agendas, and opening up new possibilities for coalition work; the audience response made it discouragingly clear that the fierce attachments to narrow agendas continues strong & that racial cooperation within the lesbian/gay world continues to be weak. But none of this is to detract from the energizing, even inspirational nature of the conference. I wrote as much the day after to F.J. & L. reiterating how much I wanted CLAGS to be a site for anti-racist work, how much I admired what they had achieved at the conference, and how much I hoped we could put hurt feelings behind us and move forward together. I hope their response is positive.

To F.J. and L., March 12, 1995: ". . . I'm so filled with admira-

tion for the extraordinary events of the past three days that I wanted
to write and say so . . . It was for me personally a deeply informing,
inspiring conference. . . . May I add one other personal word? The
process leading up to the conference was at times so difficult that
some harsh, even hurtful words were said. I hope we can ascribe
those to the stress of the moment, and let them pass. I also hope we
can continue to work together. . . . I want CLAGS to be a site for in-
terracial cooperation and anti-racist (and anti-sexist) work, and I
hope you will stick with us to help make this possible. . . ."

*[I never got a response. At a subsequent board meeting, I took my
life in my hands and asked F. why not. "Because we viewed your letter
as a typical effort on your part to control the discourse," he said. Say
what? At that point I gave up, done with the placating and breast-
beating. Each of the three, in varying stages, soon stopped showing up
for board meetings. Over time, some marginal sort of relationship was
re-established with two of the three (see pages 205–06).]*

A few curious sidelights: Chip [*Samuel*] Delany dumped me
into the élitist grabbag during his plenary remarks by contrasting our
two histories; the white man who graduated from Harvard, has always had access to the media, and got tenure decades ago, and the
black man from City College who finally got tenure six years ago. I
was miffed at being (yet again) summarily shoved into the Privileged
White Male category, with not a momentary glance at the ways in
which I've tried to use my manifold (& acknowledged) advantages to
open doors for others less well placed; or *some* awareness that I've had
a bit of pain myself; or that I *lost* my touted "access to the mainstream
media" (e.g. the *Times*) when I came out. Chip was so proud of his
formulation that he ran it by me just before he went on stage, not
pausing to let me get a word in edgewise.

Another: Joan Parkin, out of nowhere, apologized to me for her
behavior in the 1991 graduate seminar; says she feels badly about
how she & others behaved. Oh, the sleepless nights that admission
could have saved me!

Finally: dear, enigmatic T. She moderated a panel on Friday with
such curious pauses & stumblings, that I recalled what Esther had

told me just a few weeks ago: "T. is stoned on grass most of the time. Didn't you know *that?*" No, I didn't, but knowing it certainly helps to explain her unpredictability in the past, & made me guiltily retract my many complaints about her "bizarre" behavior. The terror, the inner demons, that must underlay her daily reliance on pot! Yet another lesson (still largely unlearned) not to be so damned quick to judge others. . . .

MARCH 27, 1995

. . . yet another "Multicultural PhD" meeting. The historian Colin Palmer's opposition is now out in the open; he joins with Frank Kirkland & Ed Gordon in trying to convert an *inter*cultural vision back into one where separate disciplines join *very* tentative hands. I spoke angrily against the evasions, delays and manipulations—& homophobia—that have long characterized these meetings, and made it clear that the lesbian/gay contingent was feeling frustrated and fed up—*and* had no intention of withdrawing. With the CUNY budget cuts about to descend, it's unlikely a new PhD could successfully get through the Albany bureaucracy anyway; but on the off-chance we need to keep pushing ahead.

D*uring these same months, my frustration was building over the deepening silence from Philip Cohen about the future of the Chelsea Houses series, and the ongoing complaints from authors over their mistreatment. By early 1995, with manuscripts coming in at a rapid rate for my edit, we had few commissions left in the pipeline. I repeatedly warned Philip that unless I was soon given the go-ahead to sign up additional books, a serious gap in publication would ensue. I also told him that several authors, months after the appearance of their books, had yet to receive a copy, and that several educators had written to complain about getting the runaround when making inquiries or trying to purchase books. What was going on?! If Philip wanted to cancel the project, why not simply say so? If he intended to continue it, why not clean up the act?*

When I finally heard from him, there was no explanation or apology for the various screw-ups, but only the thin excuse that "the educational marketplace" was in bad shape and ("I am totally perplexed here") the series selling slowly; and the only thing that matters is the bottom line. That seemed to me a clear enough warning that unless sales increased, there would be no additional books. In a letter the following month, Philip confirmed that Chelsea House "would commission more titles at that time when we have learned how to sell them much better." I doubted that that time would ever come, but because Philip continued to insist that "we are committed," I decided to bide my time a while longer—though I'd lost the fervor I'd originally felt for the possibilities of the series. Replacing it was the dispirited sense that the project, despite having fourteen books in print, was dead in the water. Was it killed by Chelsea House ineptitude? By homophobia among school officials and librarians? Was the caliber of the writing too high and the sexual discussion of the subject's life too explicit for high school students (and their teachers) to handle? I was at a loss for how to parcel out appropriate shares of blame.

APRIL 22, 1995

Duty-bound & drag-assed, took myself off to a party in honor of Andy Kopkind's posthumous book [*The Thirty Years Wars: Dispatches and Diversions of a Radical Journalist, 1965–1994*]. Expected multitudes, Andy-like warmth & celebration, car loads of (probably boring) old lefties—and a quick exit. Instead, a decorous, "select" group of some two dozen, chilled & dwarfed in Jean Stein's huge penthouse. Surrounded by walls of original everybodys, glasses tinkled politely as egos shrunk down to nervous, normal size. Contrarily, I seized my third wine, expanded beyond all carefully contained recent boundaries, catapulted back to the mid-seventies, my heyday of vain exuberance, cavorted through the cavernous rooms, loudly daring this one, doubting that one, in a burst of raucous, wondrously restorative bad boy vigor. The anarchic streak resurfaced. Didn't know I'd been

missing anything in my super-contained, responsible life. But I loved
the rush of amplitude. . . . "Playfully," I threatened to pocket the
small Cycladic sculpture on the mantle, while announcing that of
course it couldn't be real. "It *is*," Stein's husband said, hovering . . .
more camping, dishing, as the evening grew later & I grew younger.
John [*Scagliotti*] closest to my Peck's bad boy mood; maybe as angry
as I was [*he'd been Andy's longtime companion*] at the inappropriate-
ness of such a setting as a site to honor him. Tony K. [*Kushner*], usually so impish, seemed sweetly subdued, energy absorbed in *not*
saying yes to the passing hors d'oeuvres. Richard Goldstein, as always, stood guard in the doorway of his own warmth, blocking the
way with smart conversation. Andrew Ross wore yet another (this
time becoming) hairdo; how devoted he is to demonstrating, fash-
ionably, the fluidity of surfaces. Hilton Als insisted on a couch tête-
à-tête to find out what more I knew of Dorothy Dean & friends. I
told him to find Willie [*Dunn*] & write a book; and pointed him to
Dick Poirier as someone who knew Dorothy far better than I. Took
immediately to Henry van Ameringen, surprised at such a playful intelligence in such an upstanding Community Philanthropist. We
were getting along famously until, exuberance to the fore, I told him
that his foundation *had* to start supporting CLAGS; thereafter he
eased away. Victor [*Navasky*] told me all about his guru's assorted
grape diets & gauze wrappings—smiling throughout.

Anyway, time to go back to being 64 and the Good Mother.

APRIL 25, 1995

F. called to reprimand me for writing a thank-you letter to the Ford
Foundation's Sheila Biddle, for "poaching" yet again on the autonomy of the BNQN committee. Perhaps I would once more have swallowed the abuse if the year & a half of it had been at least briefly
interrupted. . . . I told him that it was my *duty* as director of CLAGS
to have written Sheila in thanks for a historic grant, and that I was
drawing, finally & probably belatedly, a firm line: if he, J. & L. still

found it impossible to direct anything but hostility towards me (& CLAGS) I was no longer going to sit still for it . . . they've consistently, resolutely, refused *any* share of responsibility for past errors & hurt feelings.

The "Queer Theater" conference on the whole came off well, but only the second day seemed to me first-class from start to finish. . . . During the Larry Kramer/Tony Kushner onstage "dialogue," I got so exercised at some of the badgering audience comments and questions (abetted by Kramer) about Tony's "Marxism," and his sweet willingness torturously to try & explain himself, that I stood up & said, in essence, that Tony was—more than any artist I knew—insistent on remaining connected to social justice movements & didn't deserve the hostile invitations to breast-beating, nor the glib dismissal of socialist egalitarianism. Tony called me later that evening to thank me; but of course also said he had felt "embarrassed" by my public praise.

Sobering, tho not unexpected experience at today's panel at the Jewish Museum on social protest movements. I'd been asked to represent the lesbian and gay movement, but the sold-out audience froze me out. . . . The crowd was packed with serious-minded, socially conscious, grey-haired Jews—and they wanted to hear *nothing* about gays & lesbians. Not a single question was directed to me. . . . It was as if "gay and lesbian" didn't qualify under the rubric "social protest movements." And this is Manhattan. Our issues, our lives, remain in contempt. . . . Mary Waters, next to me, got only one question. Why? She had focused her remarks on *class* divisions—another vaguely anti-American topic.

MAY 8, 1995

Its taken me two days to settle down enough to write about Saturday's board meeting. Esther had warned me the night before (I don't know who told her what) to "watch my back—F. is determined on trashing you." What began as a reasonably good-tempered go-round, each person saying the extent & reason s/he felt the board was in crisis, came to a grinding halt when F.'s turn arrived. He repeated *all* his old accusations against "the Executive Director" (refusing to call me by name), how I had *dared* to write Sheila Biddle, etc., and added a few new ones that were total inventions (e.g., I had told him the graduate school would waive its 15% on the Ford grant. Does he know he's lying? Or is that kind of ordinary ethical question inappropriate to diva-hood?) Though it was a truly nasty performance, I held my tongue in the name of continuing the go-round—for which restraint L. promptly accused me of "acting above it all—as if I had nothing to answer for." "I hardly feel above it all," I said. "I feel deeply hurt & misrepresented, & would be more than happy to respond in detail." But Mitchell [*Karp*], the facilitator, insisted we move ahead & return to the issue later. Except later never arrived: Matt, my assistant, who fielded many of the calls, was never asked to report on the actual train of events regarding BNQN, though F. was allowed to interrupt the proceedings twice more to vent additional spleen. What I did manage to say was that the founder of an organization must always, at some point, be willing to leave it, so that the organization could take on a life of its own and shape itself anew to meet the needs of those currently involved in it. I felt that point had arrived with CLAGS. It was time to replace me as director. Indeed I insisted upon it. I would stay on for a transition, but I wanted the transition to begin *now*. Having invested nine years in CLAGS and believing its existence important to lesbian & gay studies, I'll do all I can to ensure its continuing growth and health. But I'm no longer willing to serve as a lightning rod for abuse; I need to lower my level of stress & reclaim my own time. I've called for an executive committee meeting within two weeks to get the wheels in motion.

MAY 16, 1995

All the board was urged to attend last night's executive committee meeting, and a good ⅔ds showed up. I stuck to my decision to withdraw as director and discussion, beginning first in the long-range planning committee, about how & when to replace me will start within two weeks. . . . Who walks in (2 hours after the meeting started) than—F.! Oh the timing of the true diva—'tis a thing of wonder! And of course I instantly felt guilty & ashamed (though I had no reason to), and then later (campy) anger at having been robbed of a portion of my righteous rage (F. had told Matt that morning that neither he nor J. nor L. would attend). He sat silently for the remaining 45 minutes of the meeting. I'll never be his match as a tactician!

MAY 19, 1995

The panel last night at Lincoln Center on biography felt lively & focused. Frank Rich had 102 fever but kept us all nicely on target. I especially took to Joan Acocella: great reserves of forcefulness, in an edgily warm, eloquent envelope. Afterwards, a Frank Pearsall (?) from GMAD [*Gay Men of African Descent*] came up at the reception to say he had suggested me as a speaker for GMAD but had been turned down because I was white & because Duberman "sounded like a German Jewish name." If true—& I have no way of verifying Pearsall's version—how appalling that every social prejudice reappears within our own ranks, dividing them still further. . . .

JULY 11, 1995

David Dunlap took me to lunch at the Century Club to write a profile of me and/or a story on CLAGS for the *Times*. But it turns out this very morning Joseph Lelyveld, his boss, told him he wants *fewer* gay-themed articles from David & more relating to his original beat, real estate (This in response to David saying he was feeling schizophrenic in his dual roles & wasn't it time the paper had someone who *just* did the gay/lesbian beat). A sign of the conservative times/ *TIMES*. Thoroughly liked David: low-keyed, honest & honorable; a little sexy, too.

First in a series of the long-range planning committee to begin the search for my successor. I reiterated that my decision was irrevocable but I would do all I could to ensure CLAGS's future; I was willing to stay—at the outside—through this coming academic year, but hoped a replacement could be found sooner. Given the desultory nature of the discussion, my pessimism grows—not simply over whether I can get out sooner, but whether enough energy & vision exists to find—& then lend the necessary support to—the new director. But paralleling that pessimism is a growing sense of resignation: CLAGS may have fulfilled its purpose—begun the process of institutionalizing lesbian & gay studies. And its purpose fulfilled, an institution should wither away, the alternative being the creation of another bureaucracy that serves no need beyond its own survival.

SEPTEMBER 9, 1995

The full day CLAGS board facilitation went far better than I would have anticipated. I arrived full of apprehension, a residue of anger at the distorted, abusive attacks of last May, and a determination to remain self-protectively quiet. J. arrived late & left at the lunch break, consuming most of the intervening period with a fierce, one-sided insistence that CLAGS had made the BNQN committee feel insistently "other"—omitting (& possibly not even recalling) the committee's *demand* that it be treated as a wholly autonomous body. L. never showed up at all—though sent word thru J. that she had never been notified of the meeting; Matt pointed out that *every* board member had been reminded of the meeting, by mail, *three* times. . . . To F.'s credit—and particularly after J. had left—he avoided personal invective and did acknowledge that our group *might* be well-intentioned in matters of race & gender. Indeed, at the final go-round, with each person expressing positive reactions to the day & more hopeful feelings about the future of CLAGS, F. deigned grandiloquently to announce that despite his earlier intention to resign, he *might* now be willing to "run the risk of remaining on the board." I couldn't help feel a wave of affection for his swaggering peacock ways.

SEPTEMBER 13, 1995

Tim Sweeney [*the former director of Lambda Legal Defense*] here for a couple of hours to talk about the "leadership project" he's taken on for the Rapoport Foundation. It was fun—bouncing my war stories off his, sharing the puzzlement & hurt that (so Tim reports) every director of every gay/lesbian organization feels, where mistakes become cosmic crimes and no good deeds go unpunished. It gave me great comfort to feel merely one among the condemned.

SEPTEMBER 21, 1995

Nigel [*Finch*] & Ruth [*Caleb*] here to discuss (at my insistence) the screenplay draft [*for* Stonewall] they had sent but then never followed through on. And a fair amount was wrong with it historically—in particular, and bizarrely, turning Fat Tony [*one of the Mafia owners of the Stonewall bar*] into some kind of sympathetic hero! As Britishers, Nigel and Ruth apparently don't understand how the Mafia sucked money from the community and in return treated us like scum. I *think* I got through on that score, but on another I doubt that I made a dent: They seem determined on over-featuring and over-crediting drag queens in the film. The success of "Priscilla," of Ru-Paul, etc., has got them smelling a commercial hit. Besides, the screenwriter, it turns out, "likes to put on skirts." The upside of that is the often hilarious dialogue he's written for the queens. The downside is that he's pretty tone deaf on non-drag queens, the disinterest in "ordinary" gays radiating from the script.

OCTOBER 8, 1995

... the CLAGS "Lesbian & Gay History" conference . . . the two graduate student panels were filled with original, trenchant work-in-progress; it was inspiring to hear how much the field has grown, & in what good hands the future resides. . . . James Miller, on the biography panel was to me the best of a good bunch: an honest, vulnerable straight man trying hard to (publicly) explore his right to represent and his ability to empathize with a life (Foucault's) centrally dissimilar from his own.

Anyway, there was lots of audience enthusiasm, networking & mutual morale building—which alone would be sufficient grounds for calling the conference a success.

OCTOBER 27, 1995

Went to the reception inaugurating the Tom Stoddard fellowship. A wonderfully large turnout. I felt very teary by the end. A combination of things: the ghastly way Tom looked—a marked deterioration since I saw him at the LeGal awards—and the contrast of his frail physical state with his still fiery will & eloquent words. Tom & I have traveled a long road; initially turned on by his affectionate, effusive nature, I was later turned off by what I saw, as his fame mounted, as a too-frequent arrogance. But I never lost the affection, and last night, seeing him so bravely square off against extremity, brought it flooding back. Thank heaven this tribute came off in time. . . .

[*A YEAR LATER. OCTOBER 5, 1996*]

Buffet for a dozen here to celebrate Torie's [*Osborn*] book publication . . . Tom [*Stoddard*] looked beyond awful, much worse than at the party honoring him. I'd heard that he was having a hard time & wasn't reacting well to the protease drugs, but I wasn't prepared for the gaunt, hollow-eyed figure who came through the door—on his way *back*, no less, from a conference in Boston: The mystery of why some prematurely fold up & withdraw from life and others insist on plunging in beyond their current strength. He only stayed about an hour & a half, but engaged fully in the talk, always articulate, sometimes bravely funny. . . .

OCTOBER 29, 1995

Matt tells me a rumor is circulating that Barbara Smith [*founder of the pioneering Kitchen Table Press*] is "furious" at me, claiming that I personally de-railed her CLAGS Rockefeller Humanities Fellowship—& is being widely believed. Here we go again! [*Barbara had won both the CLAGS Rockefeller and a financially comparable Schomburg Library grant. Barbara wanted to keep both and asked me to intervene with both Rockefeller and Schomburg to that end. I agreed to try and had kept Barbara abreast of developments. But obviously she believed I'd been working against her best interests.*] I'd suspected something was wrong, since she hasn't returned my last three phone messages, but that she could believe such a thing—& spread it—shocked me, given our long, friendly, mutually supportive history. So I put in another call to Barbara. On my message I ran through the *actual* history of the fellowship: Schomburg had never returned my several calls. Barbara had gone to see them directly & reported they *had* agreed to let her hold *half* the Schomburg grant along with the Rockefeller. I had then asked Rockefeller's permission to accept that arrangement, but the program officer characterized it perjoratively as "double dipping." When I then asked if Rockefeller would agree, like Schomburg, to letting Barbara hold down a *one* term Rockefeller fellowship, they'd been dubious but withheld a decision until the CLAGS fellowship committee discussed the matter. When the committee met, it unanimously rejected the idea of splitting the fellowship money in half, thinking the whole amount was necessary to buy a scholar enough free time. I reported all this in detail to Barbara at the time. If she doesn't return my call this time, then the hell with it. I'm sick of trying to persuade people that I haven't been diabolically working against their best interests. . . . It feels like a fucking feeding frenzy, and this fish can't wait to leap to another pond come June 1. . . .

OCTOBER 30, 1995

Return call from Barbara. Says a member of the jury (a "she"—no name offered) told her I had unilaterally, without consulting the CLAGS fellowship committee, decided not to halve the Rockefeller award & had quickly offered the grant to Jeff Edwards to prevent the committee from countermanding my action. Why such a malignant misrepresentation? And why would Barbara—given our cordial history—accept it, and so fully as to leave my calls unanswered? Even now, she sounded steely and suspicious. When I suggested she'd been predisposed to believing the worst because of the BNQN poison that had been poured in her ears, she gave a begrudging "Uh-huh." I now come away feeling soured. . . .

NOVEMBER 13, 1995

Self-deprecation is often confused with modesty. Former is fear of acknowledging one's worth. Latter is recognition that "worth," as usually defined, is an *in*significant measure of anything of true value—like an awareness of the insignificance of us all.

NOVEMBER 28, 1995

"Public intellectual" in this culture, a Camille Paglia–like Star, is someone who *boldly* speaks his or her opinions. An intellectual is someone who tries to figure out why he or she holds them.

DECEMBER 2, 1995

Last night's CLAGS Kessler event encapsulated in a perilously satirical way, lesbian & gay studies at this moment, the academy in general (and in particular its awesome generation gap), CLAGS at its

most esteemed & picayune, and much else (like the art of catering). When I finally got back home at 11:00 p.m., I had to howl for
an hour before even beginning to settle down. Howl first at the
grotesque amount of time (an hour & a half) used up by the first two
"introducers," to their contented sense of centrality to the universe.
Sad, I suppose, that they should have to clutch so fiercely at their
moment in the spotlight, but still an infuriating misconception of
who it was we were honoring. The third introducer, Ann Pellegrini,
reading for Judith Butler, was a model of concise, *brief* intelligence.
But by the time we finally got Monique Wittig, the awardee, on the
stage, about a third of the previously packed auditorium had crept
out, and Wittig herself looked even more wan and fragile than earlier. Wan like a tiger, of course. I had vaguely recalled seeing a picture of her as a theatrical beauty some 25 years ago, but now she
resembles much more a birdlike, wrinkled little boy (or is it an old
man?) We chatted amiably enough at the pre-lecture dinner & post-
lecture reception, she imperiously shy, me playing charmed slave—
but nothing approaching animated camaraderie. I take everybody's
word for it that she's a world-beating genius (even if the excerpts read
in English from the podium of an untranslated work came across to
my tired ears as precisely the kind of abstracted, "philosophical"
prose I find repellent and grandiose).

DECEMBER 10, 1995

For once, a painless board meeting. F. attended and has apparently
decided to remain. J. did not—just as neither she nor L. had bothered to lend themselves to the full-day facilitation convened specifically to deal with their charges of "racialization." They never wanted
to resolve any organizational issues; they wanted to accuse, vent,
trash and burn—and feel infinitely self-righteous about it. Without their help, we elected seven new board members—six of them
non-white.

At 5:00, Jim Wood's Memorial Service at All-Soul's. Gifted, gentle, passionate, tender—dead at 32. We were only passing acquain-

tances, yet I couldn't staunch the tears—for Mike Ryan and Essex [*Hemphill*], too, all three gone this month, all three under forty. So much living left, so much to do and give. Poor, poor boys . . .

*B*y 1996, there were more than a million AIDS cases worldwide, 70 percent of them in Africa, and with still no effective treatment in sight (at the end of 1995, the FDA released yet another new drug, 3TC, which proved as useless as the preceding ones). At the same time "compassion fatigue" had set in: donations to AIDS organizations began to decline steadily, paralleled by the sinking sense that the disease would never be brought under control.

And then, seemingly out of nowhere, the FDA also released saquinavir, the first of a whole new category of drugs known as protease inhibitors. Two others rapidly followed: ritonavir and indinavir. It quickly became apparent that—as FDA Commissioner David A. Kessler (no relation to our lecture series funder) put it—"we now have some big guns in AIDS treatment." The year 1996 would prove a milestone in the long struggle against AIDS. A milestone—not a miracle.

Almost immediately, reports came in of how the new drugs were reducing the amount of HIV in infected individuals, sometimes to the "undetectable" level, even as CD4 cell counts—essential to a healthy immune system—were correspondingly rising. But what also became quickly apparent was that the new drugs did not work at all for some people, and worked only briefly for others. Besides, the exorbitant cost of the drugs (up to fifteen thousand dollars for a year's supply) put them out of reach for most people suffering from AIDS. In the United States, drug-assistance programs existed in about half the states—but didn't initially cover protease inhibitors. Additionally, most of the leadership in the hard-hit Latino and black communities had learned to distrust "innovative" white medicine (in part thanks to the notorious Tuskegee Experiment, which had used black sharecroppers as human guinea pigs).

Many church leaders, moreover, stigmatized AIDS as "a gay thing" and therefore—talk about massive denial—not a black (or Latino) issue. AIDS was not to be discussed from the pulpit, nor information *about its treatment made available in the lobby. Later, after it became undeniably clear that HIV had increasingly become a disease of color, after AIDS had decimated the African continent and in this country cut a horrifying swath through black and Latino communities (by 2007, African-Americans, just 13 percent of the U.S. population, accounted for more than 50 percent of new HIV diagnoses), those in leadership positions finally proved willing to engage with the issue.*

In the meantime, President Clinton, having (unlike his predecessors) directly addressed the AIDS crisis and increased funding for research and services early on in his administration, then showed little sustained interest or resolve. Despite the findings of the National Institutes of Health, for example, that needle-exchange programs unquestionably lowered the incidence of AIDS, and despite the support of his own senior health officials (including Secretary Donna E. Shalala) for such programs, Clinton refused federal funding for them. Instead, he signed the 1996 "Defense of Marriage" Act, which denied same-sex couples the right to have their unions legalized—thereby serving notice that recent progress in the acceptance of gay people (itself pretty much confined to the most assimilable segment of the gay population) shouldn't be equated with any inevitable march towards first-class citizenship—or even second-class for the truly, proudly different (which is to say, in mainstream lingo, the freaks).

Most gay teenagers didn't need to be reminded that they weren't considered quality goods, but by the mid-nineties many in the gay world, and particularly in the more tolerant urban areas, did choose to believe that equality was around the corner, bound to happen, that a little more tidying up around the edges—perhaps best done by pushing the freaks as far offstage as possible—and the struggle would be over.

Paralleling the rise of optimism about the goal of converting AIDS to a "manageable disease" was a surge of conviction that as a people we were now unstoppable. Some prominent gay leaders and organizations, and in particular Elizabeth Birch and the influential (largest and wealthiest) Human Rights Campaign, were entirely in accord with the goal of assimilation and with fostering an image of gay people that would accelerate that process. That meant replicating themselves, featuring one segment only of a diverse gay community: mostly white, educated, well-spoken folks who dressed for success and held mainstream values. Those gay people with left-wing politics saw assimilationism as defeat and deceit—a misrepresentation of the many different communities that constituted the gay world and a denial of the subversive potential of our distinctive values and perspectives. The lefties didn't want to serve openly in the military; they wanted to destroy the war machine. They didn't want to settle down into traditional marital relationships, nor give them privileged status; they wanted to challenge sexual monogamy, gender stereotyping, and traditional patterns of child-rearing.

But left-wing gays had shrunk by the mid-nineties—in contrast to the early seventies—to a small, nearly silent voice in the community as a whole. The majority of gay people chose to see themselves as "just folks"; their highest aspiration was to join the mainstream, not to challenge its orthodoxies. When Bill Clinton, the following year, spoke at a dinner for the Human Rights Campaign, the thrilled, monied crowd shouted down a heckler who'd dared to yell out "People with AIDS are dying!"—and they rose several times to give Clinton standing ovations.

JANUARY 13, 1996

Turned in the manuscript (2,000 pages) yesterday of the CLAGS Reader [*I'd volunteered, as a parting gift, to prepare selections from our first ten years of colloquia and conferences*]. Niko [*Pfund, then head of the NYU Press, the Reader's publisher*] gulped hard, said the contents looked "great," and said he felt sure further condensation will prove necessary. Having already trimmed, even as the accumulation mounted, for a year, I'd like to hold out for a two-volume work—especially since I don't want to have to now inform several dozen people who I talked into changing/expanding/rethinking their original presentations that their contributions are being dropped. But sympathetic as Niko is, he has to keep a bottom eye on sales. [*In the upshot, Nick did decide on two volumes,* A Queer World *and* Queer Representations, *both published in 1997.*]

JANUARY 14, 1996

Esther is angry at the nominating committee's agenda for the next
Board meeting, and doesn't want to attend, let alone chair it. I'm
trying to persuade her to change her mind, even as I share her opinion that they're reinventing the wheel, insisting on "re-evaluating
CLAGS's mission," even though its founding principles of multiculturalism, feminism & gender parity are precisely those that they
emphasize. But this is a necessary process, however redundant, if
they're to feel that CLAGS is *their* organization, that they truly own
it. It's not as if anyone else is standing in the wings offering to take
over. If CLAGS is to survive, those of us who are departing are going
to have to sit still for a fair amount of holier-than-thou rhetoric. I see
my essential job between now & June as saying as little as possible
and showing up with as bland a face as I can screw on.

FEBRUARY 5, 1996

I more & more make campy fun of my "infirmities" of memory. It
suddenly strikes me that what's long been fading is my *trust* of memory (of "fact"), not my memory itself. Growing older means (if one
is lucky) growing up. It means better understanding that what we
thought we knew—could uncomplicatedly verify—turns out to be
partial, shifting, contradictory, mysterious. Barring organic disease,
aging is best seen as a process of maturation rather than (as usually
described) disintegration. Or disintegration of the most necessary
kind: the inability any longer to make pat pronouncements, the loss
of easy certitude.

FEBRUARY 10, 1996

Random reflections on our two-day Gay Politics conference. Cathy
Cohen spoke eloquently against a queer politics that demonizes all
heterosexuals as not being serviceable to people of color; to realize
the radical potential of queer politics we need a better understand-

ing of the linked intersections of race, class & sexual oppressions—their shared marginal relationship to dominant systems of power (shared *across* the boundaries of "heterosexual" and "homosexual)" Yes, exactly—as some of us have been saying since the early seventies.

In my own introductory remarks to the conference, I tried to raise some related questions for the conferees to consider. Why do our organizations find it so difficult to swell their ranks and treasuries? One recent estimate puts the total membership in all national lesbian and gay organizations, including AIDS-related ones, at a maximum of 200,000, with a total annual budget of less than twenty million. By contrast, a single right-wing group, "Focus on the Family," has an annual budget of more than sixty million. *One* anti-gay coalition has three times the budget of all pro-gay organizations combined.

Why? Does the still-hostile national ethos prevent the majority of gay people from coming out in sufficient numbers? What role do our own organizations play in their failure to attract more adherents? Are they too skewed, as I believe, to the values and agendas of the already-privileged among us—too narrow, in other words, to attract the allegiance of non-whites, non-males, non-middle (or upper) class people? Is the civil-rights strategy that continues to dominate our organizational efforts too limited to effect liberation for the many, as opposed to assimilation for the few? If so, how do we re-make our movement so that it speaks in various voices and in response to a wider variety of needs?

As if that challenge wasn't enough, how do we form coalitions, both grassroots and national, with other marginalized groups? How do we make the kinds of connections across the boundaries currently separating ethnic, racial and class groupings that would allow us to combine our strength and thereby heighten our ability to produce substantive social change? But are other marginalized groups *interested* in combining forces with us? [*I was thinking here not only of the polite homophobia surrounding our efforts—by now aborted—at the Graduate Center to form a PhD program in multiculturalism, but of the many current attacks by white male liberals like Todd Gitlin on "identity" politics.*]

Others at the conference rang their own themes:

— Paul Hagland seemed excessively pessimistic about *any* human rights strategy working; I agree that the state, the chief violator, is also the chief enforcer, but public pressure *can* matter; I also agree that human rights doctrine must be shaped to fit indigenous conditions, but surely we can come out against female genital mutilation, torture, police brutality, etc., *across* national boundaries ("tradition," when used to justify violations of body & spirit, carries no automatic moral weight — as deferential cultural relativists seem to presume).

— Riki Anne Wilchins, the transgender activist, speaking entirely without notes, was remarkably eloquent, but her expressed disinterest (later echoed by Rich Tafel [*then head of the Log Cabin Republicans*] in any movement "so spiritually poverty-stricken" that it's willing to "leave behind" Newt Gingrich and Bob Dole as candidates for transformation, avoids just one or two little problems: Newt & Bob's total disinterest in being transformed, and their entrenched investment in policies of economic injustice that a radicalized movement would/should focus on (rather than "spiritual renewal"). . . .

— Not charmed by D.S.'s response to a question about Farrakhan's anti-semitism: "I'm not about to join a group of white men in criticizing a black man" (or words to that effect). This at a conference struggling to find common ground for coalitional work! S. is smart and charismatic, but needs to do more homework.

— As for dear Larry [*Kramer*] . . . the performance was as expected. He has no politics — has never had — beyond narcissistic rage. Now that "hopeful new drugs" have reduced his personal fears, his language has gone all mushy. "Love," he now tells us, is what the movement was all about, and ACT-UP fell apart because "everybody theorized so much

it made everybody sick." So the villain is not corporate America, but misguided gay intellectuals. Larry Kramer, in his
new guise of aging hippie, calls on the "brothers and sisters"
to hug more—oh, yes, and to find "the right leadership"—
a mishmash of saccharin Bonapartism. Though "I'm all
right, Jack" might be closer to the mark. He seemed genuinely startled at the suggestion from various quarters that
we need to concern ourselves with the growing maldistri-
bution of income and the accompanying impoverishment
of millions. Smug laughter from this super-romantic at the
"romantic" notion of attacking capitalism.

—Dennis Altman made infinitely more sense (as he always
does). Dennis has it right: the chief problem with the efflo-
resence of Queer Theory is that it has de-politicized sexuality. He took a step beyond Urvaishi's [*Vaid*] abstract call
for a "post-identity politics." He gave it substance: we must
start talking again about social justice—about a politics
not solely grounded in self-interest. We must return to the
call for a coalition agenda that will benefit a now-suffering
majority (and suffering not least from a still entrenched
anti-community, pro-capitalist rhetoric); and, above all,
we have to give chief priority to the least fortunate. Identity
politics *plus* old-fashioned social justice politics; *that's*
the ticket—tho where we get the needed troops seems, far
more than in the '60s, the conundrum. The troops at this
conference seemed more intent on playing softball with
the handsome, appealing Rich Tafel than on challenging
his stated belief in "the American way," the goal of assimilation, and the proud Coué-ism that free market capitalism
is *the* guaranteed path to expanded "justice."

FEBRUARY 18, 1996

Found myself standing next to L. [*one of my three antagonists over
the BNQN event*] at the party for Nan & Lisa's book. We did our

usual curt nod & I could feel myself flooding again with unhappiness. I felt regret all over again at my inability to reach her during the steamiest days of the board struggle last year. Her brilliance has always been clear, but why didn't I see what is now so apparent—her *kindness* (unlike J.)? I must have been too hurt by the assaults on my "racism," too crouched in a defensive posture. And L. did make her contribution; she never broke ranks with J. and F., sometimes even topping them in vituperation.

I took her arm & asked if we could talk for a minute. She seemed pleased. I said how much I'd admired her talk at the politics conference & how awful it was that we—natural political allies—should find ourselves antagonists instead. She shook her head in agreement—this was easier than I'd anticipated—and said she hoped I knew how much she *did* respect me. No, I said, I didn't, given the persistently fierce way she's attacked me. Well, she said with a big grin, you became a "symbol." "Why me? I'm not the enemy." She laughed again in agreement & said she thought we ought to move forward & get beyond "all that." Fine with me. We hugged twice, both beaming. I'm *very* happy at the reconciliation. With the Pat Buchanans at our throats, it's way past time we aimed our combined recriminations at the real beasts. . . .

MARCH 9, 1996

Adrienne Harris gave an unusually rich colloquium last Tuesday. Some subtle (and brave) stuff on tomboyism as *both* gender outlawry and gender conformity; on how a "boyhood"—or any—identity serves psychically to foreclose memory, and its associative fears of annihilation. She talked about her own stoicism as a form of boyhood (tho her orientation is heterosexual); she learned as a child to be "a good soldier," not to experience or express pain; as an adult that has become a mechanism in general for "not knowing."

It was a special pleasure hearing Harris grapple with the subjects of affiliation and attachment. It made me realize again how unconcerned (and thus untheorized) most academics are today, and certainly most queer theorists, with matters relating to love and intimacy—as contrasted with the fascination with technologies of the body.

MARCH 18, 1996

I'll never get over (and maybe shouldn't) the discomfort I feel at having "too nice" an apartment. "Too nice" for someone with my politics. Too nice as a signifier of disposable income and consumerism. Too nice as a marker of privilege. Is it any wonder people find my inner turmoil hard to read, when the externals are so variously gilded?

MARCH 20, 1996

My diary-keeping—my life?—has been a prolonged series of narrative presentations on the theme of "me-in-crisis." It's the theme of the privileged class. Other lives, far more crisis-ridden on the primary level of material want, go unrecorded—the erasure as full as the want. Only those with pen & pencil, and the leisure to utilize them, have the luxury to ring endless variations on their Lamentable Plight, to (despairingly) relish their capacity for torment, their conscience-stricken struggle for authenticity. . . .

APRIL 21, 1996

. . . We tried to stop in at Different Light [*the gay bookstore*] but it was jammed with fans waiting for Michael Feinstein's appearance. Light air in the Citadel of gay culture. Why do I persistently expect more—more than musical comedy—from *our* folks? It feeds my accumulating sense of disaffection, which is further fueled by my real and growing need to form larger linkages, to return to the many unresolved questions relating to race, gender and class—to *other* aspects of social justice (or rather, its absence).

APRIL 25, 1996

Great news—CLAGS has again won the Rockefeller Humanities Fellowships Award! It was unprecedented the first time around for a (non-AIDS) gay/lesbian organization to win such a large sum from a mainstream foundation; the second time around partakes of a miracle. Harriet [*Malinowitz*] gets a lot of the credit for the splendid essay she wrote that accompanied our application. Hopefully the Rockefeller's *double* imprimatur (once *wasn't* enough) will open more mainstream foundation doors (I was quick to notify Alison Bernstein at Ford, etc.). I want to pass on as solidly grounded an organization as I can. Which Eli warns me won't prevent a new team from squandering the legacy and/or blaming me for not having passed on an infrastructure solid *enough*.

APRIL 26, 1996

Sat through most of the "Future of the Welfare State" conference today at the Graduate School. The conference was both stirring and depressing. The panelists were mostly heterosexual white men over 50, all (rightly) wringing their hands over the growing global disparities between rich and poor, but all spouting mostly tired analyses and almost all (the Swedish diplomat Pierre Schori the major exception, in regard to women) showing little interest in or comprehension of recent work in feminist or gay studies. Not that such work should supplant prior emphases on class, but it might at least, if acknowledged, provide supplemental insights. The omission of any reference to gay and lesbian as either objects of concern or subjects of active agency, was especially glaring. The entire first panel was (devoutly) concerned with "strengthening dialogue with mainstream religion," & E. J. Dionne worried about the Left embracing assisted suicide. But *we* weren't even worried over it, didn't exist. True, Barney Frank was one of two concluding speakers; and he did mention his own sexuality a number of times (in a charmingly offhand way). But Barney's focus was the coming election, and his tone one of almost gleeful optimism (i.e., the Democrats will cream 'em in 1996; those of cheerful temperament need to concentrate on the short-term to sustain a smile).

Norman Birnbaum deplored the Left's "ideological stubborn-ness" in preventing new ideas from emerging — yet never mentioned the current ferment over traditional gender/sexual models as one possible source for new ideas. Joe Murphy (he who, when Chancellor in 1987, made it clear to Proshansky that he would not openly oppose but did not favor the establishment of CLAGS) seemed smugly self-congratulatory about a new Ethiopian constitution he's involved in formulating that *rhetorically* declares for the needed liberation of women — even as he freely predicts it will take "a long time" before that liberation begins to be implemented. Bogdan Denitch warned against "feel-good" politics & focusing on "cultural" issues; I am delighted, he said snidely, that Clinton favors gays in the military, "but that is (broader smile) obviously not the most urgent issue facing us." I happen to agree with him, but wouldn't have smiled.

All of which confirms the need for raising awareness — and attempting linkages. The Left needs to be kicked in the butt for its alternating ignorance, silence or flipness over gender/sexual issues. And the gay/lesbian world has to awaken to the horrendous plight of the unemployed, the homeless and the working poor. I must say, that plight, as vividly described at the conference by Katherine Newman & Frances Fox Piven (by who else? — the only women on any of the panels) is *so* horrendous, I felt less & less distress as the conference proceeded over the absence of discussion of gay men & lesbians. It's not that our plight isn't also real, or our political movement unnecessary. But the global horrors of poverty, racism & ethnic cleansing make their foregrounding essential — and reinforce my conviction that the gay movement must be reconfigured (à la GLF in 1970) to become a site for contesting, in coalition with others, established concentrations of power. It's not work I feel temperamentally well equipped for; these days especially, I want to nestle into the autobiographical cocoon; subjectivity currently draws me far more powerfully than does the public arena. On top of which, I've grown distant from the straight Left. Though I still recognized many faces from the Sixties & early Seventies, I hadn't seen—let alone worked with—any of them in many years. Barney Frank was the only attendee I felt connected enough to—though we're bare acquaintances—to exchange a few personal words. In focusing for 25 years on gay issues, I'm now chasms away from "the Left" (& the Left's indifference to gay issues bears some of the responsibility)—and am not optimistic that the needed bridge back can be built (for me & my generation of gay lefties, anyway).

MAY 3, 1996

I found our Trans/Forming Knowledge conference yesterday more engrossing than I'd expected. The audience turnout was pathetically small (30–40)—was it the subject matter? the vague title? the fact that it was Thursday?? But several of the panelists & topics proved fascinating—like the discussion of the shifting borderlines (and internal uncertainty) between vernacular knowledge and "expert" opinion; or between the super-butch (and, alternately, the "effeminate") and the trans-gendered. But "community knowledge," as someone pointed out, can be reified just as much as professional expertise— eg., lesbians are the lowest risk group for AIDS, which is based on the white, middle-class assumption that a "real" lesbian was not a druggie or a sex worker, or ever slept with men.

It was the variety of narrative voices that I found most moving. We—the gay/lesbian community, the country as a whole—need to hear these transgressive gender voices (within ourselves, too). The continuum of desire and personae would be expanded, dignified, affirmed. But as Ben Singer smartly warned, most of those in the trans-gender community do *not* want gender to go away; they remain attached (unlike the wondrously *un*-gendered Karen Nakamura) to the traditionally visual appurtenances of "male" & "female." As Singer further argued, "you can't—shouldn't—de-stabilize an identity before it's become established." He himself does *not* want to be accepted as a biological male, though apparently does want to pass visually; aware of the many multiplicities within, to survive in the outer world requires *some* identifiable general signifier.

MAY 4, 1996

My final CLAGS Board meeting. I was surprised by the amount of emotion I felt; a dysfunctional family we often were, but a family nonetheless. The organization is probably in the best shape ever— $115,000 in the bank, fellowships endowed, a series of books in the works, a pioneering Directory published and a solid network of contacts established with foundations, members & donors. The rock of Gibraltar we're not, but given the original odds & the repetitive ambushes along the way, we're far more solidly established than I would have thought possible even a few years ago.

MAY 22, 1996

On the Charlie Rose show last night, I was part of a panel of four to discuss the extraordinary *Romer* decision. [*The Supreme Court, in its 6–3 decision* Romer vs. Evans, *had just invalidated Colorado's "Amendment 2" to the state constitution, which (as approved by a majority of voters), had declared it illegal for cities, town, or counties in Colorado to pass laws that protected lesbian and gay rights. By essentially declaring in* Romer *that the U.S. constitutional guarantee of equal protection for all citizens did apply to homosexuals, the Supreme Court had provided a firewall against the enactment of antigay prejudice into law.*]

I thought the discussion went well enough, but these events are intrinsically absurd, with their rapid-fire sound bites and lack of substantive, *thoughtful* exchange. Charlie Rose's own slick shallowness compounds the problem. Plus he's rude to his own staff. In short, a '90s culture hero made to order.

JUNE 6, 1996

Chatting with R.S. [*a* New York Times *reporter*] a few minutes before taping his TV show last night, I was surprised to hear him say, "The *Times* really has it in for you, doesn't it, even though they quote you in their news sections. Do you want to talk about it on air?"

My new book, *Midlife Queer*, had just been published. The reviews were mostly favorable, but the *Times* had, as with my last few books, assigned it to an unsympathetic reviewer. As I'd written in my diary (May 13): "This time it's Walter Kendrick, bitchily aflame about—God knows what? It *seems* to be: My productivity? My activism? My self-exposure? . . . Between [*Tom*] Stoddard's rave in the *Advocate*, and what I hear is Ed White's "glowing tribute" due June 1 in the *Voice*, I'd begun to have hopes for the book—now stopped dead in its tracks. . . . The *Times* does have a genius for finding reviewers of my work who are temperamentally at odds with it."

I *was* tempted to talk about all this on air, but my instant conclusion was that I might come across as paranoid. Still, I was glad to have had confirmation that I wasn't. And R.S. *had* read the book: "After all," he said, "in this one you do attack [*Mel*] Gussow & [*Walter*] Goodman"—the raised eyebrow & twinkle suggesting that that had *not* been wise. "I didn't attack them," I said, "I told the truth about their homophobia" (a naïve distinction, as I was well aware).

JUNE 7, 1996

The opening of [*the film*] "Stonewall" last night at the Public Theater. The jam-packed audience was so enthusiastic (& Rickie Beadle Blair, the screenwriter & host so charming in his responses to audience questions) that I liked it a *little* better this time around. Finally, it remains trivializing, sentimental and (even for a "fictionalization," too high-handed about history. But hey—it was a million-dollar budget, and how much of an authentic riot scene (or anything else) can you recreate for that? So I'll aim for a philosophical tone on tomorrow's panel, *not* playing the punctilious professor.

Christine Vachon, the producer, foolishly (or forgetfully) didn't give Sylvia [*Rivera, who'd been featured in my* Stonewall *book*], Ivan [*Valentine*] & other "Stonewall Vets" tickets to the opening, and when I tried to intervene was told they were sold out. So Sylvia, Ivan & half a dozen others, with my encouragement, demonstrated with placards outside both the pre-screening party & the Public. I kept bringing them wine from the party, camped it up with them for the cameras and (as usual) stuck $50 in Sylvia's pocket (I've never seen her looking more like a *boy*: not a good sign). Eventually 6 tickets were somehow "found" but the demonstrators, with proper hauteur, rejected the last-minute appeasement. Lots of people stopped to talk to & support them, & spirits were mostly high; they *did* agree to come to the post-screening party. The one true bizarre note was not Ivan's 2-foot-tall blonde wig (she carries off *anything* she wears), but Randy Wicker carrying one of the placards; unless history has been still further rewritten, he *denounced* the riots in '69.

JULY 8, 1996

A column of protest by Todd Gitlin in the *New York Observer* over my Tomasky piece in the *Nation*. Not well-argued or even fully coherent. These straight white boys just won't get it—the "universalist" banner they're peddling really has only *their* names on it—and when you hold their nose to that fact, they howl with indignation.

*M*y lengthy review of Michael Tomasky's* Left For Dead: The Life, Death, and Possible Resurrection of Progressive Politics *in America, in which I defended "identity politics" against his attack on it, appeared in the July 1, 1996, issue of the* Nation. *Tomasky had denounced those on the Left who concentrated on demands that had "nothing to do with a larger concern for our common humanity and everything to do with a narrow concern for fragmented and supposedly oppositional cultures."*

"Note the 'supposedly,'" I wrote in my Nation *response. "Elsewhere Tomasky refers to the 'superficially radical and transgressive'*

*ulturalism. But declaring certain ideas superficial does
n so, especially since it isn't clear that Tomasky has ab-
dical redefinitions of gender and sexuality that are under
n feminist and queer circles—postulates about such uni-
versal m... ers as the historicity and fluidity of sexual desire, the performative nature of gender, and the multiplicity of impulses, narratives
and loyalties that lie within us all. This is no ersatz sideshow. . . ."*

"Many minority intellectuals," I further wrote, "are also troubled
about the inability of overarching categories ('black,' 'gay,' etc.) to
speak to the complex, overlapping identities of individual lives; uncomfortable about referring to "communities" as if they were homogenous
units rather than hothouses of contradiction; concerned about the inadequacy of efforts to create bridges between marginalized people and
then outward to broader constituencies. Yet one holds on to a group
identity, despite its insufficiencies, because it's the closest most non-
mainstream people have ever gotten to having a political home. Yes,
identity politics reduces and simplifies; it is a kind of prison. But it is
also, paradoxically, a haven. It is at once confining and empowering.
And in the absence of alternative havens, group identity will for many
continue to be the appropriate site of resistance and the main source
of comfort. . . . The legitimacy of our differentness as minorities has
not yet been more than superficially acknowledged—let alone safe-
guarded. You cannot link arms under a universalist banner when you
can't find your own name on it. Cultural unity should not be pur-
chased at the cost of cultural erasure.

"Tomasky's appeal 'to connect with those unlike oneself' is unimpeachable—but he's addressed it to the wrong crowd. Many of us involved in identity politics have been trying to reach out . . . Tomasky
claims we have 'simply written off' many potential allies. Well, our efforts at dialogue could certainly improve, but they have not been as
nothing. Yet we've been met mostly with patronization and hostility—
that is, when we really try to talk about our lives, rather than pretend
that we're 'just folks' who want to join up. It is not our interest-group
politics that turn off Tomasky's purported legions of allies—it is our
lives. . . ."

I came down as hard as I did on Tomasky because he represented what had become a mounting attack by straight, white, and left-wing male public intellectuals on an identity politics that emphasized issues relating to ethnicity, gender, and sexual orientation. Among the more prominent of these intellectuals were Eric Hobsbawm, Arthur Schlesinger Jr., Ralph Nader, Richard Rorty, Jack Newfield, and Todd Gitlin. Collectively—and curiously—they chose to focus on us, rather than on corporate America (which of course they did denounce for its greed and corruption), as the chief villain in the decline of interest in the transcendent issues of class division and economic inequity. We had abandoned the working class. We had destroyed the Left.

They did have what seemed to me several irrefutable points. Our national gay political organizations had long been woefully indifferent to class-based inequities, even among LGBT people—those within our own ranks who suffered from the mounting insecurities of blue-collar life, to say nothing of the impoverished and the unemployed. The major, partial, exceptions had been the Gay Liberation Front in the early years of the movement (1969–71), which had spoken out boldly against entrenched privilege of every kind, and the recent struggles by ACT-UP and other AIDS organizations to get drugs and housing into the hands of those who couldn't afford them.

In between, middle-class reformism (skilled lobbyists pressing for narrow, piecemeal change through traditional political channels) had reigned—though the quest for respectability was less pronounced in the separatist-inclined, left-leaning lesbian community. (I myself had long been arguing against the reformist turn. When, in a speech at the seventh annual Lambda Legal Defense Fund dinner way back in 1982, I had used the occasion to denounce the "endemic racism" in the gay world and our indifference to class-based issues, a number of white men walked out in the middle of my remarks and I was subsequently reprimanded for my "inappropriate and offensive" comments.)

When the central goal of the organized national gay movement is focused on "acceptance," then gay people, like the good, mainstream Americans they choose to emulate, will, by definition, remain deaf to class issues and in denial about the extent of ongoing racism and sex-

ism. But it needs to be remembered that gay politics is not uniquely limited in scope. The Tomaskys were certainly right in 1996 to sound the alarm against the growing disparity in income in this country, even as social services were being scaled back and more and more companies were denying benefits to their workers.

(In 1999, the New York Times would announce that it had detected "the biggest surge in campus activism in nearly two decades," most of it focused on improving working conditions for labor—on providing a living wage, an end to sweatshops, and so forth. The announcement mystified me. On my own campus, the City University of New York, I did see a marked growth in tolerance for "differentness" of all kinds, but nothing like a newly activated campaign to curb plutocratic excess or broaden the safety net for the working poor. Indeed over the next decade the gap between rich and poor would turn into a chasm.)

In emphasizing the role that identity politics had played in shattering the Left, Tomasky, Gitlin, and others failed to give anything like equal weight to a host of other, more convincing culprits: a hostile state apparatus; a news-media network that dutifully turned to conservative commentators for "expert" testimony and shunned the countervailing opinions of anyone to the left of Rudy Giuliani; a corporate culture that increasingly gave workers the choice between rejecting unionization (and collective bargaining's ability to protect them), or losing their jobs; a powerful religious right that, ignorant of Biblical scholarship, preached the Bible's literal truth (lingering lovingly over the contested Levitical passage about homosexuality being an "abomination," even while nimbly disregarding such discomforting Biblical injunctions as the need to return fugitive slaves to their "rightful" masters); and the bland textbook mill that either teaches the young nothing about the Left's history or distorts and denounces it (those "fanatical" abolitionists, etc.)

Nor were these well-positioned white male critics of identity politics close to being truthful in claiming we'd "written off" potential allies. One could argue (as Stanley Aronowitz has) that labor has long since ceased to be a progressive force; as late as the seventies, many unions had still not integrated. Traditional heterosexist norms, more-over, remain dominant on the factory floor; gay workers either remain in the closet or risk being ostracized—or physically harmed. When John Sweeney was elected president of the AFL-CIO in 1996, he pledged to push for more progressive policies; some argue that he's suc-ceeded, but others claim that the AFL's new rhetoric has still not been matched by new practices.

The story has been similar when gay people try to form coalitions with other marginalized groups. As far back as the Black Panther Party—for which GLF raised money and offered support—Huey New-ton stood alone in accepting the extended hand. As recently as the AIDS crisis, efforts by gay organizations to make information and ser-vices available to other groups were largely rebuffed, the black churches slamming their doors with particular force.

Oh—and have I somehow missed Gitlin & Co. making any re-ciprocal gestures to gay people, ever lifting a finger to alleviate the discrimination under which they suffer? (Some heterosexual women have, with a few of them—Mathilde Krim, say, or Judy Peabody—becoming genuine heroes in the AIDS crisis.) During the eighties and mid-nineties, did the Gitlin crowd ever sign a petition or join a protest in support of the life-and-death struggle for early release of promising AIDS drugs? Have I missed their banner passing by in the major D.C. marches for gay rights? Have they so much as written a small check for any gay-related cause? I've never seen the name of a single one of these humanist champions on the donor lists of LGBT organizations (and I've seen most of them). Certainly none of these prominent and pros-perous worthies has ever put a dime into CLAGS's coffers—though scholarship is often their own calling, and though topics relating to class, which they claim we don't care about, have been the subjects of several CLAGS colloquia and conferences.

Still, it is true enough, and the cause for real despair, that on the whole national gay and lesbian organizations continue to pay scant attention to issues relating to working-class grievances. And it is equally true that while some unions have improved the work climate for their LGBT members, a significant amount of fear and discrimina-

tion continues to exist. The challenge ahead is to further transform attitudes on both sides: to create a heightened awareness of class issues among gays and an increased sensitivity among unionists to the difficulties of gay life. Should that millennium arrive, we would be on our way to a revitalized politics and civil culture.

AUGUST 10(?), 1996

I stepped down as the executive director of CLAGS nearly ten years to the day in 1986 when I'd gathered a small group of friends in my living room to discuss the possibility of setting up a lesbian and gay research center. Out of that initial gathering, CLAGS had been born—though it took five years of struggling to raise money, support and visibility before we became formally established as a center at the CUNY graduate school.

By 1996 I felt strongly that the right time had arrived for me to step away, to let a new generation reconfigure CLAGS in its own image. And I really did step away. Under Eli's tutelage (he'd built Literacy Volunteers as an organization) I understood that the new director (Jill Dolan) had to have a clear field. I made myself available for information or advice—but only if asked. The break was clean and without regret.

There was much, in retrospect, to feel good about. By 1996, CLAGS, though always in need of money, had a large mailing list and had become well-known as a centerpiece and clearinghouse for the burgeoning new field of lesbian and gay studies. And the center had kept to its original mission and principles. Through a series of fellowships, publications, and a remarkable (especially for a new organization) number of colloquia and conferences on major issues relating to gender and sexuality, we'd increased the amount of reliable scholarship on the LGBT experience, and disseminated it to a general public. And—despite some brief periods of imbalance—we'd basically stuck to our principles of gender parity, multicultural perspectives, and the inclusion, in terms both of fellowship awards and board membership, of scholars who weren't academically affiliated.

Though I was proud of CLAGS's accomplishments, the daily grind of organizational work had never been particularly congenial to my scholar-hermit temperament. And sometimes—especially in the early years when I lacked even a part-time assistant to do some of the legwork—the grind had made me miserable, particularly when it coincided with one of those periods, perhaps inevitable in movement work, when heated factionalism held sway, accusations flew, tempers got frayed and feelings hurt.

When Jill finally took over the reins during the summer of 1996, I wrote in my diary: "It really is over. I've longed for that, yet the void looms large." Most people welcome free time as a chance to relax, to lie fallow, to recoup. Not me. Like most workaholics, I found repose a threat, a prelude to depression.

Immediately ahead, fortunately, was a two-week tour for my latest book, Midlife Queer. No sooner back from that, then Eli and I speed to Long Island to pick up our new seven-week-old yellow Lab, christening her "Emma" (for Emma Goldman, of course) and thus inaugurating, as I put it in my diary, "a new life of bucolic puppy happiness."

Not quite. "Ten minutes of every hour," I was soon explaining in my diary, "she's a sweet, cuddly comfort; the rest of the time, she's a whirling dervish with stiletto-sharp teeth (at last that coveted pierced ear lobe; now where to find the right earring?)." Her demolition derby, a whirlwind of piss and shit, a cacophony of barking and biting, made it impossible to get any work done unless I first ran her ragged in the park and then stuffed my ears with plugs to block out her piteous wails of abandonment.

Exhausted, demented, I called in a trainer for help in curbing her biting. "Give a high screech," he advised, "to scare her into letting go, then a warm 'good girl'"—assuming she has let go. But Emma, like her namesake, proved willful; either that, or I never learned to pitch the screech high enough. Complaining on the phone one day to Tony Kushner about Emma's untamable ways, Tony's response was, "What did you expect, naming her after Emma Goldman? Rechristen her Patient Griselda—or call in a rabbi for an exorcism."

Eli, a psychotherapist, was away at his office most days and, like a typical daddy, would return (as I angrily saw it) for happy cuddles on the floor, followed by a retreat to TV. (He was, of course, much more help than that, but martyrdom is part of my theatrical nature.) Every night, when Eli came home, I'd announce that "I can't go on, we have to give her up," and he'd coax me into trying it for "just a few more days." The days, of course, lengthened, intense love seized me, and before long no one could have pried Emma loose without my calling the cops and brandishing the kitchen knife. Emma, age thirteen, is with us still, despite five cancer surgeries, the wild young thing evolving into a sweet, little old grandma.

By fall 1996, Emma and I had achieved a modus operandi, and I was back at my workaholic ways. For a time I had to give myself over to the final stages of getting the two CLAGS readers I'd edited, A *Queer World* and *Queer Representations*, to press. At nearly 1,200 pages combined, and with more than one hundred contributors, it proved a job and a half getting the essays edited and reworked, tracking down the essayists for their input on the hundreds of copyediting queries, and doing a final close reading of the text.

The tedious chore finally done, I swore to shift gears for a while, to get off the gay dime and get back to some of the other social issues that had earlier absorbed my time and energy. I did—to some extent. But first, I somehow found myself drawn, and then immersed, in the life of "Donald Webster Cory" (Edward Sagarin), author of the 1951 *The Homosexual in America*, the first full-scale, nonfiction account of gay life in the United States—and an astonishingly positive one; in opposition to psychiatric calls of the day for "cure" and religious demands for "repentance," Cory's message to the homosexual was to "turn inward and accept yourself." Who was this far-ahead-of-his-times figure, about whom nothing substantive had ever been written? Were enough of his intimates still around to interview? And did enough source material exist to track his life—including, as I soon learned, Sagarin's later reconversion to the orthodox "sickness" view of homosexuality of the day?

It would prove quite a surprising journey before my long essay ("The 'Father' of the Homophile Movement") finally reached completion. I did find a number of early leaders of the pre-Stonewall organization, the Mattachine Society, who'd been friendly with "Cory," as well as his lover during those years—also his wife. Therein lay the painful part. In the upshot I came to wish that mutual acquaintances had never led me to Gertrude Sagarin, that she'd never (reluctantly) agreed to see me and that she'd remained a distant figure toward whom I felt no personal responsibility.

When I began researching Ed Sagarin's life, I had no idea that Gertrude was still alive. I sailed blithely ahead, and so did my agent, who sold the proposal to the *New Yorker* for what seemed to me (used to writing for negligible—or no—fees, in the gay and left-wing press) a staggering sum of money. But no sooner did I meet Gertrude, then in her eighties, than I knew I was in trouble.

FEBRUARY 2, 1997

. . . Gertrude asked me—between tough questions and angry accusations—not to "bring alarm to my family." It made me cringe. Harm [*Ed being outed in the article as gay or bisexual*] as she defines it will surely follow: her circle of friends will fully know, as they now do not, the details of Ed's double life. By what "right" do I inflict that kind of pain? "In the name of historical truth"?—not good enough, not when reclamation becomes tantamount to invasion: the historian as scavenger . . . Besides, I like Gertrude enormously—direct, warm, real. She even served me salad & cheese, for God's sake!

FEBRUARY 6, 1997

. . . We talked for three hours. Her main fear is *The New Yorker*: "everybody reads it, all my friends will know, I can't cope with the stress." . . . How can I justify making her final years so miserable?

Which is another way of saying, I have so much trouble living with myself that I couldn't tolerate not thinking well of myself morally.

It became clear to me that Gertrude doesn't know the full dimension of Ed's gay past—sexual and political . . . I made a decision on the spot: not to publish the article in *The New Yorker*. The clincher came when Gertrude told me that . . . she's been so upset she can't even read at night. Analyzing his life is hardly worth hastening her death. She did give her blessing to my publishing the essay in a non-mainstream journal; I specifically mentioned the *Harvard Gay & Lesbian Review*. [*It appeared there in the fall 1997 issue.*] Now Gertrude can sleep at night, & I can return to my tumultuous (preferred) state of agonizing over where & when I'll find my next project.

MARCH 1, 1997

I notice I've been getting lots of moral mileage out of telling everyone in sight that I've canceled *The New Yorker* contract—and why. Much praise for the integrity of my position; which I modestly slough off, thus earning more praise . . .

While searching for a new project that would truly consume me— ultimately it would turn out to be a novel (Haymarket, *published in* 2003), *I spent part of late* 1996 *through* 1997 *getting my collected essays ready for publication* (Left Out, 1999), *writing short pieces on various themes, and hatching a few (failed) plots. One was to break the stranglehold that conservative gay white men (like Andrew Sullivan and Bruce Bawer) increasingly had as mainstream reviewers and media "experts" on LGBT lives.*

It started one day at lunch with the writer Sarah Schulman, the two of us grousing away about how mainstream publishers, once convinced (the so-called "crossover" phenomenon) that some heterosexuals would actually care to read about LGBT lives—a nonsense notion, if ever there was one—had mostly given up, dropping many LGBT authors altogether and providing those remaining with such reduced ad-

vances that they had to take on sideline grub work to survive. From
that shared outrage it was but a lighthearted step away to stoking each
other's indignation about the conservative gay monopoly of media out-
lets. We decided to invite a few like-minded gay lefties to ponder fur-
ther with us.

MARCH 10(?), 1997

Dinner last night with Sarah, Tony [*Kushner*], Urvaishi [*Vaid*] &
Kate Clinton to plot strategy for getting radical voices heard more
in the mainstream media *and* in our own communities . . . we bat-
ted around various issues & strategies for 2–3 hours. In the upshot,
we're adopting a three-pronged approach: (1) a "manifesto" ("we *are*
different—especially from the Bruce Bawers—& have much to tell
you"); Sarah will write the first draft. (2) An attempt to get a "Queer
Issue" of *The New Yorker* as a natural follow-up (so we will argue) to
the recent "Black Issue." Tony will contact Skip [*Henry Lewis*] Gates
& John Lahr [*theater critic for the* New Yorker] for advice on how to
approach Tina Brown. (3) My idea, deriving from my prior, vague
thought about doing a book on how the Left doesn't understand us, is
to put together an anthology on that same theme, a variety of off-
center voices contributing their perspectives.

　　All, of course, is in the follow-through. With such busy folk, with
their multiple projects & jammed time schedules, I'm skeptical of
ultimate results. Still, its been an energetic beginning, and we can
hope. . . .

MARCH 17(?), 1997

Tony K. has had a long preliminary talk with John Lahr at *The New
Yorker* about our idea for "a gay issue" & Lahr is enthusiastic ("a
great idea"). He warns of the amount of work that would be involved
(their special issues take up to a year to put together), and of Tina
Brown's demanding ways. None of which is a surprise, but Tony today sounded daunted over the phone & more inclined for the five of

us to invest our immediate energies in getting out our planned Manifesto, possibly as a *Times* op. ed. piece. There's the real & additional danger that Tina could take our idea & run with it straight into the arms of Camille Paglia, Sullivan, Bawer, etc. All true, even likely, but risks that I feel strongly should be run. Tony & and I came down on moving simultaneously on *both* the New Yorker & the Manifesto — but more talk is needed, especially before Tony, as a next step, proposes lunch with Brendan Lemon (which was Lahr's suggestion for a strategic step two).

S arah did come up with a first draft of the Manifesto, which (along with my edits) read in part as follows:

> . . . *The elevation of gay Republicans and other gay conservatives by the national media is mindless and dishonest. We differ with these safe and official homosexuals on questions of gender, sexuality, race, class—and the broader national agenda. And we challenge their manipulation by the dominant press as a way of avoiding the hardest issues at the core of the struggle of all minority—not merely gay—people in America today.*
>
> *"We believe that homosexuals* are *different and have something rich and profound to offer this country from our place of difference. While gay people deserve the same legal rights and protections as heterosexuals . . . an insistent assimilation and conformity to the institutionalized inequalities of the status quo is not in the best interests of any of us. . . . Like many people who have fought for gay liberation, we are Socialists and we're not afraid to say so. We believe that every person by virtue of being born deserves a home, a competitive education, quality medical care and meaningful employment. We are sickened by the disparities of opportunity and wealth, and by the corporate-driven politics of this country . . . gay conservatives do not represent us. When the national media uses them*

to comfortably fill a token slot, they are cynically reinforcing mainstream conformity as the standard . . .

I draw a complete blank as to what happened next. I don't recall (and didn't record) any further meetings of "the five." I know for sure that we never met with Brendan Lemon; my guess is that the idea of a "gay issue" of The New Yorker *was early on thrown in somebody's waste basket. Nor was the Manifesto ever submitted to the* Times, *or published anywhere else. I have a vague recollection that, as I'd feared, schedule conflicts and lack of time prevented any one of us from pushing the agenda and carrying the organizational ball. Too bad. Down to the present day, the voices of gay lefties remain under-represented, their views largely unheard, even within the gay world.*

Another failed "plot" during this period was my attempt to get approval from the National Endowment for the Humanities to lead one of their six-week summer seminars for teachers—mine to be on the subject of "Gender and Sexual Nonconformity." I designed the course as an overview of the challenges queer studies were currently offering to "regimes of the normal"—to traditional definitions of "maleness" and "femaleness," and to the use of "gay" and "straight" as oppositional categories. Through the prism of historical and cross-cultural evidence, I wanted to question the traditional notions that gender and sexual categories were objective, universal, binary realities, or whether, through time and across cultures, they've been regarded in radically different ways. I wanted to explore how and why being "different" and being "authentic" were becoming linked, along with "marginality" and "creativity" (with the center being destabilized as merely the site of traditional authority). I wanted to place under scrutiny the tenets of a sex-gender system that privileged white, heterosexual males, relegating others to some subcategory of being.

Utterly galvanizing! (sez I to me) as I carefully prepared a twelve-page essay and syllabus, confident that when combined with my cre-

dentials in the field, the proposed seminar would win a standing ova-
tion from the judges. Thus doth hubris wipe out empires (and hedge
funds). The NEH turned me down flat, and didn't encourage me (as it
often does) to reapply. I asked (as was my right under the rules) to see
the five reviewers' comments, which on a second request were finally
sent. None were enthusiastic; only one of the five found the proposal
"worthy of further consideration."

With varying degrees of subtlety, all the referees found the merit of
queer studies suspect, and its challenge to mainstream norms dubious.
All, of course, used the polite language that has traditionally served to
conceal the ferocious bigotries of academe. One reviewer vaguely complained that my proposal "was repetitive and lacked focus" (it was, if I
may say so, concentrated to a fault).

Another disliked my "heavily theoretical approach, not sufficiently
concerned with historical fact"—precisely the opposite of how queer theorists themselves tended to view me: "fact-haunted"; "theoretically soft."

A third reviewer, intriguingly, deplored my lack of provision "for
any activities" aside from the seminar meetings (an orgiastic hot tub
outing? a "Dress in Drag" party? a visit to the headquarters of Dykes
on Bikes?). Another juror feared that a seminar about gender and sexual nonconformity, topics "considered by many citizens as morally ob-
jectionable . . . could cause considerable harm to both NEH and
NEA at a time when they are already under attack." And, finally, the
rare (in academia) flat-out animosity sounded by academic juror #5:
"I regard this as a sort of missionary summer camp to spread the word
of queer theory . . . preaching to the converted. . . . All of the purported
'science' is from The Journal of Homosexuality"—which was fla-
grantly untrue.

I suspect that this view of me as a proselytizing zealot had been
underscored by two recent pieces I'd written, one in the New York
Times on Robert Rauschenberg's major 1997 retrospective ("Is There
Room For Privacy on the Canvas?"), and the other a lengthy review
("Bloom Buried") for the Nation of Lawrence W. Levine's The Open-
ing of the American Mind.

In the Rauschenberg article I picked up on a new trend among

younger art critics to uncover the significant amount of homoerotic im-
agery in his work—to the displeasure of a curatorial-museum estab-
lishment more comfortable with decoding Christian symbolism. I asked,
in the article, why some aspects of an artist's biography were consid-
ered relevant to a discussion of his/her art, but not others. The argu-
ment that Rauschenberg hadn't chosen to "come out" publicly had to
be weighed against the fact that he'd loaded his work with same-sex
iconography that he must have known would some day be "read."

Besides, Rauschenberg was, by any definition, a Famous Person,
and that status carries with it, in our celebrity-obsessed culture, a pre-
dictable amount of invasion of privacy. He was "public," moreover, in
other senses as well: "He displays his products," I wrote, "for the pub-
lic's gaze, response, critical commentary—and sale. And he displays
them, moreover, in museums that rely, to varying degrees, on public
support." Rauschenberg himself had long been upfront with friends
(as several had told me) about his sexuality and had even gone to the
edge of publicly coming out: in 1990 he'd told Interview *magazine*
that he didn't see "any sin or conflict" about the fact that he and
Jasper Johns had at one period been "the most important person in the
other's life. . . . It was sort of new to the art world that the two most
well-known, up-and-coming studs were affectionately involved." In say-
ing as much, Rauschenberg was clearly in advance of the curatorial-
museum establishment—to say nothing of academic reviewers for the
National Endowment for the Humanities.

The NEH referees could easily have found additional ammunition
for regarding me as an evangelist for cockeyed subversion in my review
of Lawrence Levine's The Opening of the American Mind. *Utilizing*
Levine's rigorous, lucid scholarship, I joined him in arguing that those
who disapproved of "ideological" multiculturalism entering the uni-
versity were indulging a shallow nostalgia for an earlier curriculum
they wrongly regarded as "apolitical."

Far from being apolitical, the 1950s humanities curricula through-
out most of academe had been dominated by Western Civilization sur-
vey courses parochially taught as the triumphant Anglo-Saxon
march across the Earth's surface—without reference to entire cultures

*or epochs. And the professoriate teaching these courses—a homog-
eneous group of mostly conservative white males—were hardly engaged in a value-free enterprise. When an undergraduate at Yale in the
early fifties, I remember enrolling in (the then-well-known) Samuel
Flagg Bemis's diplomatic history course. Arriving at the subject of
our land-grab from Mexico, one brave undergraduate asked if our actions had been entirely justified. An exasperated Bemis shot back,
"Why? Would you like to give the land back?" Much laughter. End of
discussion.*

*In contrast to this sort of narrow arrogance, the multicultural im-
pulse represents an effort—belatedly—to tell the truth about our
country's past and present. It seeks to broaden understanding of our
peculiarly variegated society by paying attention to the diverse cultural threads and interactions that have created our national character. By labeling this effort "political correctness," conservatives have
converted an opening up into a closing down—just as they've tried to
reduce multiculturalism to an exercise in feel-good therapy. But it's
the conservatives who are insisting on "correctness." In an effort to
erase various cultural distinctions and contributions, they champion
the static view that "universal" values exist that always have and always must form the basic fabric of society, and which can (must) be
transmitted to the young through certified texts that "correctly" portray
our heritage.*

*Our is the key word, and its definition is not self-evident. The ba-
sic struggle here is over ownership and legitimacy. Previously silenced
minorities, having recovered their voices, rightfully insist that they be
heard. To disdain their claims is to ignore or discount the process by
which our dynamic society has continued to renew itself. Official, traditional culture may be loath to acknowledge the fact, but a variety of
races, ethnicities, genders and classes—plus some charming folks who
fit none of the standard categories—have long been making profound
contributions to the country's life. Diversity is not a curse but a
blessing—the source of much that has given U.S. culture its distinc-
tively robust, vibrant, ever-revolving character. America's strength is its
heterogeneity.*

APRIL 1, 1997

The media is awash and agog with the "crazies" of Heaven's Gate who killed themselves last week. I've yet to read or hear a word about the absolutely analogous craziness of believing in the Virgin Birth, Papal Infallibility, or the Resurrection of Christ. All religions are based on faith (non-reason) and one set of mythologies is no more "irrational" than any other. The same TV news commentators who speak in hushed, pious tones about the glorious worldwide celebrations of Easter, hee-haw over the Heaven's Gate fools who senselessly abandoned their bodies. Is there some historical reason I don't know for the propinquity of April Fool's Day to Easter?

APRIL 10, 1997

I'm thinking of doing my next book on Alger Hiss and spent an afternoon with his widow, Isabel. We got on instantly and her radiance and beauty, despite age and a stroke, dazzled me. But Alger's son, Tony Hiss, is sitting on the only known manuscript materials relating to his father that scholars haven't already combed through, and Tony, understandably, is saving them for his own book [*which he did write*].

But I do still want to revisit some of those nongay topics that earlier absorbed much of my attention, and especially issues relating to race [*I'd started my scholarly life as a historian of nineteenth-century slavery and antislavery.*] By the mid-nineties, two widespread assumptions seemed to have taken hold among whites: "Blacks have achieved a great deal of progress (though few of them, judging from their continuous whining, seem willing to admit it)"; and, "We're sick of the whole damn issue; if anything more is to be done, it's up to blacks to do it—to get off the streets, to get themselves educated and employable, to properly parent their children."

Two weighty books are out that are receiving widespread attention, and drawing nearly opposite conclusions about how much progress has in fact been made and who should be held most responsible for any further advances. One of the books, Stephen and Abigail Thern-strom's massive *America in Black and White*, all but drove me up the wall. The other, David Shipler's *A Country of Strangers*, all but made me weep.

For those whites suffering from "race fatigue," the Thernstroms' tome will become something of a Bible, and Abigail especially is beginning to appear regularly on talk shows (where the media's idea of "diversity of opinion" ranges from retired admirals to retired generals). In their book, the Thernstroms several times reiterate their antiracism, but they could certainly have fooled me. They denounce the policy of affirmative action and reject any notion of "preferential" treatment. They argue that if blacks wish to retain the support and confidence of whites, they need pull themselves up by their bootstraps (what we might call the Booker T. Washington solution). After all, white racism has become so diluted, the Thernstroms claim, that it can no longer be held accountable for the remaining disabilities under which some African-Americans suffer.

David Shipler knows better. In his wise and humane *A Country of Strangers*, he agrees with the Thernstroms that in some areas (more blacks in college and holding public office) the situation has improved, but in others has worsened. One-third of black men in their twenties are in jail, on probation, or on parole. One-quarter of all blacks lack even a high school diploma — and the income of more than a third of all African-American households is below the poverty line (which in 1997 is fifteen thousand dollars for a family of four). The gap between whites and blacks in asset ownership is even more pronounced. The nation's schools, moreover, are becoming resegregated at the fastest rate since the *Brown v. Board of Education* decision in 1954.

As for white racism, it has indisputably declined, though there is still quite enough to go around: one careful study last year concluded that 57 percent of nonblacks regarded blacks as "less intelligent than whites" (what whites say in public is not the same as what they feel in private). And whereas the Thernstroms insist that housing segregation has declined, that's in fact true only for metropolitan areas with small black populations; three-quarters of all African-Americans continue to live under highly segregated conditions.

Liberal whites often see "color blindness" as the ideal social goal — in much the same way that they're unable to find any features of the so-called gay subculture worth protecting. But "color blindness" is in fact a surrogate phrase (and goal) for asserting the superiority of white (or straight) ways. It represents in essence a refusal to acknowledge the genuine difference, and value, of black (or gay) experience and culture. It's tantamount to declaring that such subaltern identities aren't distinctive enough to be worth preserving. But many blacks (as well as left-wing gays) find their unique culture a source of great solace and pride, and they're uninterested in surrendering it for the blessing of being wholly swallowed up by a soulless mainstream. "How shockingly misguided," most whites, including most liberals, would respond, resolutely refusing to entertain the possibility that if the mainstream would open itself to assimilating some of the values and perspectives of minority cultures, its own desiccation might lessen.

APRIL 18, 1997

I'm reading Cary Nelson's excellent *Notes of a Tenured Radical*, and it keeps jolting me into renewed awareness of my uncommon good fortune in life. I arrived in academia just before it began the slow decline into what is now a desert of unemployable PhDs and ruthlessly exploited adjuncts — and with even tenure under siege as a concept (free speech) worth preserving. And here I sit on top of the hill, morosely brooding about the color of a book jacket or the shape of a review. And of course always will. Awareness of good fortune doesn't guarantee the experience of it.

MAY 4, 1997

I heard some smart things said at the CLAGS conference on gay families, things that confirmed my own discomfort with moving family and marriage issues to the center of the movement's agenda. In privileging the needs of those who've chosen coupledom and parenthood, we're downplaying the importance of meeting the needs of the *un*-paired, the *non*-monogamous, the *non*-child-centered—that is, those whose life styles carry forward more of the radical potential for disrupting (rather than joining) sanctified social behavior. And wouldn't the centering of traditional families further alienate those non-whites who've typically resisted being placed in a position of exile from their families of origin, and resisted, too the long-standing notion that those African-American families with women as heads of households and kinship-focused were somehow "not normal?"

Yet when John D'Emilio spoke (smartly) of the need to lay claim to *non*-traditional, non-nuclear family structures associated with portions of the working class and some minorities (kinship networks, god-parenting, etc.), how can that organically be accomplished, or legitimately claimed, when a white élite still dominates the movement? Most of our "leaders" seek not a revision in traditional models of coupledom and child-rearing, but rather extending its blessings (and there *are* many social and economic ones) to gay people. Few in the gay mainstream want to destabilize the gender norms that traditional marriage continues to typify and underscore. LGBT people rightly demand to share in the many social and economic benefits that accompany legal marriage (like securing Social Security survival benefits). But those benefits should be extended to every individual, regardless of his or her relational status.

Tellingly, after Massachusetts legalized gay marriage and some six thousand gay and lesbian couples, in the single year of February 2004 to February 2005, took advantage of the new law, the percentage of Bay State voters who supported gay marriage jumped from 35 percent to a remarkable 56 percent. Clearly, as they saw it, the sky hadn't fallen nor—something of a pity perhaps—had the superstructure of Western civilization been threatened, let alone destroyed.

Two years later, some twenty queer activists hammered out in a two-day conference a document ("Beyond Same-Sex Marriage") that was subsequently signed by hundreds of movement people (myself included). It offered a clear, densely argued challenge to current strategies for "marriage equality" being pursued by the major LGBT organizations. In a detailed and brilliant brief, the authors of "Beyond" set out to honor the diverse ways people actually "practice love, form relationships, create . . . networks of caring and support, establish households, bring families into being, and build innovative structures to support and sustain community."

The document reminded us that a majority of people in the United States do not live in traditional nuclear families; diverse households are already the norm and range from kinship networks and extended families, to senior citizens living together, to single-parent households. Marriage and the nuclear family, "Beyond" argued, are "not the only worthy forms of family or relationship and should not be legally and economically privileged above all others." The call is for a new vision of human relatedness and a civic commitment to recognizing and securing the wide diversity of household arrangements that actually characterize the country's domestic topology.

Putting the issue of legalizing gay marriage to one side, a growing body of scholarly evidence (as reported in the New York Times, *on June 10, 2008) suggests that same-sex couples significantly diverge in behavior from their heterosexual counterparts—and in ways (as the* Times—*remarkably—puts it) that "have a great deal to teach everyone else."*

Whether the relationship is between two men or two women, same-sex couples are "far more egalitarian than heterosexual ones" in sharing responsibility both for housework and finances—unlike heterosexual relationships, where women still do much more of the domestic chores (and live with a lot of anger) and the men are more likely to pay the bills. *Perhaps as a result, gay and lesbian couples "have more relationship satisfaction."*

Certain features are apparently common to both gay and straight couples. When one partner—usually the woman, in heterosexual relationships—makes demands for change, the other reacts by withdrawing. Also, the amount of conflict that arises in couples is roughly comparable, whether gay or straight. Yet even within these commonalities there are significant differences. "Belligerence and domineering" are less frequent when gay couples fight; the partners make fewer verbal attacks on each other, are better at using humor and affection to defuse confrontation, and show much greater ability at "seeing the other person's point of view."

Such findings aren't set in concrete; they need replication, lots of it, before they approach truisms. Still, as they stand the studies are highly suggestive. And—time for some immodest gloating—confirmatory of several positions I've taken over the years. First, that gender differences we've been trained to view as biological in origin ["Men are from Mars, Women are from Venus"—and other assorted crap], may well not be. "Demand-withdraw" interactions are common to both gay and straight relationships and thus do not rely on supposedly deep-seated, ineradicable differences between the genders. This is grounds for optimism—assuming we really do want to create an egalitarian society.

Second, as I've been repetitively, perhaps tiresomely arguing, there really is a gay subculture, a way of looking at life and coping with its joys and sorrows that has much to offer the straight world—if we can somehow get it to open its ears. Further, the multitude of gay people who prefer to claim that we're just like everybody else, are not only deluding themselves but in the process helping to destroy a distinctive set of values and perspectives that could do much to inform—and reform—mainstream patterns.

NOVEMBER 14(?), 1997

The ever-mounting avalanche—unimaginable a mere two decades before—of gay-themed articles, monographs, courses, conferences, books, and journals has made it difficult for even specialists to keep pace. Which isn't to say that resistance to the rise of gay studies has disappeared. A member of the University of California's board of regents recently condemned the new field as lacking any "educational value." On National Public Radio, Harold Bloom, he of the mournful countenance, has charged that queer studies had "helped destroy literary study in all the universities of the Western world." And gay conservative Andrew Sullivan, he of the shrieky pitch, chimed in to denounce queer (not gay) studies as "a sect restricted to the academy, which they control as a cartel."

Though "gay studies" and "queer theory" are often conflated, they're in fact quite distinct, and often antagonistic, enterprises. Queer theory, derived from cultural studies and utilizing the difficult vocabulary of the French deconstructionists (most influentially, Michel Foucault), regards gay and lesbian studies as old-fashioned, as primitively innocent in its glorification of "facts," and blind to their cultural production and use. Queer theorists also dismissed as simplistic and sentimental the idea of a core "gay identity," rejecting the notion of a "true self" of any sort that awaits discovery and affirmation. As a countermodel, they insist on the multiple, shifting, and overlapping identities that characterize most people ("The fact that I'm lesbian is much less important to me than the fact that I'm black"; "My working-class background defines me to a far greater extent than my skin color," etc.).

Gay and lesbian studies, in turn, denounced queer theory as unintelligible, apolitical "jargon." Even the very word queer—so redolent of past humiliations—is often seen as arrogantly deaf to its ugly past usage. (I myself prefer queer as an umbrella term that puts out the welcome mat for all those who are different). Gay studies has always addressed itself (unlike queer theory) to a general audience and is proud of the yeoman work it's done in excavating the historical roots of a recognizable gay "identity." An economistic Marxism has added further fuel to these debates by assaulting both queer and gay studies as intolerable bourgeois distractions from the serious work of class struggle.

As a historian whose work has always been deeply rooted in archival research, I tend to be seen as hostile to queer theory. There's some truth in that. I am intrinsically a nominalist, resistant to generalization (theory), and primarily interested in the intricacy and texture of individual life (thus my attraction to writing biography). But at the same time, I feel that I've personally learned a great deal from queer theory's anti-élitism, its reclamation of silenced voices and scorned "low" art products, and its emphasis on the fluidity of sexual and gender identities. Some of its texts, in particular Michael Warner's *Fear of a Queer Planet*, et al., have proven iconic for me, clarifying jumbled, disconnected views I've long held but hadn't seen as unified.

Since I feel some affiliation with the perspectives of all three (gay, queer, socialist) combatant groups, I can't summon up the zealous partisanship needed to participate centrally in the escalating debate. Besides, I've had my say on some of the key issues at stake. I've long since, and in a variety of venues, called for far greater awareness within the gay world of how class privilege distorts our agendas, clouds our vision, and fails to address the fundamental needs of the poor among us. And as far back as my 1972 book, Black Mountain, I've challenged the historian's ideal of "objectivity" as deceptively naïve, as obscuring the fundamentally ambiguous, fragmentary—and class-based—nature of evidence, as well as the historian's inescapable subjectivity in interpreting it: "Every historian knows [or should know] that s/he manipulates the evidence to some extent simply because of who s/he is (or is not), of what s/he selects (or omits), of how well (or badly) s/he empathizes and communicates."

I also feel that the charges and countercharges in this latest academic dustup have been overdrawn, and that the intellectual enterprises currently under debate aren't as incompatible as some make them sound; each could well profit from heeding some of the insights of the others. As I said in a private letter, "there's no necessary contradiction between research and theory, though many teaching in the field of LGBT Studies proceed as if a choice must be made between the two. And the choice, lately, has been to highlight theorizing (with particular emphasis on popular culture) and to downplay the historical context. In my own opinion, this has been unfortunate because theory, when not grounded in detailed, substantiating evidence, not complicated by a historical perspective, tends to become thin, trivial and entirely focused on contemporary life. . . . 'Factual' materials, on the other hand, are always subject to scholarly interpretation—to theory—which amounts to an individual scholar's decision (conscious or not) to privilege certain aspects of evidence over others. . . ."

Given the general uproar, one might have thought that gay (or queer) studies had taken over American universities. Hardly. The City College of San Francisco still stands alone in offering a major in gay and lesbian studies, and only a handful of schools offers a minor. On the graduate level, not a single university has a doctoral program (our own efforts at the CUNY Graduate Center to create a PhD in multiculturalism, which would have included a gay component, has come a cropper, the victim (in my view) of subtle and insidious homophobia).

Many straight faculty and administrators on college campuses continue to regard the study of homosexuality, in whatever form, as an unseemly enterprise that meets no organic scholarly necessity. The number of courses with lesbian and gay content has proliferated over the previous decade, but even when taken together, they hardly represent the "explosion" of interest sometimes claimed. Nor do they begin to rival in stability the state-funded programs, complete with faculties and research grants, that characterize Utrecht University and the University of Amsterdam in the Netherlands.

If I steered away from directly entering the lists in the gay versus queer versus Marxist controversy, I did have more to say—and more free time for saying it (now that I was no longer bogged down in administrative duties with CLAGS)—on other disputed subjects.

Late in 1997, John F. Kennedy Jr.'s relatively new magazine, George, decided to put out a book, 250 Ways to Make America Better, *and invited a diverse group of Americans to share their views. They only gave us five hundred words each, so I tried to be concise:*

How to make the United States a better place? It's simple (though not easy): Redistribute the wealth. For starters, guarantee a minimal annual income—$25,000, say—to every American.

The gap between rich and poor has gotten shockingly wide—and there are many more poor than rich. "God's will," some will say; the Bible tells us that "the poor you shall always have with you." Not being biblically-inclined (nor God-privy), I can't help but doubt the self-serving banality of the explanation. Besides, I've known too many people with brilliance of various kinds who never had the chance to convert talent into tangible assets. No, the poor are not dumber than you and me; they haven't had our access to privileged headstarts.

The Social Darwinists among us—and 19th century values are alive and well in much of the land—would insist that those who win the race for wealth are those who are the most "deserving." But the personal qualities that usually translate into economic success are often the least attractive ones, humanly— qualities like avarice, connivance, manipulation, ruthlessness. Not that everyone who makes a bundle is a bastard. Some simply inherit their stash from wealthy families. We're a nation that purportedly believes in "earning one's bread by the sweat of one's brow," yet such protest as we hear about "giveaways" relates to Aid to Dependent Children, not to corporate welfare.

Nobody needs three houses and five cars. But lots of people need a clean, dry apartment, enough food on the table, basic medical treatment and education. So the downside of guaranteeing everyone an annual income (since the economy is unable to guarantee decent jobs) is that a few of the rich might be taxed down to two houses and four cars. Tough.

FEBRUARY 20, 1998

Jane Gallop, a prominent feminist theorist and a distinguished professor of English and comparative literature at the University of Wisconsin at Milwaukee, had been accused by two female graduate students back in 1992—though she'd long been in a monogamous relationship with a male film professor—of sexual harassment. A university committee appointed to investigate found that Gallop and the students had engaged in sexual banter, flirtation, and, in one case, a passionate and public French kiss, but concluded that the behavior hadn't amounted to harassment. In 1997 Gallop published a small book (*Feminist Accused of Sexual Harassment*) in which she revealed that as a graduate student she herself had slept on separate occasions with two male professors, and as an assistant professor had slept with several of her own students. She further argued in the book that sexualizing the classroom atmosphere and eroticizing (on a consensual basis) relationships with students helped to level the power differential between them and led to a freer, more inventive climate in general.

I myself had never kissed, slept with, or attempted to sleep with a student. As far back as the sixties ("An Experiment in Education"), I'd become profoundly concerned about the authoritarian structure of the college classroom (exams, grades, and The Professor as the oracular fount of Truth). That atmosphere, I felt, induced immobilizing fear and professor-pleasing dishonesty in students (and a God complex in professors), preventing any free-spirited, dynamic exchange of views—any true learning. For much of the sixties and seventies, I'd experimented with a variety of ways to reduce the clogged tensions of the classroom—everything from encounter-group exercises to dispensing entirely with exams and grades.

But I'd never thought that the solution to a repressive classroom environment lay in openly erotizing teacher/student relations (student-student ones played out privately). Well, maybe I'd thought about it, but I never dreamed of acting on the fantasy. I was fully aware of the presence of unspoken erotic desires between a variety of people in any given classroom—and felt that in some utopian future these might be responsibly explored, at least verbally. And I was certainly aware that an occasional student in one of my classes did turn me on, and that if we'd met in some other context, I'd have been delighted to become his bed partner.

But because we'd met as teacher/student, I'd never attempt to act on, or even hint at, my attraction; it would risk too many negative consequences, psychological as well as professional. Perhaps I simply lacked Jane Gallop's imagination. Perhaps I was too cowardly, fearing exposure and an end to my career. Perhaps I'd heard too many analogous horror stories about the disastrous consequences of therapists having sex with their patients.

In my twice-yearly course at CUNY on "The History of Sexual Behavior," I'd seen how explosive even the distantly historical topic of Greek Love could be. Just saying aloud the word cross-generational produced dropped jaws and sometimes a literal shriek—and I made it clear that we were talking primarily about late teenagers and a partner often but a few years older (with literal "boys" strictly off-limits).

When I would carry the topic into our own day and raise the general question of what the so-called "power differential" between two people, whether heterosexual or homosexual, consisted and how it could most accurately be identified, initial puzzlement would give way to widely shared, immoveable—and culture-based—assumptions. Sex between a sixteen- or seventeen-year-old and an older—say forty-five-year-old person? Uniform horror. Why? "No sixteen-year-old is mature enough to give informed consent, to reach a reasonable, logical conclusion about what is in their own best self-interest."

Is that equally true for young men and young women? "Sure." But aren't young women more likely to have been socialized (if less so than fifty years ago) to please men, especially men in positions of authority, and to defer to their wishes? If so, can we really say that even a forty-year-old woman in this culture is "mature" enough to know her own interest and to follow it? As for young men, here I'd cite some of the (limited) scholarly literature, particularly an article based on extensive interviews with young gay hustlers that quoted a majority of them as insisting, years later, that they had felt in control in their relationships with infatuated older men ("You buy me that sound system or I'm outta here"). Come to think of it, how about all those forty-year-old straight men who are constantly making irrational, self-destructive—that is, "immature"—decisions (like staying in a dead-end job, like abandoning their families, like constantly drinking to excess)? Is anybody ever "ready" for sex according to the necessary precursors and narrow definitions we've set up?

In short, I knew some of the minefields connected to discussing sex with college students, let alone actually having it with them. And I certainly felt experienced in trying to overcome some of the barriers that the university structure set up to any education worthy of the name. I felt fully prepared, in other words, to exchange views with Jane Gallop.

Early in February 1998, CLAGS arranged for a panel discussion ("Anxious Pleasures") featuring Gallop and her book *Feminist Accused of Sexual Harassment*. I found the evening fascinating, but ultimately frustrating. As I wrote in my diary the next day:

> . . . Jane Gallop & the panelists were all impressive, and opened up an intriguing set of issues. . . . Why have we been trained to see "inconsequential fun" (Gallop's term) as a power move? She argued (the panelists agreeing) that a "romantic joining" is (or should be) intrinsic to pedagogy, and that our current conflation of sexual harassment and voluntary pleasure produces a thin, dreary vision of what is possible between student and teacher. Yes . . . but. I'm on the side of iconoclasm and "excessiveness," but Gallop's assumptions are too narrowly and righteously perceived. Neither she nor any of the panelists challenged the terrorizing structures that remain in place in the university (the set of sadistic rituals, for example, at the heart of "professional training"). All the central questions raised in the '60s about education were ignored by the panel: What is a true "learning environment"? What is "professional training" really about or for? How can we stop perpetuating the hierarchical (and patriarchal) structures of the university and replace them with a more collegial/communal spirit?

Later, at the reception, Gallop volubly insisted that her concern was to protect the university from the Right, not to challenge the university as an institution. To which I said that I couldn't understand how someone like herself, "blissfully in love" with her students, can remain uncaring and unconcerned about the humiliating, damaging "training" to which they are subjected—and the borderline poverty which further assails their esteem. We got nowhere with each other. . . . Yes, let's explore play and desire in student/teacher relations, but so long as the university's superstructure remains intact, the "fun" (for students) will be minimal.

*F*ew *of my Lehman students think it was honorable to have been on the left during the McCarthy years; even fewer feel any sympathy for or would support rehabilitating those known to have been actual members of the party. Yet many Americans who did take out Communist Party membership did so out of idealism, out of the quite reasonable belief—at a time when blacks were still being lynched in this country—that the Party was the likeliest vehicle for improving life for the underclasses. It wasn't their fault that Bolshevism's initial vision was later betrayed by the Soviet leadership itself.*

My feelings about all this have been further reawakened by having reviewed Ron Radosh's Commies *for the* Nation. *He focuses particularly on the case of Julius and Ethel Rosenberg, executed in 1953 for what J. Edgar Hoover called "the crime of the century"—stealing the secret of the atom bomb and giving it to the Soviets. By the end of the Cold War, it was generally understood that there hadn't been any single secret central to making the bomb, that the Soviets' own scientists had already made headway toward producing atomic weapons, and that the spy who had most helped them was not Julius Rosenberg, but the British physicist Klaus Fuchs.*

But what has never been widely conceded is that the Communist Party USA wasn't, even in the 1930s, primarily a recruitment agency for spies. Rather, the Party attracted a broad spectrum of compassionate left-wingers whose reasons for joining had nothing to do with espionage. The argument has become more detailed and intricate with the publication of John Earl Haynes and Harvey Klehr's Venona: Decoding Soviet Espionage in America, *an analysis of nearly three thousand pages of deciphered cables between Moscow and its U.S. agents—some 350 people in Haynes and Klehr's estimate.*

When Venona *appeared, it was widely hailed in the mainstream press as having conclusively demonstrated that the CPUSA was indeed a significant "fifth column" working against our country's interests, with the added implication that the anticommunist crusade undertaken by McCarthy and others had been justified. But as someone who worked with FBI files for my biography of Paul Robeson, and also in researching the early years of the gay movement, I can testify to the frequent inaccuracy of agents' reports, and their sometimes laughable distortions (which doesn't make them any less dangerous). In regard to the gay movement, I've read FBI reports that rendered "gay" as "gaye," defined transvestites as "a militant group of women," referred to the early 1970s countercultural university "Alternate U." as "Ultimate You," and mislabeled the gay Marxist study group Red Butterfly as prototypically anarchist.*

In regard to Robeson, FBI headquarters learned from its various agents that Robeson had taken out formal membership in the Communist Party (which he never did); that he and his brother Ben "do not get along too well" (it was Robeson's wife, Eslanda, who didn't get along with his brother); that the union members who volunteered to form a cordon around Robeson during his dangerous Peekskill concert, and who held various political allegiances, were all "Communists . . . endeavoring to recruit delegations." One FBI agent even managed, during the run of Othello *on Broadway—in which Robeson co-starred with Uta Hagen and Joe [José] Ferrer—to report that he hadn't been able to identify the "Joe" mentioned in a phone log, though he thought "Joe" might "possibly [be] associated with Paul Robeson's show."*

None of which is to say that the FBI didn't often get things right, but only to say that its agents were and are human, with blind spots, prejudices, areas of ignorance, and ambitions to make a mark or please a boss. Too often Radosh and Joyce Milton relied in their earlier The Rosenberg File *on a single agent's report, uncorroborated by independent evidence, treating it as the full story, unblemished and unbiased.*

In Commies, *predictably, Radosh hails the release of the Venona files as conclusive proof that Julius Rosenberg committed espionage; "all doubts," Radosh writes, "have been laid to rest." Probably, but Radosh is strangely mute about whether or not Ethel should also be regarded as guilty; far too often he writes about "the Rosenbergs," lumping husband and wife together as co-conspirators, whereas many lefties I know feel that although Ethel may well have had knowledge of her husband's work, the evidence that she directly shared in it is weak; that she may in fact have been framed by the U.S. government; and that given the limited extent of her involvement, in any case, she hardly deserved the death penalty.*

As to Julius, the Venona evidence has changed minds on the Left. Victor Navasky, for example, told me that he's shifted "from agnosticism to the belief that Julius did something." And as for Eric Foner, whom Radosh portrays as Julius's rigid defender, he's never claimed that Julius was innocent but only that the case against him had not been proven. Since Venona, Eric's opinion has, he told me, "to some extent changed," but only toward accepting the possibility that Julius (not Ethel) may have engaged in some sort of low-level espionage.

We can't even be sure of the nature of the Venona information: We still don't know what portion of the total number of documents transmitted to the Soviets by U.S. espionage agents has in fact been released. Nor do we know how or why particular code names in the documents have been linked to given individuals like Julius Rosenberg. So we can't be sure what Julius Rosenberg did, or may have tried to do. Radosh and others feel entitled to declare that the Venona material has "proved conclusively" Julius's guilt, but they can't tell us precisely what sort of "secrets" Julius was guilty of passing to the Soviets.

In addition, if we put aside nationalistic fervor, we might dare raise a broad question that Radosh, the zealous patriot, refuses to go near: Why do we seem unable to feel some compassion and extend some understanding toward those who chose, often at enormous personal sacrifice, to give primary allegiance to a country which they believed—however mistakenly, we might today feel—stood alone among the great nations in the 1930s and 40s for antiracist, anticolonialist principles? (In the United States, gleeful crowds were still enjoying the community spectacle of a burnt, lynched black body.)

The principles, we now know, were mostly window-dressing; and beyond the windows stood the most ghastly horrors. But the point remains: if someone managed to produce a statistical study of those Americans who became espionage agents in the 1930s or '40s, my guess is that the motivation of the larger portion by far would turn out to have been not material considerations but humanitarian ones.

Paul Robeson assuredly fell into the ranks of those who saw in Bolshevism and the Soviet Union the best hope for advancing the rights of people of color and for putting an end to Western colonialism. The centennial of his birth in 1998 produced an ironic assortment of tributes — as well as a resurgence of Paul Robeson Jr.'s animosity toward me.

I indicated something of what I meant by "ironic" in an article for the New York Times:

> Hounded in his day by the guard dogs of civic orthodoxy, Robeson is about to be praised within the halls of some of the same institutions that once locked him out, denied him an audience, helped to destroy his career. Caution is therefore in order. As is usually the way with public anointments . . . his story is likely to be smoothed out and polished up for mainstream consumption. The breadth and tenacity of his challenge to the status quo, to say nothing of his transgressive personal history (his difficult marriage, his multiple affairs, his problematic parenting) will likely be blanketed in a surfeit of hollow hallelujahs.
>
> Among the more glaring ironies looming ahead is the participation of the Academy of Motion Picture Arts and Sciences in honoring Robeson's film career. Under the Academy's dazzling auspices, viewers will be invited to forget that Robeson managed to make exactly two Hollywood films: the "pictur-

esque" "Show Boat" and the awesomely bad "Tales of Man-
hattan" (two of his nine other movies were also made in the
United States, but by independent producers). Nor was Robe-
son ever invited to put on film his historic performance in
"Othello," which opened on Broadway in 1943 . . .

The big studios did (and do) little to represent the range
and richness of black life . . . black performers in Robeson's
day were largely confined (as the historian Donald Bogle has
amply documented) to playing loyal, subservient Uncle or
Auntie Toms; goggle-eyed buffoons; tragic mulattoes; primitive,
violent African savages; rotund and devoted mammies; or,
mostly in the '70's, powerfully muscled, sexually threatening,
cunningly criminal, big black bucks.

There were limited strategies available to black performers
for circumventing the constricted roles offered them. They had
to "smuggle in," as James Baldwin once put it, a "contraband"
reality. Robeson was particularly adept at it. Even when "per-
forming the primitive," he often succeeded in adding layers of
emotional depth and dignified intelligence to the intended im-
agery of debasement. Through the force of his own personality,
he so overpowered his mostly demeaning roles as to come
across more as archetype than stereotype . . .

Robeson's breaking point with Hollywood came in 1942,
with the release of "Tales of Manhattan." In accepting the role
of a sharecropper in the film, he'd been led to believe that he'd
have considerable say over the script and that it would realisti-
cally depict the plight of the rural black poor. But in the end—
though he was allowed a few lines in praise of a world with "no
rich an' no mo' po"—his sharecropper reprised the familiar
simple-minded darkie who'd already disfigured so many Holly-
wood films. When the movie was shown in Los Angeles, Robe-
son joined the picket line of protesters.

In addition, he called a news conference to announce that
he was abandoning Hollywood for good. He advised other pro-
gressive performers henceforth to lend their talents to low-budget,

*independent film projects not reliant on maintream bigotry
and big-studio profit margins. Robeson promptly followed his
own advice, offering his services as the off-camera narrator for
"Native Land," a feature-length film documenting civil-rights
abuses. But it never got more than limited exposure. Some denounced it as subversive of the war effort, and an F.B.I. agent
called it "obviously a Communist project."*

In his important book Framing Blackness, *Ed Guerrero argues
that it's really only in the 1990s that a wave of black filmmakers
(Spike Lee, Julie Dash, Marlon Riggs, Bill Duke, Charles Burnett,
etc.) have managed to take the reins firmly in their own hands, returning to a tradition established in the 1920s by black filmmakers like
Oscar Micheaux. In Robeson's day, black artists had more limited
choices. For a time, he primarily relied on his own dignified and commanding presence to humanize—sometimes even overpower—the cardboard creations of the scriptwriters. But finally, he could satisfy his
conscience and his politics only by leaving Hollywood behind. He
proved one of the rare celebrity figures—one thinks also, and immediately, of Muhammad Ali's and Eartha Kitt's outspoken opposition to
the war in Vietnam—willing to place their careers in outright jeop-
ardy to call attention to the bigotries and barbarities of the age.*

There wasn't a peep of objection from Paul Robeson Jr. about my
Times *piece. But when, early in 1999, I published "Writing Robeson"
in the* Nation, *in which I struggled with the issue of whether it was appropriate for a white man, let alone a gay white man, to write the biography of a black hero, the house fell in. Both he and Lloyd Brown
(who'd helped Robeson Sr. write his autobiography* Here I Stand) *sent
in screeds of denunciation to the* Nation, *and both were published.*

*Brown's letter made no effort to conceal his homophobia: "I
formed the opinion that Duberman was a sick writer when he asked
people if my close relationship with Robeson might have been more
than collegial—me, a lifelong one-woman man, openly heterosexual!*

Not even the many investigations made of me by J. Edgar Hoover,
whose concern about the class struggle was equaled by this fixation on
the ass struggle, did such probing."

In a second, private letter to the editor of the Nation, Katrina van-
den Heuvel (who sent me a copy), Brown reiterated his high-minded
theme: "Shame on the Nation for having a man with an obsessive
anal fixation write your centenary article on Paul Robeson. I cannot
believe that you would ever do something that demeaning if you were
observing the centennial of a white American of Robeson's historic
stature."

In my printed response in the Nation (to Brown's first letter), I referred to the "stupefying vulgarity" of his homophobia and his "ad-
dlepated" insistence that I'd been persistently asking interviewees
about the possibility that his and Robeson's relationship had been a
romantic/sexual one. In fact I'd never once brought up the matter — "it
never even crossed my mind. That bizarre notion is wholly a figment of
Brown's own imagination."

Paul Robeson Jr.'s protest required a more detailed reply. In his
lengthy letter to the Nation, he insisted, among a variety of charges,
that on beginning his father's biography I'd "formally consented to
suspend" my "gay activism for the duration of his work on the book";
that my "attempts to include" an itemization of Robeson Sr.'s "actual
sexual behavior" weren't in the book because "such materials were rejected both by me and by his publisher"; that I had "deliberately omitted a 'list'" he'd given me of his father's "black female lovers"; that,
preferring to dwell on matters sexual in the book, I'd said very little in
the biography "about the artistic life of one of the great performing
artists of the century."

I'd endured a dozen years of Paul Jr.'s misrepresentations and abuse
and had refrained from any public response. But this time I'd had it.
the Nation, after all, was home base for me; it was read by people whose
politics I mostly shared, and I also wrote for it occasionally. Enough of
swallowing his slanders silently. Load up the old blunderbuss.

"I never agreed," I began, "I never would have considered *agreeing* to the preposterous, homophobic notion that I suspend my gay activism for the duration of preparing the biography. . . . As is easily demonstrated—and as Robeson Jr. was well aware at the time—my active involvement in the gay movement continued throughout the eighties: I wrote a regular column on gay and lesbian history for the [gay paper] The New York Native, began work on establishing the university-affiliated research center on gay and lesbian life . . . that became CLAGS, and answered the phones one afternoon a week at the office of the People with AIDS Coalition. It is mystifying how Paul Robeson Jr. can equate this amount of activity with 'withdr[awing] from the public gay scene for seven years.'"

As for the claim that I'd tried to include as much clinical detail about Robeson's preferred habits in bed and had been stopped only by the superior morality of Paul Jr. and my publisher, I'd never made any such attempt in the first place. If I had, Paul would have had no way to stop me: In a formal legal agreement he'd surrendered all control over what I might ultimately choose to say in the biography. He had zero power to reject or include material, sexual or otherwise.

The assertion that my biography was primarily concerned with Paul Sr.'s sex life [for more detail on this aspect of the exchange, see pages 54, 58–60] and said little about his artistic life, I wrote, "is preposterous." His artistic and political lives are "far and away the dominant topics—as a glance at the index will prove." It was no less preposterous—"given the overwhelming historical evidence to the contrary"—for Robeson Jr. to deny that his father's "most intense, longlasting affairs were nearly all with white women." His further claim that he'd given me a list of his father's black female lovers—which he never had—and that I'd suppressed it, was a flat-out lie.

I never lost my respect for Paul Jr.'s sharp intelligence and for the admirable way he'd devoted himself to salvaging and organizing his parents' papers. Nor did I ever completely lose my empathy for the unlucky hand he'd been dealt in being born to parents who weren't much interested in raising a child and whose father in particular no more than distantly acknowledged him as a youngster. The wounding ef-

fects of such nonparenting have, I believe, been profound and, curious as it may sound, help to account for his odd decision to ask me to become his father's biographer.

From the beginning, I'd puzzled over his choice. The reasons he cited at the time—my "nuanced prose," my "complex understanding of personality," my left-wing politics and my experience in the theater— never seemed to me a sufficient explanation. There were any number of black, heterosexual scholars with left-wing politics and nuanced prose. I was unconvinced that his stated reasons for inviting me to do the biography were the sum of his motives; but since I wanted to do the book, I had taken him at his word and accepted.

It was only two or three years into researching the biography that a more complex account began to dawn on me. It may strike some as too convoluted and outlandish to be believable—but, then, one has to know Paul Jr. He's one of the least self-analytic people I've ever known; perhaps he's had too much pain in his life to tolerate any exploration of its origins and manifestations; denial, after all, can be an essential tool for survival.

In any case, as Paul's periodic mentions of his daughter's "imprisonment" by a lesbian and the need he'd felt to burn his mother's "lesbian letters," etc., multiplied, it became increasingly obvious that despite his occasional "progressive" remark, he held a negative view of gay people. The more I thought about it, the more curious it seemed to me that on the very first day Paul and I met, he would bring up the subject of his father's "affair" with Sergei Eisenstein; it suggested that high on his agenda was planting the seed of Paul Sr.'s occasional sexual propensity for people of his own gender.

I had of course hoped that was true, and diligently set out to research the matter. I'd located and interviewed Eisenstein's sister-in-law, and also a gay man who'd lived in Moscow during the 1930s and known Robeson. I also made a point of bringing up the matter with a host of Paul Sr.'s intimates (Revels and Lee Cayton, Freda Diamond, Helen Rosen, etc.), all of whom greeted the question with a unanimous howl of derision at the notion that Paul Sr. had ever had a sexual encounter, let alone an affair, with Eisenstein, Marc Blitzstein, or any other man; he was, all hands agreed, as single-minded a hetero-sexual who ever lived. When I told all this to Paul Jr., he angrily de-nied ever having mentioned a Robeson/Eisenstein affair. But my agent had been in the room during that first meeting between us and she confirmed that Paul had said exactly that. When I phoned to tell him about the confirmation, he hung up on me. And I got a silent, angry stare from Paul Jr., and no thanks, when I later firmly discredited the unsubstantiated claim of two different writers in two different publica-tions that Paul Sr. had been "bisexual."

So what was Paul Jr. up to? An explanation gradually began to dawn on me. His resentment against both his parents ran deep, and with good reason. But in the case of his father, he was unable con-sciously to acknowledge it. In a classic reaction formation, he speaks of his father as a man of unparalleled shrewdness, wisdom, mastery, a man without character failings or personal inadequacies. To compen-sate, he dumps his anger against both parents solely on his mother, who was in fact the more attentive of the two; she becomes everything from a double agent to a secret lesbian.

Paul Jr. may deny any anger toward his father, but the uncon-scious isn't so easily silenced. It will have its say, in however devious, even unrecognizable, a form. Poor little eight-year-old Paul Jr., turned over to the harsh embrace of his grandmother while his father goes off to pursue his career, will get back at him some day, even if his motives and methods remain concealed—including to himself.

Time for the gay historian to make his entrance. Homosexuality may not be the very worst item in Paul Jr.'s negative hierarchy, but it ranks right up there. High enough up to serve nicely as a covert vehi-cle for trying to sabotage Paul Sr.'s reputation and lay waste his fan base. But alas for even the most wily of psyches: the gay historian doesn't bite. Instead of seizing on the disinformation planted in his path (Sergei Eisenstein et al.), he examines it skeptically and discards it as false. So guess where Paul Jr.'s rage goes now? And guess how much this account will heighten it?

Let's return to the world where gay people are gay (or at least, if you're a follower of queer theory, think they are). Not that it's necessarily a more peaceable world. No, disputes can become even more heated because the storehouse of anger many gay people carry around as a result of familial or social mistreatment can get inappropriately dumped on any disagreement, and heighten it. I'd seen plenty of that during my ten years with CLAGS, and since resigning as director had been living in a comparatively tranquil (never serene—not my nature) landscape.

Still, the late nineties were a time of considerable contention within gay male circles and I was occasionally part of the argument. These were, praise be, essentially battles fought through words, rather than the more bruising face-to-face confrontations that had sometimes characterized CLAGS. Words can hurt—badly—but shouts and threats delivered six feet away are scarier still for us cowardly lions (Leos).

The most heated dispute in the late nineties circled around the growing phenomenon of "barebacking"—having unprotected sex. The gradual proliferation of new drugs to fight AIDS—though they certainly didn't work for everyone, and plenty of suffering, and death, remained—had helped to produce the widespread notion that AIDS had become a manageable disease, not an automatic death sentence. Accompanying that view was a growing rebellion against the so-called "condom code," the insistence that safe sex be practiced on all occasions. The rebellion, predictably, was most pronounced among the young, who hadn't lived through the worst years of the plague and who, like the young everywhere, viewed mortality as some abstract concept that somehow didn't apply to them.

Back in 1995, the psychologist Walt Odets had written a subtle, deeply empathic book, In the Shadow of the Epidemic, *which had picked up on the new attitude and sexual practices that were beginning to spread. In it, he put "the emperor has no clothes" in a new context: the AIDS establishment hadn't been telling the truth: sex was not just as pleasurable with a condom as without one. Gay men, moreover, had grown psychologically weary of always having to play by the rules, of never being able to abandon themselves to the passion of the moment, of never being allowed, unless monogamous, the intimacy of sharing semen with a partner.*

The late Eric Rofes, a well-known activist, had soon after followed with two books (Reviving the Tribe *and* Dry Bones Breathe) *in which he went beyond Odets — and ironically joined hands with the gay political conservative, Andrew Sullivan — in declaring that we'd entered a post-AIDS era in which the disease itself may not have been conquered but gay men had ceased to see it as the centerpiece in their lives, the source of enormous anxiety and the ruling element in their erotic behavior. The gay sexual revolution of the 1970s, it seemed, was making a comeback: monogamy was bourgeois nonsense; emotional commitment and sexual fidelity were not organically linked; a multiplicity of partners was a necessary source of pleasure, self-exploration, and adventure.*

Not so fast, argued Gabriel Rotello in his hugely controversial 1997 book, Sexual Ecology. *He charged that the "brotherhood of promiscuity" (anal sex with multiple partners) among a small percentage of gay men in bathhouses and sex clubs had been a—perhaps the—major factor in producing the AIDS epidemic. Yes, it remained true that there were other culprits as well: the government's failure to issue warnings or to fund research; the scientific and pharmaceutical establishments' early indifference; the media's absence of reporting; and the mainstream's homophobic indifference all shared in the blame. Yet what was long overdue, Rotello argued, was an acknowledgment of the role gay men themselves had played.*

And they still continued, in Rotello's view, "to shy away from analyzing . . . our own ecology, including our desire to preserve what appear to be toxic aspects of our hard-won sexual freedoms." Reliance on the "condom code" wasn't a sufficient solution, Rotello agreed, simply because condoms tear roughly 10 percent of the time and besides, only about half the sexually active gay male population used them consistently — for the same reason people of all stripes find it so difficult to exercise regularly, to stay on a diet, or to permanently quit smoking.

To avoid a resurgence of the epidemic (rates of seroconversion were already beginning to rise again in the United States, though selec-

tively; globally, they'd begun rapidly to escalate, especially in Africa),
Rotello advocated abandoning a multiplicity of sexual partners and
always using condoms for anal sex, which itself should only cautiously
be indulged and preferably with a known partner. Even unprotected
oral sex, he warned — contra the advice of the AIDS establishment —
carried some risk of infection, though much less than receptive anal sex.

In my mixed review of Sexual Ecology *in the* Nation, *I pointed*
out that although Rotello "never overtly preaches the inherent superi-
ority of monogamy and lifetime pair-bonding . . . that seems to be where
his heart is." Despite my own long-standing resistance, expressed in
print many times over, to the view that monogamy was best suited to
satisfying human needs and promoting human happiness, my insis-
tence that eroticism and romantic love were not equivalents (despite
what the official culture taught), and my argument that erotic zest
hinged to a significant degree on mystery, tension, and even anony-
mity, I nonetheless praised Rotello's book (to the surprise of several
prominent sex radicals) for its "strenuous courage," and its "immensely
conscientious, caring effort to think about what has for too long been
unthinkable."

Not that I didn't find a lot in Rotello's analyses and prescriptions
to worry about. His entire argument lent credibility to those on the
Right who'd long argued that gay men were sick sexual compulsives
who'd brought on their own destruction and—even in the face of
death—were unable to control their behavior. I also predicted that
Sexual Ecology *would produce an "explosive and protracted" reaction*
among gay sex radicals, that they'd view this call for "a more bal-
anced" set of sexual practices as a reflection of that squeamish, uptight,
middle-class value set that gay men had devoted their transgressive
lives to testifying against.

My prediction proved short of the mark: there was in fact an ava-
lanche of venomous reaction to Rotello's book. It was widely viewed by
radicals as an absolute betrayal of what was most unique and revolu-
tionary about gay sexual liberation. Michael Warner, whose own book,
Fear of a Queer Planet, *I'd admired so profoundly, led the charge.*
Continuing to believe that the condom code was the best way to con-

trol AIDS, Warner denounced Rotello's argument that sex clubs produced a rise in HIV infection; to the contrary, he argued, they responsibly promoted condom use and were safer than such meeting places as gay bars.

Like Warner, Eric Rofes praised those gay sex radicals who refused to surrender the transforming bliss of multipartnered sex to the threat of nonexistence. One wants to add mere nonexistence, since their paeans to unbridled passion are unmatched by encomiums to physical survival. It's as if a life without unrestrained libidinal pleasure couldn't possibly be a life worth living, as if sex alone provided human beings with meaning and pleasure. Both Warner and others have said so almost directly: gay men have "few ways besides sex to feel connected with one another"; "without a sexual culture . . . we have almost nothing else that brings us together."

If this be true, then some of us have been misguided in peddling the notion of a multidimensional gay subculture—and I don't believe we have been. We share a unique past that has provided us with a special set of perspectives—including the sexual, but not confined to it. I have my doubts, too, about the claim that any curtailment (condoms, illogically, somehow don't seem to count among some of the sex radicals) of physical pleasure is tantamount to a betrayal of gay liberation. But wait. Lesbians, bisexuals, and transgendered people are also part of that liberation, yet none had (or have) a sexual culture that glorifies the pre-eminent importance of randy indulgence (there have been lesbian sex clubs from time to time, but none have caught on for very long).

Besides, wasn't the chief importance of gay liberation, and its ongoing necessity, to end the oppression that often made gay life wretched and insupportable? It isn't even as if constant, unbridled sexual expression is something all LGBT people want, or want as a steady diet. Some prefer the occasional revel, or monogamy, or even celibacy. Call that "false consciousness" if you wish, but that puts you in a position of claiming to know more about their "real" needs than they do. Besides, they would say the same about your claim to an overriding need for constant, ungoverned sex.

———————

Neither the debate over barebacking nor the antagonism between single-issue gay assimilationists and multiple-issue social justice queers died down in the late 1990s. Nor had AIDS ceased to be a concern of worldwide proportions. In this country, many ACT-UP chapters had ceased to operate by the late 1990s and others had refocused their efforts on the global issue of getting affordable versions of the new drugs to poor countries. By this point the gay movement as a whole had drifted decidedly to the right, with the issues of gay marriage and gays in the military leapfrogging to the top of the agendas of the most powerful movement organizations (and especially the Human Rights Campaign). As early as 1994, during the celebrations of Stonewall's twenty-fifth anniversary, one of the top fund-raising events—to the disgust of everyone one inch left of center—was held on the deck of the aircraft carrier Intrepid; *for weeks before, ads for credit cards with rainbow flags appeared in the gay male press. That press, incidentally, was itself becoming unrecognizably different from the politically aware publications* (New York Native, QW, *etc.) that had once held sway. By the late nineties the popular favorites were* Genre *(specializing in poolside swim wear) and* OUT, *which as late as 2008 boasted a five-man* fashion *department, but not a single literary, theater, or politics editor.*

My own energy, more limited than before, remained centered on the—many would say foolhardy—effort to augment the decimated ranks of gay lefties, to link the gay movement to a broader agenda of social justice issues and organizations, and to get a largely indifferent heterosexual Left to become aware of the widely relevant insights and concerns of a gay perspective they consistently patronized. My efforts would prove as minuscule as were the opportunities to employ them.

A few paragraphs from a review I wrote in June 1999 of Dudley Clendinen and Adam Nagourney's valuable Out for Good: The Struggle to Build a Gay Rights Movement in America *will serve as an introduction to my activities in those areas:*

Those working for progressive social change in this country tend to fall into two camps: liberals struggling to integrate increasing numbers of people into what is viewed as a beneficent system, and radicals struggling for a substantive restructuring of the system itself. Social justice movements in this country are often started by radicals who are then, and usually in short order, repudiated and supplanted by liberals. The Garrisonians give way to the Free Soil Party (a call for the abolition of slavery sliding into a refusal to allow its further expansion); the Knights of Labor ("One Big Union") mutates to the AFL, catering to skilled workers and denying admission to blacks; the broad-gauged Seneca Falls declaration of grievances gets transmuted into the suffragists' single-issue right to vote.

Now and then a special set of circumstances will provide a renewed opening for radical voices in a given movement, but the deeply conservative undertow of American ideology soon silences them once again. Activists who self-identify as leftwing have never been able to solve the double conundrum of how to prevent a radical impulse from degenerating into reformist tinkering, or how to mobilize a constituency for substantive change when most of its members prefer to focus their energies on winning certain kinds of limited concessions, like civil rights legislation, and show little interest in joining with other dispossessed groups to press for a broader social reconstruction.

Thus it has been—for several cycles now—with the gay rights movement. The bold analysis of the Mattachine Society at its founding in 1951 gave way within a few years to the patient placations of later Mattachine; the anarchic, visionary demands of the 1970 Gay Liberation Front were soon abandoned in favor of orderly lobbying for legal reforms; the fervor and fury of ACT-UP in the eighties had by the mid-nineties yielded the organizational spotlight to the Human Rights Campaign, with its surreal 1998 endorsement of Republican Alphonse D'Amato in the New York Senate race.

It isn't at all obvious why a gay rights movement should ever have arisen in the United States in the first place. And it's profoundly puzzling why that movement should have become far and away the most powerful such political formation in the world. Frequent same-gender sexual acts have been documented throughout history and across cultures. Today, to speak with surety about a matter for which there is absolutely no statistical (though some literary) evidence, more adolescent male butts are being penetrated in the Arab world, Latin America, North Africa and Southeast Asia than in the West.

But the notion of a gay "identity" rarely accompanies such sexual acts, nor do political movements arise to make demands in the name of that identity—though this is beginning to change. It's still largely in the Western world that the gender of one's partner is considered a prime marker of personhood, and among Western nations it is in the United States—a country otherwise considered a bastion of conservatism—that the strongest political movement has arisen centered around that identity.

We've only begun to analyze why, and to date can say little more than that certain significant pre-requisites developed in this country, and to some degree everywhere in the Western world, that weren't present, or hadn't achieved the necessary critical mass, elsewhere. Among such factors were the weakening of the traditional religious link between sexuality and procreation (one which had made non-procreative same gender desire an automatic candidate for denunciation as "unnatural"). Secondly, the rapid urbanization and industrialization of the United States, and the West in general, in the nineteenth century weakened the material (and moral) authority of the nuclear family, and allowed mavericks to escape into the welcome anonymity of city life, where they could choose a previously unacceptable lifestyle of singleness and nonconformity without constantly worrying about parental or village busybodies pouncing on them.

OCTOBER 1999

Two disheartening events within three days. Speaking at one of the *Nation*'s regular luncheon/seminar meetings, two of the magazine's leading male honchos had at me about identity politics. Then today, at Beth Simchat Torah [*the gay synagogue*], I felt as if back at a Mattachine meeting in the 1950s: deeply conservative people, with a few younger, more liberal types mixed in. Everyone wanted to give a speech in answer to my speech, and I was serially chastised for "caricaturing" the American Right, for not understanding that socialism equates to Stalinism, for having dared to speak positively about the Palestinians. Being baited at the *Nation* for adhering to identity politics and at the synagogue for being committed to left-wing politics, makes for gloom. A stony path this bridge work of encouraging straight leftists to pay attention to the insights of feminist and queer theory, while encouraging middle-class white gays to open their ears to issues of race and class. The takers on all sides seem few. The sole hope lies with the new generation, with young people whose views aren't cast in concrete and who seem encouragingly *bored* by the tired ideological formulas and loyalties of their elders.

2000s

So the Socialist Scholars Conference finally invites an openly gay person—me—to participate and, feeling I *must* accept, I agree. Then for three weeks, I'm unable to get a return call giving me the precise title and meeting place of the panel and telling me whether the format will be brief presentations or entirely informal discussion. Finally at 8:00 this morning—the panel is due to convene at 1:00—I find a message on my machine telling me the room number (it later turns out to be inaccurate), the names of my fellow panelists (an entirely different set of names than originally given me), and the title of the session: "What's Radical About Identity Politics?"—but still no word as to whether or not to prepare an opening statement. At 1:30, with some thirty people gathered in the BMCC Faculty Lounge (somehow, they'd managed to discover that the panel was not in the Faculty Dining Hall, as announced), I was still the only panelist present. I thanked the attendees for their patience, told them I was as mystified as they as to where the other panelists were, and said that I would be glad to discuss the announced topic with them if they were willing to settle for a single presenter. They were, and off we went. At around 2:00, H.B., the purported chair of the session, noisily arrived (the other two panelists never did), interrupted me in the middle of a sentence, started in on some blustery explanation (but no apology) about his daughter's homework (or something like that), and seemed all set to speechify at length. I said I was in the middle of making some remarks and, swallowing my anger, simply went on with what I'd been saying. The audience salvaged what little was left of the day. Their sympathy toward me was palpable and their smart response to my remarks produced, miraculously, a lively discussion (with the charismatic H. continuously interrupting to deliver canned, semi-relevant harangues; the man is clearly used to *commanding* center stage). This event will doubtless go down in SSC annals as "outreach to the gay community." Should there be a round two, I'll leave it to someone else from the community to reach back.

NOVEMBER 8, 2000

Up half the night watching election returns. Results still not known, though I have a sick feeling in my stomach that nincompoop Bush is going to squeak through. . . . I could cheerfully kill the smug Mr. Nader and his *culturally* conservative followers (who think they're radicals). *Nach Hitler uns*, they smilingly announce—the jackasses!

DECEMBER 14, 2000

. . . Gore's concession speech. It was poignant—and infuriating. Gore won the election—the future will confirm that—and it took the political intervention of the Supreme Court to snatch it away for Bush. Now we have to stare at that smug, smarmy puss for at least four years, and suffer the consequences of his policies. Ralph Nader has announced he has no regrets, which confirms he has no soul either.

AUGUST 30, 2001

For a considerable time now I've been searching for ways to connect with like-minded people politically—& suddenly it came to me today: contact the editors of *Out at Work*, which I recently reviewed for *The Progressive*, and ask how I might contribute to the crucial work of building a gay/labor alliance. Patrick [*McCreery*] was the one I reached, and he couldn't have been more pleased and gracious. He, Kitty [*Krupat, the co-editor*] & I are going to meet for drinks next week.

W*hat had struck me so forcefully about the essays in* Out at Work *was their straightforward statements of some mind-bending facts about gay people and class, and their tentative suggestions for a more inclusive social justice movement.*

Some of the facts (as I wrote in the Progressive*):*

—*Most gay people are working-class (whether "class" is defined by income, education level, or job status).*

—*Everyone's place within the economic order is deeply inflected by their race, ethnicity, gender and sexual orientation.*

—*Most people in this country, including many with poverty-line incomes, identify themselves as "middle-class."*

—*In a majority of states, employers can still legally fire workers simply because they are gay.*

—*The workplace remains strongly defined by heterosexual norms. Most straight workers believe that gender comes in two, and only two, packages: male or female. And most would claim to believe (at least officially) that lifetime, monogamous pair-bonding is the best guarantee of a contented, moral life.*

—*Within some segments of organized labor, there's been a growing awareness of the effect of homophobia on gay workers, and a willingness to address it.*

—*There's been no comparable growth in understanding within national gay organizations about class issues. Nor have they expressed any notable concern about the economic plight and working conditions of many within the LGBT community itself.*

What the essays in Out at Work *collectively argued was that progressives active in class, gender, and sexual politics need to recognize more than they do the linkages between their struggles, and to find ways to act together collectively, at least in regard to certain issues. The official LGBT movement needs to broaden its agenda to include workplace problems that directly govern the lives of many gay people. For its part, the union movement has to take greater responsibility for the oppressive, even dangerous conditions that make daily life at the work-place so miserable for gender and sexual nonconformists.*

Much *easier said than done. The traditional gay agenda focuses primarily on the needs of the comparatively prosperous, marginalizing less privileged (and less conforming) members of the community, and working through traditional political channels like electioneering and lobbying to win (much-needed) civil rights. To service the needs of everyone else, a few financially fragile, understaffed radical groups (like Esperanza or FIERCE!) have surfaced in the last few years, but so far lack the resources to tackle, other than marginally, the gargan-tuan issues facing the large LGBT underclass of unemployed and working poor.*

The traditional union agenda, for its part, needs to aim for a work-place environment where LGBT people can feel protected against ha-rassment, comfortable in being open about their lives, and represented in contract negotiations on such issues as domestic partnership bene-fits. Certain recent developments provide grounds for limited opti-mism. Within several unions, gay caucuses now exist; and some union leaders—such as the AFL-CIO's John J. Sweeney—seem firmly com-mitted to putting gay rights and gay safety on their agendas. In 1998, Pride at Work, a national caucus of gay, lesbian, and transgender trade unionists, become an official constituency group of the AFL-CIO. Gays have become somewhat more willing to come out at work, and their straight counterparts somewhat more supportive when they do.

The pessimists would stress that homophobia at the workplace and within union hierarchies remains profound. They would point as well to the bitter truth that the national gay organizations are powerful for the simple reason that their assimilationist goals accurately reflect the values of most gay people—who've expressed no wish for a radical analysis of class nor a radical alliance with straight left-wingers. No, they want to win the right to mimic the institutional straitjacket of state-controlled marriage, and to openly join the armed forces in state-sanctioned killing.

The optimists would respond by pointing to the (slowly) growing number of unions (AFSCME and SEIU, for example) that actively support the formation of strong gay caucuses and are making a significant effort to educate straight workers about the fear that homophobia engenders in their gay counterparts. At the same time, an increasing number of gay workers are throwing off their long-standing doubts about the value of unions and are beginning to recognize that organized labor could become a significant ally in their own struggle. A reconfigured working class could conceivably recognize the varied lives and the amalgams of identity that unions, like it or not, do represent. The struggle for better working conditions and higher wages would continue, but in the future would be linked to the race, gender, and sexual struggles in which they're embedded.

Imagine: an economic-justice movement that included gay people, and a gay movement that concerned itself with a more equitable distribution of wealth. In tandem they could create a revitalized workplace and a reinvigorated politics. Even pessimists might dance the tiniest jig.

[In November 2007, the House would pass a bill (the Employment Non-Discrimination Act, or ENDA), giving broad protection in the workplace to LGB (but not transgender—which kicked up a serious division within the movement) people. ENDA, if passed, would provide some defense—that is, for LGB people—against bigoted employers, but not against the abuse of fellow employees. Not, that is, unless local or state legislation existed that would allow the abused worker to bring suit, or unless a gay-friendly union existed that would itself haul the assailant(s) up on charges. As of 2008, nineteen states, Washington, D.C., and numerous cities had passed laws providing various sorts of protection against anti-gay discrimination. No comparable federal legislation yet exists. Even should ENDA pass, its failure to provide gender identity protection will make it a decidedly mixed blessing. The Human Rights Campaign, the largest—and most assimilation-minded—gay rights group in the country, has sanctioned the omission. But left-wing gays especially have strongly denounced the lack of any protection for transgendered people.]

SEPTEMBER 5, 2001

Met with Patrick [*McCreery*] and Kitty [*Krupat*] last night for drinks. It went wonderfully. They're terrific people—affable, bright, committed warm-heartedly to something beyond their own egos & careers. It turns out they had hoped all along that the book [*Out at Work*] might lead to some kind of organization-building, and my call therefore delighted them. They asked lots of smart questions about how I put CLAGS together and were especially taken with how it originated—a few people sitting around my living room trying to figure out what was needed & how to go about creating it. They think the same low intensity "think tank" approach is right for inaugurating a labor/gay alliance. We're going to have dinner soon at Kitty's to go over potential names to invite—agreeing there shouldn't be more than a dozen for starters . . . this time around I want to work in the trenches, not lead. I'm so grateful to connect again to useful political work, that I don't require any star turn as a further incentive.

SEPTEMBER 12, 2001

It's 24 hours since the attack and although (so far as we now can tell) we don't personally know anyone killed or injured, our minds and hearts are reeling. I can't shake the particular image of those still trapped beneath the rumble, able to use their cell phones—the horrors of consciousness—yet not able to lead rescuers to where they are. The numbers lost are not yet revealed, the individual tragedies mostly unknown. Eli & I brought water bottles down to those on line yesterday waiting in the hot sun for boats to Jersey, and are searching today for some way to volunteer. He's a whirlwind of energy; I feel mostly numb, hunkered down. . . .

What we most have to worry about now, I fear, is bully-boy Bush's response. The culprits need to be caught and punished, of course, but what we don't need is a Dresden-like carpet bombing of Afghanistan for "harboring" the villains (if, indeed, they did). Bush is quite capable of a brutal massacre of innocents; and what's more, the country would applaud it.

SEPTEMBER 16, 2001

Like most New Yorkers, I'm still dazed and spacey. As more and more stories emerge about the individuals lost, I constantly fight back tears—so many young people with so much ahead of them. The only time I feel awake is when Bush or one of his masters pops up on the screen spouting, with smirky resolve, their militaristic, knee-jerk patriotism. What makes it all still scarier is that the country and the Congress have given the hawks a green light to inflict maximum punishment. May the name of Barbara Lee, the one person in Congress to vote against giving Bush carte blanche, go down in history as the hero she is.

We need urgently to ask ourselves why so many people around the world hate us. But we won't. We'd rather be outraged that anyone could be so blind or insane as to attack "the land of freedom."

SEPTEMBER 21, 2001

Bush delivered his "speech to the nation," written by somebody else of course, with surprising (for an empty-headed adolescent) poise and equally surprising self-assurance. The country is widely hailing him for having "risen to the occasion," and the press is uniformly ignoring the offensive religiosity in a speech that dares xenophobically to claim that ours is "civilization's" fight, that "God is not neutral." The unfathomable, triumphalist arrogance—the country's as much as the man's! Why are we hearing almost nothing in the mainstream media about our own foreign policy atrocities of recent years that have generated so much rage against us?—our destruction of one of Sudan's two pharmaceutical factories, our indifference to the slaughter in Rwanda, our daily bombings of Iraq, our support of the autocratic, patriarchal regimes in Kuwait and Saudi Arabia, and so forth.

All in a context of an appalling greed that wallows in luxuries created on the backs of millions of the world's illiterate, poverty-stricken, despairing people—who will shortly be feeling, in addition, an avalanche of militaristic destruction. None of which excuses for a second the barbarism of the September 11 attack. But it does help to explain it.

SEPTEMBER 30, 2001

Dinner last night at Kitty's, with Patrick and Tami Gold [*who'd made the* Out at Work *film*]. We were all so over-excited at having found each other and needed political work to do in common, that conversation was like a cascade of fireworks and, as we drank more & more, hilariously loud. My face was fire-red with the worst attack of roseacea I've ever had, but not even that dented my spirits. We didn't finally get around to talking about who to invite to our next meeting until nearly 11:00—past my bedtime these days, but who cared. Patrick's working on a draft letter to some 20 people we finally settled on, which the rest of us will then edit.

OCTOBER 10, 2001

Fourth day of the bombing. Almost no detailed information from the Pentagon, other than acknowledgement that "ground troops" (meaning illiterate teen-aged boys) are being directly assaulted. As for civilian casualties, we hear not a word—though the Pentagon couldn't conceal the death of some aid workers. And now the major news media have caved in and agreed to self-censorship; an ominous reflection of what the new Department of Homeland Security (ugh!) may have in mind for muzzling civil liberties. Even while denying that we're involved in "regime-building," Bush has clearly decided to enter, massively, into the Afghani civil war—to the benefit of a Northern Alliance that (judging from the shards of information that do get through) is only *somewhat* less repressive than the Taliban. Peaceniks here seem mostly paralyzed (certainly I am), without any clearcut alternative strategy (the UN? The Hague? An Arab summit?) to offer. The war-lovers have a pretty clear field. At least thus far.

OCTOBER 18, 2001

The CLAGS conference today on "Labor, Class & Queer" (life does, somehow, go on). It drew, at maximum strength, only about 50 people, but the crowd was largely non-white and working-class—a constituency rare, needed & welcome in the Graduate Center. I found Bill Fletcher the most interesting of the first set of panelists, especially his warning that progressive union leaders often get elected *despite* their progressivism and *can't* necessarily bring along their membership on controversial issues (like homosexuality). Miriam Frank, on the second panel added some other cautionary notes: the legacy of the bitter fight to unionize at the Gay Men's Health Crisis (GMHC) is still with us; only 12 states have legislation to protect lesbian and gay workers against discrimination (and only 2 protect transgender people); and the need to recognize the hazards of relying excessively on legislation (like ENDA) to protect us—it's almost always narrowly conceived, difficult to get passed and easy to repeal. That leaves, I suppose, local organizing and educating to raise consciousness both within the unions (on gay issues) and the gay community (on class ones), the optimal channels for change.

OCTOBER 24, 2001

On the war grinds, now clearly aimed at the "regime-building" that Bush initially eschewed. Rumsfeld (wasn't he saying this 30 years ago about the Vietnamese?) expresses surprise at the tenacity of the Taliban, apparently still under the impression that high-tech weaponry "should" be able to decimate recessed caves—as it now unapologetically is decimating civilians (all the while obscenely claiming that our minuscule high-altitude food drops are a "humanitarian" gesture, instead of a transparent sick joke).

NOVEMBER 6, 2001

I moderated a panel last night at the Public Theater on one of those chestnut topics, "The Artist as Sexual Outlaw." So who's an "artist?" So what's a "sexual outlaw?" These days, as I said in my brief introductory remarks, in much of Manhattan anyone committed to the model of lifetime monogamous pair-bonding would, as representative of a deviant minority view, be today's true "outlaw."

NOVEMBER 10, 2001

I told Kitty & Pat that I was picking up lots of ambivalence from them about continuing to try and get our new group off the ground — understandably, given their multiple commitments and limited resources. I certainly didn't want them to feel they had to move ahead from some misplaced obligation to me. They confirmed the ambivalence, and we had a good talk about what our realistic expectations can or should be. In the upshot, we *are* going to convene a first gathering of some 12–15 people, but on the understanding that *they* need to want this to happen and be willing (preferably eager) to take the lead. I like both Kitty & Pat a lot, but I don't want the potential friendship to get tainted at the start with feelings of obligation.

DECEMBER 15, 2001

A mostly dreary year drawing to a sodden close. So many lives cut short, American, Iraqi and Afghani; a foul regime toppled abroad, but its remnants even now re-grouping; a glib domestic patriotism scarily rampant even as the unemployment rolls increase and low-paid ex-welfare workers (whose gruesome reality Barbara Ehrenreich has so brilliantly captured in *Nickle and Dimed*) are abandoned without a minimal safety net, or a sigh.

As I'd feared, Kitty and Pat, already swamped with completing their doctoral theses and meeting a host of other commitments, have withdrawn from our effort to put together a new organization. We'd gotten only as far as agreeing on a list of some 20 invitees to attend an initial discussion. We'd also drawn up a statement of purpose to send to them:

> We write to you as people interested in making the LGBT movement more responsive to class issues, and unions more responsive to LGBT issues. We believe a more profound alliance between the two constituencies could spearhead a larger social transformation—one desperately needed. In recent years, we've seen some gains in civil rights and workplace benefits for LGBT people. . . . Nevertheless, few academics, LGBT activists, or labor leaders are focusing their attention on examining the ways people understand, acknowledge, and express their sexuality in relationship to their working lives. Nor do these groups necessarily see the workplace itself as a site of struggle for LGBT rights or for challenging heteronormativity as the standard against which discrimination or non-discrimination is based. . . .
>
> When attention is given to these issues, the focus is usually narrow. Academics typically study changing notions of gender and class and the ways these identities intersect with sexuality. Progressive labor leaders look to incorporate non-discrimination language and domestic partnership benefits into union contracts. And LGBT activists seek to achieve legislative and judicial protections. While all of these efforts are necessary and worthwhile, they are, from our perspective, too limited, often disconnected, and sometimes rooted in misconception: LGBT people are not—as many LGBT organizations seem to imagine—largely white and middle-class. And their work is not—as many unionists seem to believe—

limited to niche industries. LGBT people are overwhelmingly of the working-class: they are represented across the
spectrum of industries and workplaces; and (if the workplace
can be made congenial) they offer a potentially significant
increase in numbers for the labor movement. These facts
suggest powerful if unexplored connections between the
LGBT and labor movements.

This organizing manifesto, alas, never got sent. . . .
With Pat and Kitty leaving the project, it doesn't seem feasible
for me to try to carry on alone. There are several reasons for this.
Even if I had lots of additional energy in reserve—and at seventy-
one, I don't—I wouldn't have been willing to again take on the role
of Maximum Leader, with the predictable arguments and angst. And
especially since I'm in the middle of an unusually crowded writing
sequence—completing a novel (*Haymarket*), preparing a new collec-
tion of my essays (*Left Out*) for publication, and revising my play
about Emma Goldman (*Mother Earth*) for an upcoming workshop at
the New York Theatre Workshop.

Besides, the climate within the national gay movement isn't congenial to a left-wing turn. In 1999, when a range of progressive organizations came together to protest the policies of the World Trade
Organization (WTO)—of which the "Battle of Seattle" in November 1999 had been the high watermark—none of the major LGBT
national organizations joined in and left-wing gay people participated as individuals only.

Similarly, the Human Rights Campaign and the United Fellowship of Metropolitan Community Churches—neither known for
their vanguard agendas—has apparently decided, without consul-
tation with other LGBT groups, to cosponsor for the next year a
so-called "Millennium March" on Washington. With its corporate
sponsorship and its emphasis on gays being "just folks," the apolitical
nature of the March is to some of us in shocking contrast to the three
previous marches (1979, 1987, 1993). Certain that this one provides

no hint of a challenge to "regimes of the normal," most gay left-wingers are staying home.

"At this point in the GLBT movement's evolution," as the activist Liz Highleyman has put it, "it's worth asking whether gay, lesbian, bisexual, and transgender people are in fact a progressive constituency. . . . As GLBT people gain mainstream acceptance, many feel a decreased need or desire to align themselves with marginalized groups or radical causes. . . . Does it make more sense to join forces with the progressive multi-issue movement [*the Battle for Seattle, for example*] rather than trying to influence the GLBT movement? . . . Who are our best allies—mainstream and conservative GLBT people, or progressive and radical homosexuals?" Those questions need asking, but the receptivity of most progressive straights is decidedly in doubt; for me, it boils down not to "either/or" but, alas, "neither/nor."

The University of Chicago political scientist Cathy J. Cohen, who is African-American, has beautifully expressed my own view on all this. As she's pointed out, in 1998 alone the Human Rights Campaign endorsed D'Amato for the Senate; the Log Cabin Republicans honored a black politician who'd worked against affirmative action in California; the National Gay and Lesbian Task Force accepted (though later did return) a sizable contribution from Nike, which employs sweat-shop labor; and the Gay and Lesbian Alliance Against Defamation accepted (and did not return) a gift from the union-busting Coors corporation. Cohen's disgust with the national gay movement's efforts to "sanitize, whitenize, and normalize the public and visible representations" of the gay community—to accentuate assimilation as the path to acceptance and power—has led her to write, with justifiable anger, "Can I have my [radical] politics and be a part of this [gay] movement? Increasingly, I am sorry to say, I'm not sure."

When Kitty, Pat, and I had originally come together around the idea of a greater gay/labor alliance, we already shared a gloomy view about where the recruits for such work would come from. Was there a constituency for it? We knew it was pure fantasy to think that we'd get even marginal support from the leading LGBT organizations, but thought we had a much better chance with the rank and file (working-class and gay), with younger gay people—and also a meaningful number of straight youth; the 18–30 age cohort, gay and straight, has shown every sign of being more progressive than their elders; they're the chief beacon of hope on our dreary political landscape. Still, part of our long-range hope had been to pressure the national LGBT organizations to address class issues in a more substantive way.

W*hile mulling over what more, if anything, I could or should do to somehow keep the project alive, I was unexpectedly given direction, in a chance conversation with my friend, Terry Boggis. She told me about yet another group of progressive queers involved in the "Economic Justice Network," and invited me to the Network's next meeting. I went, and met Joseph DeFilippis, a dynamo in his early thirties. We talked about the importance of setting up a nonprofit centered on the needs of the gay poor—people in shelters, prisons, unemployed, on welfare, without health care.*

These were not people (unlike the hoped-for recruits for the aborted project with Kitty and Pat) available for taking on liaison work with organized labor—their survival needs were simply too great. But they were people whose desperate situations were being largely ignored by the national LGBT movement. Joseph and I found that we were very much on the same wavelength politically, and we both wanted to move full steam ahead in setting up the new nonprofit. Joseph, forty years younger than me, had the much fuller head of steam; my impulse was intact, but my follow-up drive less so. Anyway, Joseph and I had both learned from painful past experience that not everyone appreciated the locomotive pace, nor the expectation that every task would be completed on the promised date.

Still, by May 2002, thanks mostly to Joseph's untiring efforts, we were actually holding our first planning meeting. Spirits were high, but attendance disappointingly low. Only a dozen or so people had shown up out of thirty-two who'd expressed "strong interest." Of most concern was that many of the no-shows were people of color; Joseph, who'd done almost all the groundwork for the meeting, was deeply puzzled: he thought he'd had firm commitments. The people at the meeting I didn't already know profoundly impressed me; most were in their twenties, urgent, radical, and already devoting their lives to full-time work for a variety of social justice organizations (such as Coalition for the Homeless).

But we all agreed that we couldn't proceed to a second meeting until (as I wrote in my diary), "a good representation of people of color is invited to tell us whether this new enterprise really does feel congenial to them, and if not, how we can make it so." A number of people, with Joseph again taking on the bulk of the work, volunteered to sound out those who hadn't shown up. The soundings proved fruitful, and in July we held our second meeting—with eight of the fourteen attendees people of color. Two months after that, we had a full-day retreat; this time, only five of the fourteen people were white, though the gender breakdown was less good (nine to five male).

It was an exhilarating day. We started to form committees, put some structural building blocks in place (Joseph, by acclaim, became "coordinator"), and chose a name for ourselves: "Queers for Economic Justice" (QEJ). Consensus was rapidly achieved on nearly every issue, and goodwill was endemic (inevitably, the honeymoon would give way to occasional squabbles, but many fewer than I'd experienced in other organizations).

During the course of the meeting, concurrence quickly developed over the scandalous avoidance in society at large and within the gay community itself of issues relating to welfare reform and prison conditions, LGBT homelessness, lack of access to health care, and antigay violence at low-paying work sites. The uniform view was that poverty is most acute among the LGBT young, the transgendered and the elderly.

I left the retreat, as I wrote in my diary, "full of enthusiasm for the work ahead." In the upshot I'd stay on the QEJ board for three years, until I finally had to turn full-time to completing The Worlds of Lincoln Kirstein *(published in 2007). QEJ remains alive and well, its budget and projects slowly growing year by year. Compared with the giant gay organizations (the Human Rights Campaign has eight hundred thousand members and an annual budget of $40 million), QEJ* *is still barely known, and woefully underfunded and understaffed. Yet in serving a poor, silent and otherwise ignored segment of the LGBT community, it holds, in my view, the commanding moral ground.*

FEBRUARY 26, 2002

Sylvia Rivera, the transgender pioneer, died early in 2002. At her memorial service, I tried to pay tribute to her special qualities:

> Like most of you, I loved and admired Sylvia dearly and still find it hard to believe that she's gone. I loved her fierceness, her outrageousness, her refusal to bow to authority, to deny who she was, to abide by someone else's definition of what it means to be an "acceptable" person.
>
> I first met Sylvia a decade ago when I was researching my book on Stonewall, in which she's prominently featured. We grew to like and trust each other, though we came from very different worlds, and we'd talk for long, long hours about her life, its many difficulties and obstacles, and how she'd managed to survive against awful odds. . . .
>
> Sylvia was in my view a shaman, a mystical, magical creature. If she'd been born into a culture that valued its gender nonconformists, she'd have been as revered as were the Native American berdaches, the Polynesian mahus and the Indian hijras, valued for their gifts of transcendence.
>
> But alas, Sylvia was born into *this* culture, with its narrow understanding of gender, its menacing insistence on what is and isn't "proper" male and female behavior. As a result Sylvia's life was full of brutality and suffering. But she was indomitable, and over and over again rose above the indignities heaped upon her. She leaves us a model of tenacious courage against which we must all measure ourselves, just as we must work to keep alive her vibrant legacy—for we will not see Sylvia Rivera's like again.

APRIL 2002

Friends have been calling me a "self-hating Jew" for being *more* critical of Sharon than Arafat. But it drives me crazy to see Jewish soldiers bulldozing Palestinian homes and reading about signs going up
all over Jerusalem urging employers not to hire Arabs—and crazier
still to read about polls showing that upward of 80% of the Israeli
population applauds such barbarism. . . . I'm assuredly no fan of
Arafat; if he hadn't walked away from Barak, we might well have
avoided these current horrors. And I *do* understand Israeli fears of
underlying Arab animosity—what with only three Arab countries recognizing Israel and the rest apparently refusing to put Israel on their
maps! The only speck of pleasure in all this is watching our semi-
literate president sputtering away at the Israelis ignoring his "order"
to withdraw—though they damn well should.

*In an essay in the spring of 2002, I elaborated on many of the views
on gay life that I'd been developing over the previous decades, and
have often sounded in this book. I started the piece with a quotation
from Herbert Marcuse (in* Eros and Civilization) *nearly fifty years
ago, that had long been a kind of mantra for me: because of their
"rebellion against the subjugation of sexuality under the order of procreation," homosexuals might one day provide a cutting-edge social
critique of vast importance.*

*Marcuse's prophecy, I continued, may be coming to pass. Or so
some are claiming. There is mounting evidence that a distinctive set of
perspectives has emerged among gay people (despite enormous variations in their lifestyle) in regard to how they view gender, sexuality, primary relationships, friendships, and family. One even increasingly
hears the claim that gay "differentness" isn't just a defensible variation
but a decided advance over mainstream norms, that gay subcultural
values could richly inform conventional life, could open up an unexplored range of human possibilities for everyone. That is, if the mainstream were listening, which it isn't.*

The mainstream's antennae remains tuned to a limited number of frequencies: that heterosexuality is the Natural Way; that (as we move right of center) lifetime monogamous pair-bonding is the likeliest guarantee of human happiness; that the gender binary (everyone is either male or female, and each gender has distinctive characteristics) is rooted in biology. Those queers who look and sound like "normal" people (or are at least able to fake it) are being welcomed into the mainstream in mounting numbers. But the armed guards at the gates continue to bar admission to the more transparently queer. The mainstream somehow senses that the more different the outsider, the greater the threat posed to its own lofty sense of superiority. Fraternizing with true exotics can prove dangerously seductive, opening up Normal People to possibilities within themselves that they prefer to keep under lock and key . . .

In allowing increasing numbers of the clean-cut variety of gay white men into the clubhouse, there's a widespread assumption that at least these people are "normal" in their masculine values and behavior. But evidence to the contrary is building. According to one large-scale study, gay men volunteered 61 percent more time to nonprofit organizations than did their heterosexual counterparts. Moreover, they consistently score higher than straight men on studies that attempt to measure empathy and altruism. We perceive discrimination against others more readily than other men do, and we're more likely to have friends across lines of color, gender, religion, and politics.

Many gay men, moreover, put a premium on emotional expressiveness and sexual innovation; we've reworked the rules governing erotic exploration, friendship, and coupledom. In the latter regard, for example, the community ideal (even if only approximated in practice) is one of mutuality and egalitarianism—which again sets us apart from stereotypical straight men, some of whom spout egalitarian rhetoric but few of whom carry their fair share of domestic responsibilities.

All of this can easily be overdrawn. Hugh Hefner, after all, made some considerable contribution to "erotic innovation." Going back further, experimental patterns in sexual behavior and partnership relations date at least from the countercultural 1960s—not to mention the nineteenth-century Oneida community, the Bloomsbury crowd, or the *bohemian Greenwich Village of the 1920s. It's also vital to acknowl-edge notable shifts in attitude among many of today's younger gener-ation of heterosexuals (especially in urban areas): a "what's the big deal" view of same-gender sexuality, and a willingness to ask "what constitutes a 'family' or a 'good' relationship?"*

That doesn't mean differences between gay culture and that of the mainstream don't remain considerable and consequential. Many in the LGBT world prefer to believe that those differences are hardwired, that biology, not culture, is the root source of the gay community's "tougher" women and "gentler" men. Yet even the notion that lesbians are "tougher" and gay men "gentler" than their straight counterparts needs complicating.

Gay men, having been subjected for generations to street bashing and police brutality, have learned, out of prudence and fear (not genes), to restrain their anger publicly. Tellingly, it does show in pri-vate: The rate of domestic violence among both gay men and lesbians approximates heterosexual violence. (The latest of many studies to confirm that is No More Secrets, by Janice Ristock.) We're not devoid of rage; as a survival tactic—especially before Stonewall—we became adaptively passive-aggressive (a central ingredient in classic camp as well), taking out the aggressive side in the comparative safety of our homes—or on ourselves, through the abuse of drugs and alcohol.

At any rate, the widely and stubbornly held view that sexual orien-tation is hardwired flies in the face of most of the known evidence. A number of "scientific" studies (like Simon LeVay's on the hypo-thalamus, or the various hormonal and twin studies) have proclaimed themselves "proof" of the genetic theory, but on further inspection have turned out to be unduplicative or based on shoddy metho-dology. As the biologist Joan Roughgarden has put it, "Nature abhors a category."

Just as there's no single, proven, causative path to homosexual behavior, so too there's no fixed gay—or for that matter, straight—identity through time and across cultures. There have been huge var-iations in what constitutes proper (or improper) female and male activities, attitudes, movements, costume—even eating habits; cul-

tural taboos or mandates have differed radically in human history in regard both to gender and to same-sex relationships.

Yet in the face of overwhelming evidence to the contrary from science, history, and anthropology, gays and straights alike remain addicted to the shaky notion of a predetermined sexual pattern and a fixed identity. Which is one reason the younger generation prefers "queer" to "gay": it's a more inclusive term that potentially embraces a wide variety of "differentness" and is more suggestive of the complex, fluid, contradictory nature of our actual impulses and fantasies (anyone who pays attention to their dreams can readily see that we all have a pronounced undomesticated, anarchic side).

Why then the general preference for fixed, genetic explanations for human behavior? It simplifies a number of matters, and offers a variety of comforts. If there are predetermined states of being—categorical, airtight, distinctive (and therefore not susceptible to change)—it becomes far easier to accept oneself: "I was born this way, it's my essence, my destiny." Under the banner of a fixed identity, it's also easier to justify creating a political movement aimed at achieving the rights of those who share that identity.

The genetic explanation for sexual orientation also serves heterosexuals well—thus the huge coverage of LeVay's claim that gay brains were "different" from straight brains and the media's absolute failure to report the inability of other scientists to duplicate LeVay's findings. Most heterosexuals are delighted with the suggestion that homosexuality is inborn. It then becomes a trait confined to a small number of people who are distinctly Other, wholly unrelated to oneself (last night's half-buried dream about sucking the garage mechanic's cock was due to food poisoning).

This is a convenient self-deception, but not objectively sustainable in the face of the known evidence. Way back in 1979, in Homosexuality in Perspective, *Masters and Johnson published their preliminary findings from twenty years of studying sexual fantasies. They concluded that among gay men and lesbians, overt heterosexual interaction was their third-highest fantasy; to an only slightly lesser degree, straight men and women fantasized about overt homosexual interac-*

tion. What made the latter finding especially remarkable was that the heterosexual cohort all ranked zero ("exclusively straight") on the famed Kinsey scale and during personal interviews had described same-gender sex as "revolting" and "unthinkable."

Though Masters and Johnson recoiled from their own findings, it's plausible to argue that the widespread (if deeply repressed) existence among confirmed heterosexuals of same-gender sexual fantasies suggests (as had Freud) that almost everyone is potentially receptive to bisexual contact, that even when we've grown up in a homophobic culture that emphasizes the genetic separation of "straight" and "gays," the wish to be both retains a strong subterranean hold.

If we can say nothing definitive about the origins of sexual orientation (not to mention those who develop fetishistic attachments to "water sports," leather, big breasts, small breasts, whipping, or ladies' high-heeled shoes), the same is true about gender nonconformity and its possible link to homosexuality. Recent research findings are complex and controversial—though it's become increasingly clear that we need to emancipate ourselves from a binary view of gender that restricts possibilities in both women and men.

Commonplace assumptions ("women are more emotional, men are more aggressive") are, as with stereotypes about sexual orientation, grounded in a presumed hardwiring that is in fact much contested. Earlier, I pointed to the Talmudic scholar Daniel Boyarin's brilliant work (Unheroic Conduct) on traditional Ashkenazic culture and its definition of ideal masculinity as one that stressed the qualities of gentleness, nurturance, emotional warmth, nonviolence, inwardness, and studiousness. Boyarin's reclamation of a radically different—and socially constructed—model of masculinity wreaks havoc with simplistic biological determinism (as does the work of many other scholars, especially in anthropology, primatology, and history).

I suspect that if we really do care about breaking down the gender binary, the place to look for inspiration is not Gold's Gym but the increasingly visible transgender movement, offering as it does a radical remodeling of traditional "masculinity" and "femininity." "Gender-discordant" behavior hasn't been a front-burner topic since the early

1970s, when radical gay liberationists championed an androgynous ideal. ("Gender-discordant" is a necessary but troublesome term, implying as it does that we know what a gender-concordant model looks like, that it exists cross-culturally and should be viewed in a superior light.)

I myself ascribe to the queer theory argument that "male" and "female" social roles are not to any significant degree intrinsic—that is, biologically determined—but are primarily, and perhaps even exclusively, the products of learning and repetitive performance. In this context, "gender discordance" becomes something of a non sequitur: where all boys are capable of (perhaps even, in the earliest years, inclined toward) a female-identified—which may be the same as saying transgendered—self-image and presentation, then no particular gender configuration can legitimately be seen as "deviant." Boyarin's Ashkenazic Jews—men whose avoidance of what we call "rough and tumble" play would, by contemporary standards, be branded as "sissies"—were in their own culture esteemed as ideal representatives of maleness.

This model of manliness has nothing in common with the currently fashionable incantation—itself harking back to Jungian twaddle about "anima" and "animus"—that men "need to get in touch with their feminine side." No, it's about the need to reinvent for everyone, male and female, more fluid, expansive self-definitions; it's about moving beyond gender conformity, beyond gender itself, to molding individually satisfying selfhoods.

Currently, gender-discordant boys and girls, taunted at school and berated at home, internalize the view that something is "wrong with them," that they're "not okay." And most of them, from an early age, struggle to divest themselves of the disapproved behavior. The psychic cost is high. In repudiating aspects of the self that could be read as "discordant" for traditional gender behavior, these children do deep injury to their affective lives; many, as adults, avoid relationships that might evoke any resurgence of the "wrong" gender traits.

As regards the ongoing debate about whether gay male "promiscuity" is meretricious or praiseworthy, we need to begin by remembering *that there is enormous variation in how gay men lead their sexual lives. Even before AIDS, only about 20 percent of the gay male popu-lation pursued "sexual adventuring" in any sustained way—about the same percentage as those who chose celibacy. Still, roughly three-quarters of gay male couples do define fidelity in terms of emotional commitment rather than sexual faithfulness—a much higher percent-age than is found among either lesbian or heterosexual couples.*

Chalk it up to the onset of old age and the loss of vital fluids, but I've become a less zealous defender of the uncomplicated joys of sexual adventuring than I once was—though that does not put me in the camp of those who celebrate the transcendent pleasures of monogamy, or make claims for its "naturalness" by citing the universality of the practice among other species. The latter simply isn't true, as the latest researchers have made abundantly clear; monogamy exists in the ani-mal kingdom, but is rare—unlike homosexuality which, as we've also learned recently, is rampant. Far from being universal, monogamy doesn't even exist among birds, those previous exemplars of domestic-ity and mating. Which is not to say, either, that so-called "open" rela-tionships provide, among humans, any greater measure of happiness (as I also once argued). Apparently the safest guideline here is "differ-ent strokes for different folks," so long as partners to any relationship are honestly committed to its boundaries.

It's difficult, given our puritanical traditions, to argue against pleasuring the body. That isn't my point. My main concern is that too great a focus on glutes and orgasms often seems yoked to an under-nourished political sense and seems, ultimately, a kind of provincial-ism, an indifference to the survival issues that dominate and defeat most of the planet's inhabitants—including most of its gay people.

Celebrating rather than apologizing for gay male sexuality is a needed antidote to generations of negative stereotyping. But celebra-tion alone can become incantatory, a repetitive chant that ultimately forgets precisely what we're glorifying and why. At which point some competing perspectives might serve to reclarify our vision. I think, here, for example, of the writings of Stephen Mitchell, one of the founders of relational psychoanalysis (and among the very first to challenge the once-standard view of homosexuality as pathology). I've grown fond of citing Mitchell's view that we separate sex and love because otherwise the stakes would be too high—too likely to heighten dependency and vulnerability.

One gay writer has defended promiscuity as "diffuse intimacy." "Diffuse" it certainly is, but does that enhance intimacy or spare us its embrace? We need to be on guard against the temptation to replace the apologetics of the past with an era of too easily bestowed, and perhaps unwarranted, self-congratulation.

Glances: 2003–2008

My political novel, *Haymarket*, about the police-instigated 1886 Chicago riot, is published. It's gotten only a limited number of reviews (historians aren't supposed to write novels; if they do, it can be comfortably assumed they're not worth much). The dozen or so reviews divide about evenly between praise and dismissal, much of the latter transparently based on political hostility (e.g., the *Chicago Tribune* reviewer's claim that I "over-sanctified" the workers shot down by the police or hanged by the state). Having been this route before, especially with my Robeson biography, I loftily announce that I am unaffected. And then proceed, of course, to brood endlessly about being underappreciated.

We are no longer depicted on TV as psychopaths. Now we are jokesters. Out of the suicide wards and into the sit-coms. The American twin poles, the diametric journey. 2003 sees the cable debut of "Boy Meets Boy," soon followed by "Queer Eye for the Straight Guy." The former (along with "Will and Grace") foregrounds wit and sex, the latter fashion: the prime roles long assigned to gay men. The new trend is widely applauded for challenging traditional stereotypes, but in fact underscores them. I suppose it's better to see gay men consumed by fabric or tossing off one-liners than destroyed by fantasies of ritual murder—or literal lobotomies. Lesbians and bisexuals remain largely invisible on the tube, and transgendered people continue to be portrayed as psychotics. That's still not good enough for the Parents Television Council. Its president, L. Brent Bozell, has called "Queer Eye" the "Gay Supremacy Hour" and denounced the program as suitable only for those "earning an advanced degree in Sin Acceptance."

2004

On his death, the mainstream media is sanctifying Ronald Reagan as a man of compassion, grace and kindness.

Go tell it to the many thousands dead from AIDS because Reagan wouldn't lift a finger to foster research or to combat the mounting epidemic in any way. Mr. Compassion couldn't even say the AIDS word. And he's on public record, when Governor of California, as declaring that homosexuality was an affliction and a disorder.

Go tell it to the thousands tortured, mutilated and dead as a result of his support for the contras in Nicaragua.

Go tell it to the minorities in our own country, and in particular to African-Americans, whose civil liberties he did so little to protect, and whose opportunities so little to expand.

You needn't tell it to the world's corporate heads, generals and dictators. They felt in full Ronald Reagan's beneficence.

Historical truth matters. As a nation we care little for it, much preferring simplistic distortions that sustain our national myths about "freedom," "opportunity," and "democracy." You can't grow into adulthood when you're fed pabulum all your life. And that's why we remain a nation of adolescents, with a culture concerned far more with celebrityhood than with suffering.

F or 2004 the total income for Queers for Economic Justice was a little under $90,000. That allowed us to employ Joseph de Filippis as "Coordinator," Jay Toole as a part-time organizer to work with LGBT people living in shelters, plus a part-time consultant to help us generate additional funds. Our ambitions are larger than our budget; high among our priorities are developing "Know Your Rights" programs for LGBT people who are homeless or in need of public benefits; holding community forums on neglected issues like providing shelter for transgendered people and LGBT youth; doing outreach to other small LGBT groups (FIERCE!; Al-Fatiha; the Neutral Zone; Latino Gay Men of New York; SONG; the Queer Immigration Rights Project, etc.) attempting to do comparable work; and teaching people to advocate for themselves.

In September 2004, Eli and I gave a fund-raiser in our apartment for QEJ. The main point was "cultivation"—letting wealthy individual donors know that we exist—and we did collect nearly seven thousand dollars. But no thanks to the prosperous—exactly one prominent gay philanthropist attended. And no straight lefties, wealthy or otherwise. None of them even bothered to RSVP, let alone send a check. I guess I should stop being surprised at how little the heterosexual left incorporates us into their vision of a better future; we get the lip service of tolerance, not the embrace of comraderie. Anyway, the following year, QEJ became officially incorporated and—thanks to the support of a few small gay or left-leaning foundations (North Star, Open Meadows, Paul Rapoport, RESIST, Open Society, etc.) has continued to survive, with a slow rise in its annual budgets and its offerings. For QEJ actually to thrive would require a considerable transformation in national values, and I include gay ones.

NOVEMBER, 2004, KERRY'S DEFEAT

Copycat centrist Democrats are the real villains. The only hope of reclaiming our country is for the Democratic Party to stop trying to imitate the Republicans, to start telling the truth about corporate greed and malfeasance, about the increasing immiseration of the working poor, and the mounting despair of the unemployed and homeless. The next Kerry needs to express less sympathy for the comparatively well-off "middle class" and far more for the millions of those living at desperation's door—to say nothing of ceasing to mouth duplicate words of agreement with macho war-making and arrogant jingoism.

O*n the occasion of the thirty-fifth anniversary of the Stonewall riots in 2004, I sat for an interview with the* Gay & Lesbian Review *and said, in part:*

> *The common message of the various protest movements—antiwar, feminist, the black struggle—of the 1960s was "Don't Trust the Experts." From indicting the Southeast Asia "specialists" who got us into Vietnam, it was a small psychological step to indicting the psychiatric authorities who'd long preached that homosexuality was a pathological character disorder. The black struggle conveyed a complementary message: We don't have to go on apologizing for who we are and trying to conform to standards outside of ourselves—that is, white, middleclass standards of what is viable behavior or a "decent" lifestyle. . . .*
>
> *There were significant numbers of young gays and lesbians in the '60s who were already working in assorted radical organizations, groups, movements. They'd been turned off by what they viewed as the bourgeois nature of the tiny "homophile" movement that preceded Stonewall, dismissing its members as essentially assimilationists and apologists. And to some degree they were. But in the context of their day, they were also bravely self-assertive. Without crediting the pioneering work of the homophile movement, the young radicals of the late '60s simply dismissed it as irrelevant; they were determined on a far more basic assault against American institutions. The five days of rioting at Stonewall excited these young radicals and they seem, literally overnight, to have shifted most of their organiz-*

ing energy into fighting for their own rights. Within days they'd formed entirely new organizations, preeminently the Gay Liberation Front; it called for an alliance of the oppressed and proclaimed a general indictment of American capitalism and colonialism (they weren't—in contrast to the gay movement in 2004—focused solely on gay civil rights).

Does that mean that they represented a greater potential for producing significant social change than does the movement today? I believe so. I think the central potential of the gay movement relates to (but isn't confined by) redefining gender and sexuality. The early movement tried to grapple with questions like: "Are there any properties intrinsic to maleness or femaleness (other than the obvious physiological differences), any innate psychological or intellectual or emotional differences, capacities, qualities?" I, for one, have never been persuaded that there are, and regret the lack of dialogue on the issue that now characterizes the movement.

Gay people have long experimented with different ways of being "male" or "female." But the whole glorification of machismo that began to typify the gay male style in the late '70s ("we're just as tough and emotionally unavailable as you are!"), and is still very much with us, is based, consciously or not, on a scorn for gentleness, nurturance and kindness—for all those qualities traditionally assigned to women (or to "effeminates"). In clamoring to be seen as Real Men (i.e., to be the closest possible relative to the chimpanzee) we've gone a long way toward destroying the gay movement's potential to redefine gender (though the transgender movement has in the last decade stepped into the breach).

Much the same could be said about sexuality. Before AIDS, some radical redefinitions of "acceptable" sexual behavior had begun to take root. Gay men had stopped using the pejorative word "promiscuous" and had begun to substitute the more affirming notion of "sexual adventuring." The new

vocabulary reflected a new tolerance for a wide variety of sex-
ual practices and venues, validating back-room sex, and bath-
house sex, and sex in the backs of trucks or on the piers, any
and all kinds of unconventional ways of coupling and having
orgasms. But with the onset of AIDS, centrist gay men and
their mainstream mindset took over the limelight. It was time
to "grow up," they said, "time to embrace the 'maturity' of a
committed, sustained relationship." Maybe so. But maybe, too,
people are different in their needs. Plus the same person at dif-
ferent stages in life can shift priorities radically. To deny that
the life course involves shifts in personality and attendant
changes in desire and need, is essentially to pretend that we're
immutable, that we inhabit fixed states of being—to pretend
that our passionately vibrant, youthful selves never existed (or,
more egregiously, still do).

JANUARY 20, 2005

We gave our apartment for a fund-raiser last night for the Sylvia
Rivera Law Project. Moderate turnout. Only raised about $3,000. Of
the two dozen or so invitations I myself sent out, not a single person
(mostly prosperous gay white males) showed up or sent a check.
They just don't get it. Gender non-conformity frightens them. To
me, it's the cutting edge of evolutionary change. The trans people
here last night seemed a warmer, more caring and sensitive bunch
than any collectivity I've known—certainly more than the gay white
men who didn't show.

OCTOBER 15, 2005

During the past few months, miseries from hurricanes to deadly pan-
demics & earthquakes have been sprouting up. One likes to believe
they're Bush-induced epidemics of evil. Have we ever been cursed
with such a disastrous "leader"? His intelligence, when reduced

to essence, is mere manipulative sh
genuine, are a compound of faked (
righteousness. I loathe him. He sprea
tude Johnny Appleseed scattered his se

is liberal, not rad

even found

cuts on

me

294

The 2005 NGLTF "Creating Change" co
year of LGBT activists and organizers to (
gies] gave off more than a few glints of hope ...y again
be turning, that the number of progressive \ ...s within the LGBT
community could shortly become a ringing choir (well, maybe an a
cappella mini-chorus). The hope resides almost entirely with the
younger generation, and with activists working outside the national
LGBT organizations—like those from Queers for Economic Justice.
Discontent with the narrow scope of the gay agenda—with its pre-
eminent issue of gay marriage—is notably on the rise. The Human
Rights Campaign may currently dominate the LGBT political scene
but its grip on the future no longer seems assured.

HRC's legions represent the older, more prosperous segments of
the LGBT community, those who grew up under terrifying threats of
punishment, disclosure and criminalization. They're understandably thrilled at the recent change in climate—at being normalized
by clinicians and *courted* by straight politicians. They want more of
the same and don't want their new status threatened by association
with advocacy for the homeless and the poor. It's like the history of
immigration: the newly assimilated want nothing to do with the
newly arrived.

The surge in progressive values is taking place among the 17–29
age group regardless of sexual orientation, providing hope that not
only the gay movement, but the country, can be reclaimed from the
self-seeking avarice of recent years. Every new poll shows an increasing percentage of the young taking up progressive positions. Among
other issues, they're more likely than the general public to favor a
government-run universal health care system, an open-door policy
on immigration—and, yes, gay marriage (okay, so progressive youth

ical). One 2005 NBC News/*Wall Street Journal* poll
that 53% of *all* Americans disapprove of the Bush tax
the grounds they'll lead to further curtailments in govern-
t social services. None of which means that major social change
is around the corner. The corporations still go unchecked. The gap
between the rich and poor continues to widen. Membership in labor
unions continues to slide. The feminist movement seems in disarray.
Etc. But how good to know we can (nervously) discard the fantasy of
fleeing to Canada.

Who, if anyone, has the "right" to kill? And from what source does
the right derive? When does (or should) taking another life bring
honor, and when disgrace? Is there such a thing as a "just" war that
merits medals and heroes—the American Revolution? The Fight
against Fascism?—or is slaughter always slaughter, and never worthy
of praise? Do certain circumstances mitigate murder? Is "self-defense"
the chief of these? On what grounds would one deny the right of
Jews ear-marked for the gas chambers violently to resist? Or the right
of black slaves, their lives stolen, their bodies brutalized, to slit the
throats of their self-designated masters? Does the same exculpation
extend to Revolutionaries (American? Algerian? Cuban?) who take
up arms to topple tyrannical laws and rulers? To a woman fighting
off a rapist? A gay person being fag-bashed? A sex worker threatened
and abused?

These conundrums are prompted by reading David Reynolds's
new biography of John Brown. His life exemplifies the issues at stake.
Most African-Americans have always regarded Brown as a heroic figure, but few whites have. Until the civil rights movement produced
a limited shift in attitude, very few white historians have written with
any sympathy for the violent tactics John Brown employed during
the mid-1850s war to make Kansas a free state, or for his subsequent
attempt to lead a slave insurrection at Harpers Ferry, Virginia.

Though Nat Turner, too, has often been dismissed by white historians as some sort of crazed religious fanatic, too addled to tote up

the overwhelming odds against the success of h
somewhat more favorable press derives from the fact tha
and those who joined his uprising, were blacks, direct victi
system they hoped to overthrow. Fighting on behalf of one's ow
eration has been treated as more legitimate than fighting, as a
John Brown (or the International Brigades in the Spanish Civil War,
or the freedom-riders during the civil rights era) for the liberation of
somebody else. According to this canon of judgment, itself derived
from capitalist ethics, morality is defined as devotion to one's own
interests. . . .

In all the long years preceding the Civil War, there was little if
any evidence that the institution of slavery was weakening, let alone
moving toward extinction. To the contrary, those white Southerners
who at the beginning of the nineteenth century had qualms about
an institution so at odds with their own ringing Declaration of Independence from Britain had, by mid-century, and even in the border
states, been silenced or converted to a pro-slavery ideology. . . .

The non-violent antislavery movement has, over the past several
decades, finally been rehabilitated by historians. But not so John
Brown, purveyor and defender of violence as a necessary instrument
for dislodging the deeply embedded, unyielding, unreformable institution of human slavery. Brown has continued to be denounced as
everything from an incompetent business man, to a tyrannical father
and husband, to a dangerous sociopath. The distinguished and influential historian C. Vann Woodward portrayed him as a "monoma-
niac," a man whose family history was riddled (it wasn't, in fact) with
insanity, thus presumably proving Brown's own. Part of the ongoing
discomfort with John Brown is due not solely to his advocacy of
violence to free the slaves, but also to his own remarkable lack of
racism—exceedingly rare in his own day, in the North as well as
South, and hardly commonplace in ours.

For John Brown, equality was not a theoretical stance but a daily
practice. He forbade his family from ever discriminating in any way
against people of color, had close friendships with many black
people, deeply admired their culture, and insisted on social integra-

Brown family moved to North Elba,
ny of black people who cooperated in
nomy. . . .

ial episode in Brown's career were the
sas, in 1856 during the height of the
those struggling to bring the territory
e or slave state. David Reynolds does a
the episode, of making it clear that dur-
od, violence was everywhere employed.
Thousands of Missourians (the so-called "border ruffians") had poured
into Kansas in a determined effort to swing the area, when it came
time to elect a territorial legislature, into the proslavery column.

The border ruffians showed no hesitation in terrorizing polling
officials, employing massive electoral fraud, using outright violence
to silence antislavery settlers (one free state leader was hacked to
death in front of his wife) and, once finally in control of the legislature, passing "black laws" that mandated sentences of years at hard
labor for anyone who dared to write, or even had in their possession,
antislavery literature. President Franklin Pierce and his administration overlooked such proslavery atrocities and publicly announced
that nothing either illegal or immoral had taken place in Kansas;
Pierce even declared the fraudulently elected proslavery legislature
as unquestionably legitimate and denounced the opposition to it as
treasonable.

As if to emphasize the point that the federal government was determined to defend the institution of slavery, it was at just this time
that South Carolina Congressman Preston Brooks approached the
desk of the outspoken antislavery orator, Massachusetts Senator
Charles Sumner, on the floor of the United States Senate and caned
him so viciously that Brooks's hard gutta-percha walking stick broke
into splinters and left a seriously injured Sumner unconscious. Preston Brooks's violent act made him an instant hero throughout the
South, where the culture of vigilante justice, including the slow
burning of offending slaves over a banked fire, had long been associated with "chivalric" manliness. The South's leading newspaper, the

s rebellion, his
t he himself,
ms of the
m lib-
id

Richmond Enquirer, in hailing Brooks's murder
that "impudent" antislavery Senators were "a pack
"must be lashed into submission."

It was at this point, and in this climate, that an outraged John
Brown decided that the time for retaliation had come. As a contemporary journalist put it, he "brought Southern tactics to the Northern side." Along with a small band of supporters, including several of his sons, they singled out five men who'd been active in terrorizing antislavery settlers, dragged them from their homes, and killed them. John Brown claimed, and David Reynolds persuades us that "by the best evidence" his claim is true, that Brown himself did not participate in the killings. But he did direct them.

Retaliatory violence is violence nonetheless. There can be no prettifying the fact that John Brown, deliberately and proactively, saw to it that five people were slaughtered at Pottawatomie. To the principled pacifist, for whom the taking of human life is never acceptable, that must remain the bottom line and disapproval must remain unqualified. I myself feel closer to that position than to any other. But then, I've never been a brutalized slave, a concentration camp inmate, an abused prisoner of war or a hunted Native American. But nor was John Brown. The chief indignity he'd suffered had been to his Calvinist conscience and to his compassion for the suffering of the oppressed. Reynolds concludes that "the Pottawatomie affair was indeed a crime, but it was a war crime committed against proslavery settlers by a man who saw slavery itself as an unprovoked war of one race against another."

I myself can't do better than that, though I do wish Reynolds had taken the argument to another level, had at least posed some of the difficult questions that are intrinsic to any discussion of the utility and morality of violence as a tool for producing desired change. I can't but wonder whether Reynolds, who calls John Brown's action at Pottawatomie a "crime" would apply the same label to anyone who participated in the Warsaw Ghetto Uprising? Or the fight against Franco in Spain? Or, during the colonial period, to anyone who joined Toussaint L'Ouverture in fighting the French in Haiti?

st of the time to let the State
ified; state-sponsored wars pro-
t by what authority, human or di-
ch countries are to be invaded, what
viduals tortured or executed? And why
ix of relief and disinterest, willingly leave
ands of those who rarely suffer any personal
nem?

s Reynolds puts it) was a man "too honest to suc-
ceed a   list," too attuned to the suffering of others closely to
attend his own, too principled ever to be recognized as an American
hero. He's more comfortably dismissed as a madman or an egoma-
niac. But those who hold to that view can never explain Brown's no-
bility of behavior in jail, on trial, and awaiting the gallows. His
astonishing eloquence and spiritual grandeur in the face of death argues instead for a flawed but deeply impressive figure, one who makes
the moral midgets currently dominating our national discourse appear, by contrast, the ignoble specks they actually are.

DIARY ENTRIES FROM 2006

The crude, convenient equation of iconoclast and cynic. The iconoclast challenges pieties in the name of progress. The cynic mocks
the very notion of progress.

On Arthur Schlesinger Jr.'s death: The uninflected encomiums to
him make me boil. Is the left suffering from collective amnesia?
Case in point is Eric Alterman's column of unadulterated praise of
Arthur in the current *Nation*. Someone needs to point out to Eric
that some people — including gays and feminists — *do* bear the Bowtie
enmity, and that a significant number of historians do *not* feel that
Arthur's historical works have "brilliantly borne up though time."

There are no ordinary people. There are just people, lots of them, given ordinary opportunities (or none at all).

Peter Pace, head of the Joint Chiefs—openly, at a press conference— has declared homosexuality "immoral." I never doubted that homophobia was alive and well, but I thought we might have reached the stage where its casual public expression was no longer considered advisable (just as racism is alive and well but whites can't now get away with *open* assertions that "blacks are just plain dumb"). Nope, we're not there yet (if ever). It'll be interesting to see how the "liberal" presidential candidates react to the incident. [*They didn't; neither Clinton nor Obama spoke up. In 2008 Pace was given the Presidential Medal of Freedom, the nation's highest civilian award.*]

But oh my, how Don Imus has gotten hit in the head for uttering that rap staple, "nappy-headed hos." Imus has long been an all-purpose bigot and deserves what he got (even if one trembles for the first amendment). Besides, blacks should be the sole owners and arbiters of such phrases. Gays, however, are *far* from being the sole owners of nasty slurs about themselves. It's still only slightly less offensive than it was forty years ago to say, *in public*, pretty much anything negative you might feel about us. General Pace was as bland as a head of lettuce; why how could anyone take offense at so obvious, commonplace a truth?

LESBIAN ROCKER QUESTIONS DEMS

Yup, that's the headline on web coverage of last night's [2006] televised presidential forum devoted to (some) LGBT issues. The event *was* significant; a mere twenty years ago, after all, Reagan refused to utter the word AIDS, let alone do anything about the disaster. So yes, unquestionably a historic marker, even though the questions from the panel were lamentably limited and the content of the candidates' responses boringly predictable.

The three panelists were Jonathan Capehart, conservative African-

American columnist for the *Washington Post*, Melissa Etheridge
(LESBIAN ROCKER) and Joe Solomonese, director of the Human
Rights Campaign. Taken together they represent mainstream, majori-
tarian gay opinion, but do not represent either right-wing Log Cabin
Republicans or left-wing Queers for Economic Justice.

The three panelists were competent and self-possessed. They focused on the issues (marriage and the military) that the large majority of gay people would have wanted them to. But to left-wing gays
the lack of any reference to issues relating to poverty, health care,
employment and education which bedevil so many Americans, gay
and straight, was lamentable. And lamentable, too, was the often
evasive, centrist responses of the leading candidates to the limited
questions asked them.

Among Obama's slicker platitudes: "When truth-telling is involved, people respond." Oh really? You mean like the Holocaust
deniers or the still ardent defenders of Stalin? As an African-American,
wouldn't Obama feel like a second-class citizen if denied the right to
legal marriage? (*I* don't happen to want it, but lots of gay people do,
and anything less—civil unions, etc.—becomes the equivalent of
second-class citizenship).

The issues for gay Americans and African-Americans, Obama
tells us, "are different." Which issues? And in what ways "different?"
No clarification followed. He's passionate about extending all the
benefits of marriage to those entering into civil unions, but insists
that the sanctity of marriage belongs to THE CHURCH. Why does
religion own marriage? By whose authority was the church (*and*
state) given ownership? Doesn't the hallowed doctrine of church/
state separation add some additional complexities to the issue?

John Edwards's performance diminished my respect for him. He
acknowledged that LGBT material ought to be taught in the schools,
but when asked at what age it should be introduced, he lamely said,
"I don't know." The better answer would have been: "at whatever
point gender and/or sexuality come up—*and the earlier the better.*"
On marriage, he was embarrassingly evasive. When Joe Solomonese
asked him about an earlier remark he'd made opposing marriage

equality because of his faith, Edwards shot back: "I was wrong to say that" (or words to that effect). The TV audience gasped: Edwards was unexpectedly changing his opinion. But no. A minute later he explained that he had been wrong to mention his faith. So where does that leave us? Is he now saying that his opposition to gay marriage is *not* based on his religious belief? If so, what *is* his opposition rooted in?

On the (tedious) marriage issue, Hillary did no better. "It's a personal position" was how she grounded her opposition. Meaning? She seemed to want to delegate the question to the states, which is reminiscent of the position white racists took on segregation. Still, I've never seen her so warm and relaxed; my opinion of her went up a tiny notch.

Gravel and Kucinich were progressive perfection on every LGBT issue. Gravel is the more humanly attractive of the two; Kucinich is far too immodestly pleased with himself. Melissa E. told him "You're totally evolved!" No, not by a long shot; nor is she.

I felt sorry for Richardson, though I have little wish to defend the man. He could barely get out an articulate sentence, and kept stumbling badly. "Civil unions are achievable," he announced, "marriage isn't"—as if that settled the morality of the issue (it does if one equates political expedience with morality). On another matter, he used the word "choice" in regard to homosexuality. That really roused Melissa's ire. She *knows* that homosexuality is inborn— "God-given"—and trashed Richardson for his uneducated response. (He meekly replied, "I'm not a scientist.") All he needed to say was that no one can currently explain the origins of sexual orientation with any confidence; *that* would have been the educated response— though the vast majority of gay people, without question, prefer Melissa's answer.

Though everyone referred frequently to "GLBT" (not LGBT, mind—the difference between foregrounding lesbians or, as per usual, gay men), the actual word "bisexuality" never once crossed anyone's lips—let alone prompted the needed discussion of its potential ubiquity. Not that we get such discussions within the gay community either. The ancient either/or dogma of gay *or* straight holds firm root in the American consciousness.

By spring 2006, I'd completed the book on which I'd been working for five years (Knopf would publish The Worlds of Lincoln Kirstein *in 2007). Immediately, I was in search of a new writing project, having long felt that I had only two options in life: being consumed with a project or being swallowed by depression. What about gardening, you say? Travel? The simple joys of everyday life? Ah, easy for Leonardo . . .*

Two parallel developments—the increasing wrinkles on my face and the growing movement (particularly among the more privileged elements in the lesbian and gay community) to develop retirement communities, combined to start me thinking about doing a book—"Sunset Dreams," I tentatively called it—on the general topic of gay aging. Embedded in the topic, I felt, were a number of intriguing questions, and in particular, why it was that so many gay seniors (or so the preliminary studies tell us) don't feel comfortable in a predominantly heterosexual environment.

What's the nature of that discomfort? Have they always felt this degree of alienation from the mainstream heterosexual world, or is it a function of the aging process itself, a time in life when a familiar, unstressful environment becomes all-important? Or perhaps no distinction between older and younger should be made in this regard. Perhaps gay people in general are so culturally different from their heterosexual peers that they can fully "be themselves" only when surrounded by their own?

Underlying such questions is the much-debated issue of gay "identity." What are its chief features, and which of those become emphasized or minimized during the aging process? In regard to planned retirement communities, will men and women want to live together or separately? If together, is the expectation that the disagreements and distaste that have historically divided gay men and lesbians will, with aging, somehow disappear—the result perhaps (as many studies suggest) of gender distinctions declining with age?

More broadly still, who gets to live in these planned communities? Will they be narrowly élitist (as the early trend suggests) or will they attempt to represent the reality of an exceedingly diverse gay world? Who will be financially and psychologically able (as well as "permitted") to live in these communities? Will they be consciously designed — as are so many mainstream gated communities (fortresses, really) — to exclude people on racial and class grounds?

As I started to explore such questions, I decided to become a member of SAGE (Services and Advocacy for GLBT Elders). Along with gathering information about the attitudes of older gay people, I also hoped to make a few new friends; my own circle had recently become diminished through shifts of residence, disaffection, or death.

Among the many services SAGE provides are an assortment of rap groups loosely organized around age: the youngest is 40+, the oldest 75+. The structure varies from group to group, though in most a member of the SAGE staff, usually a trained social worker, serves as the facilitator. After everyone has given his or her first name, a second round-robin produces possible discussion topics. The group as a whole then votes its preference; starting with the top vote-getter, often three or four topics are gotten through before the hour and a half expires.

From the very beginning, I sat in on a variety of groups, sometimes going to four or five different ones during a given week. For the first three or four months, I'd write up an extended account of a session as soon as I got home. Below are excerpts from those notes. All names have been changed.

AUGUST 2006

The 50+ group: all male, all white (with a single exception). The atmosphere far distant from the interactive quasi-therapy group I'd expected. On the first go-round, after we'd said our names, people described an activity of the past week. Uh-oh, I thought, a literal return to being five in kindergarten: "What I did on my summer vacation." Not impressed with varied accounts of afternoon movies seen, museums visited, etc. Several spoke too long; half the group simply "passed" or were very brief ("I had dinner one night with a friend, that's all"); several went on and on, omitting only their breakfast menus.

On the second round, topics were suggested for discussion. "Joe Lieberman" was the top vote-getter. Everyone who spoke, with one exception, was pro-Lieberman; several were lively and well informed in their defense of him. (I'm trying hard to get off the negative dime.)

50+: Chosen topic: "Is the head of Iran deliberately trying to provoke a U.S. invasion so that it can cut off oil and destroy the American economy?" A clear invitation to windbag pronunciamentos—and they followed in abundance, delivered with maximum dogmatism backed by minimal information. I myself suggested the only gay-themed topic: "Gay Retirement Communities," and was met with blank stares—and a low number of votes. By the time we came to the topic, only a few minutes remained. I was asked to introduce it, and briefly did. I described my own mixed feelings about the developing movement: on the negative side was that most of the communities seemed aimed at the already privileged, since the costs were far too high for low-income people; on the positive side was my conviction that frequent, varied human contact was the best stay against depression; and as we aged, depression was common.

That elicited several comments. One man threw up his hands in a campy way and said, "The only such place I've heard about was *sixty* percent dykes! Who would want to live with all those lesbians?" I couldn't resist saying, "I think it would be lovely." He stared blankly at me. Another man haughtily announced that "those of us who live in New York don't need anything like that; thanks to SAGE and our other friends, we're already part of lively communities." Oh sure, I thought—but didn't say—like all those lonely, housebound folks in their eighties, desperate for contact and diversion.

I like and admire quite a few people in the meetings. But I've been taken aback at their tight self-enclosure, sometimes amounting to smugness, the general air of "Aren't we terrific?! We get out to these meetings, go to movies, see each other on the outside, and continue to engage with life." Yes, all that *is* admirable. But the general age range is 50s to 70s (with a sprinkling of people in their forties or eighties). And few seem physically disabled. What sometimes gets me angry is that they seem to feel that anyone their age could be as active as they are. ("They'd rather sit in front of their television sets," one man said, "and complain about how unhappy they are.") So much for the afflictions of depression or limited mobility that keep many of them locked inside their apartments.

40+ group: I feel I'm walking a fine line. I happen to have, from years of reading and teaching, a lot of information about the kind of topic that was chosen today: "Are there genetic differences between men and women?" As people exchanged doctrinaire, over-stated views and outmoded theories—everyone who spoke thought male/female differences were not only profound but could be fully explained by genetic and hormonal factors—I had to bite my tongue not to intervene too often with counter evidence. I spoke only twice, once to say that "it was my understanding" that traditional gender theories stressing significant innate differences were currently under challenge, and to share recent findings by primatologists about previously unobserved female dominance within a given troop.

That much alone may have sounded too superior. I don't want to set myself apart. I don't want to come across (as Allen—also a professor—does) as a patronizing, dismissive schoolmarm. That could end up isolating me. And my isolation as a writer with profound hermit instincts is part of what I hope these SAGE groups, a version of community, will bring to an end.

It's a real bind, and dilemma, for me. Most of the group members don't seem to have had my educational advantages, don't seem to read widely and are eking out retirement on limited, fixed incomes. Politically, most sound like centrists leaning a little left—which I feel sure sets these SAGE groups apart from any comparable, ran-

dom bunch of heterosexual seniors. But if political sympathies
somewhat link us together at SAGE, class lines set me and a few others apart—and in all three senses of class: educational level, income
and job status. People tell me I'm not a condescending, arrogant
type, but I *can* be a contentious one. I like to argue—and that I have
to watch.

Case in point: today's topic in the 50+ group was "The Causes of
Homosexuality." Everyone who spoke expressed certainty that the
explanation resided in genetics: "We were born this way." It was all
too unanimously dogmatic for me to sit *entirely* still. I finally spoke
up to say, "Almost all the so-called science on the subject has been
sharply scrutinized in recent years and I don't think it's any longer
possible to claim that any one theory had been proven correct." The
moderator eyed me suspiciously, as if to say that the establishing of
truth isn't our objective here; the real point is simply to *have* a rap
group where people can gather. Fair enough: contact *is* the chief
purpose, not a thoughtful dialogue.

OCTOBER 2006

To my first meeting of the 75+ group. I expected people in various
stages of distressing decay, physical and mental, uncomfortably re-
minding me of my own imminent demise. So much for preconcep-
tions! Of the eight people gathered only one was in bad shape, in
a wheelchair, shaking from Parkinson's—and even he softly contributed to the conversation. The others were more alive and engaged than any cluster in the two younger groups. For the first time
I thought I might actually make some friends. I especially liked the
diminutive, feisty Martha, and Joanne, who's active still in NOW;
both are 75.

Earlene, 84, was the true knockout: black, elegant, radiating
charm and good-humor. She started the group off—this one,
hooray, has no moderator and no set topics—by asking for feedback
about something that worried her. The "something," it turned out,
was her orgasm last night. Not only was it uncharacteristically quick,

but it felt "different in quality" from what she's been used to. Her concern was that this "strange" new orgasm, if it continued, might set off her serious heart arrhythmia. Was the pleasure worth the risk? Lively discussion followed, the consensus being that Earlene, in the end, had to consult her doctor. I was wowed several times over. Here were people primarily interested in discussing their own lives—rather than newspaper headlines—and here was an 84 year old who took it as an obvious truism that people had active sex lives into old age.

I was also delighted that there were roughly equal numbers of men and women in the group, even if I found some of the men less appealing. (Why in the hell were the other groups segregated by gender? Absurd. I'm going to bring that up.) I wasn't happy that Allen, a mere child of 63, turned up in the group, and proved as obnoxious as during our earlier encounters. He's a non-stop talker, full of bombastic, patronizing platitudes. "You *have* to learn," he announced at one point, "that every problem has a solution! It's a matter of having the right attitude." That prompted my sole contribution. I said that his view seemed to me "very American"; some problems don't have solutions, pain and grief aren't simply a product of one's "attitude." Try telling that to someone with inoperable brain cancer. Allen scowled angrily and swept onto a lengthy tangent about how proud he felt to have strong opinions and to stick by them. I let it go, but he and I aren't done. I haven't come to SAGE to indulge in confrontation, but Allen does set my temples a-throb.

In sharp contrast to the 75+ group, that same evening's 40+ meeting was full of windy complaint, a lack of direct engagement with—or even *hearing*—each other, plus noisy, rambling, narcissistic descriptions of their own plights that neither connected to what the previous person had just said nor responded to it. They're young enough still to trouble deaf heaven. In the 75+ group, acceptance has (mostly) replaced grousing, and I find far more concern and caring for each other—a greater capacity for intimacy—than among the "youngsters."

———————

Allen got the 75+ group going by announcing, his tone smugly self-congratulatory, that he "never feels guilty about anything anymore"; he's now "an adult." I could feel my temperature rising. At the least, I thought, he should feel guilty about sucking up all the air in the room. As he went on and on, I finally spoke up and said something about how guilt can sometimes be creative. If you feel guilty about your out-of-whack privilege, for example, you might be more inclined to reach out, to give money and time to those less privileged.

Allen was instantly inflamed, and for some reason focused on his corollary that only children, not true adults, are self-doubting and eager to please. My own tone went up a notch. "Child-like" and "adult," I said, aren't separate categories of being. Every adult retains child-like qualities—and usually to the good, since the child is inquisitive and imaginative. Besides, what does "adult" mean? What are its properties? Who gets to define them? On and on. Later, in the corridor after the session was over, I went up to Allen and put my hand on his shoulder: "Allen," I said, "we will find our peace." He seemed startled, angry; quickly shutting down, he began yet another rambling lecture—about what, I've forgotten.

Today was the first time I felt let-down in the 75+ group. Uncharacteristically, the session focused on the headlines, on the gruesome Bush administration. Since the group ranges politically from liberal to radical, most of the discussion was preaching to the choir, sharing tired denunciations of our "moronic president." I'm no less interested in politics than I ever was, but I'm less tolerant of generalization. My nominalism increases with age. I find Mies's "God is in the details" more profoundly true than ever. It's the details that convey the actual intricacy of life, the multiple strands that make it up.

———————

I've learned there are two other SAGE groups for both men and women. I'm going to give them a try and stop going to the all-male 40+ and 50+ meetings; too much whining and disconnection for my taste. Maybe I'll go back to them later on, when I have more time (right now the copy-edit of *Kirstein* has arrived and is consuming both eyesight and energy). The initial mixed gender group proved appealing. The topic "Why *do* people love New York City"—suggested by someone who declared he doesn't—won the day and I prepared myself for much lamentation about dirty subways, rude people, noisy restaurants and impossible rents—i.e. "it's a great city for rich people."

Not at all. With only a sprinkling of oy-veys, person after person waxed eloquent about the wonders of living in NYC, including a number who described themselves as poor (couldn't afford to go to theater or opera, for example), but have found a huge variety of inexpensive or free events to more than occupy their time. One man said that for years, he simply got on a subway and arbitrarily exited, walking around diverse neighborhoods that proved endlessly fascinating ("You'll never exhaust New York").

Others added humor: "Do you know why some New Yorkers get depressed? It's because they find out that the light at the end of the tunnel is New Jersey."

Given my own tendency to kvetch, I was stunned at the near-uniform and buoyant optimism. These are just the people I need in my life! But surely they can't be representative—either of gay or straight seniors. Two people did use canes, but most looked decidedly healthy—not at all like the many shut-aways who are dependent on other to bring meals, to visit, etc. But *if* unrepresentative, in precisely what way(s)? Is it mostly in their acceptance of the limitations that come with getting older, and their determination to maximize whatever opportunities for pleasure and creativity remain? And that determination surely hinges on the luck of the genetic draw and the kind of family culture they come from. Whatever the explanation, this group is wondrous, and I'm eager to return.

Went to the other "mixed-gender" group. About 20 people, more women than men. Lively. Everyone went for my suggested topic of "gender segregation at SAGE." I said I preferred the mixed groups by far and tried to explain why: something along the lines of the men tending to deliver self-enclosed monologues, with the sad result of accentuating the atomization of our city rather than serving as an antidote to it. Several of the women warmly supported my feeling that gender-segregated groups should be abandoned; years ago they may have represented a real need, especially among women, but our organizations and our politics are far more integrated than they once were and SAGE needs to catch up with the times. But a couple of women dissented. Bea, for one, said that she identifies first and foremost as a woman, and not as a lesbian. Jeff, oppositely, thinks of himself as gay, not male—a Radical Fairy, a "third thing," as he put it.

75+ group: This is the only forum—and that includes the *Times*, NPR radio, and the *Nation*—where I've found a discussion of some of the *basic* issues at stake in the Mark Foley case. [*Foley was the congressman forced to resign over his "involvement" with a youthful page.*] As 85-year-old Harry asked at the start of the meeting, "Would someone please tell me what crime Foley committed?" 84-year-old Earlene piped right in: "None. But he is a dope to have risked his career over such silly stuff." I enthusiastically agreed.

But some of the other, more centrist members, were vocal in their rebuttal, often spouting the simplistic outrage that's blanketed the media. "How can you defend the molestation of children!" "Foley used his powerful position to corrupt and harass minors." Foley is "an alcoholic sicko, a pedophile." Etc. Paul [*a 65-year-old radical black professor*] joined in, demanding to know how I'd react if the minor had been, say, my own daughter.

I said it would depend upon whether I felt my daughter was as mature as (so I find) many 16- and 17-year-olds today. "They're far more savvy and aware than we were at that age." That converted no one. So I pressed the case harder. "A 16-year-old today is not a 'child.' We need to distinguish between a pre-pubescent child and a post-pubescent adolescent. Coveting the gorgeous, mature body of a 16/17-year-old is not pedophilia nor, in my view, is it 'sick'—as the ancient Greeks well understood. Besides, the age of consent in most states—*and* Washington D.C.—is 16; nature's age of consent, you could argue, is when the body is post-pubescent, which these days is often lower than 16." Groans and outrage. Even Earlene furrowed her brow in doubt.

Paul, more worked up than anyone (he has two daughters), insisted that the "readiness" of the body isn't the same as the ability of an immature mind to make a considered choice. Maybe, I conceded, "but I think that varies enormously among 16-year-olds. Besides, aren't many 40-year-old women socialized to 'give in,' perhaps just as susceptible to the wiles of a powerful man as many hip 16- to 17-year-olds? Should we also deny 'immature' 40-year-olds the right to have sex, or subject them to some sort of screening—to be done, doubtless, by that same expert psychiatric profession which for so long pronounced homosexuality a pathological character disorder?"

We were all having a thoroughly good time, though seriously committed to the positions we took. Joanne, toward the end, put her finger on what may be the key observation: "in this country we've elevated sex into a category of nearly mystical importance. And it isn't. No more than sex is the same as love." What we need to worry about is why so many 16-year-olds dangerously conflate the two, and why as a culture we don't cite compatibility, sharing, compassion, and companionship as the really important ingredients in any relationship worthy of the name.

NOVEMBER—DECEMBER 2006

Mixed-gender group. The first topic was like a junior high school exercise: "Who was your favorite president? Who was the least favorite?" Protracted tedium followed. Everyone picked the same predictable names: FDR, Kennedy and Truman for "best," Nixon and George W. for "worst." And the usual classroom half-truths offered: eg., Kennedy "pushed for civil rights." Oh really? I kept my mouth shut, but I wanted to say, "It's our own lives we're most expert about; can't we focus on those?" After 45 minutes, Jane finally had the guts to say that if the group wanted to continue with the topic, she'd simply leave, no hard feelings.

Went back to the 50+ group after a month of going entirely to "mixed"-gender meetings. It proved something of a shock—and deeply annoying. The meeting started with the usual go-round of "how I spent my summer"—or in this case, week. The two or three culture-hounds in the group exchanged, at length, opinions on the Met's new production of "La Gioconda" (the half hour intermissions were "outrageous," and due entirely to "the overly elaborate set changes").

That was followed by—yet again—the topic of Mark Foley. Ted—who'd impressed me back in August and who I thought might become a friend—led the charge, denouncing Foley for all the harm he's done to the gay community by confirming the ancient stereotype of gay men as child molesters. Though a smart man, Ted sounded for all the world like the mindless columnists and TV broadcasters who've uniformly spouted the official (i.e., sex negative) view. I took up the cudgels, pointing out, along with the arguments I'd used in the 75+ group, that some of the pages' emails to Foley were more than a little responsive. Groans and catcalls rent the room.

They were as nothing compared to the angry hoots that greeted the final topic: "the comparative merits of mixed or gender segregated SAGE groups" (which I'd suggested, with a deliberate eye on provocation—and change). As we went around the room, nearly every man present said something and what they said was uniformly derogatory: lesbians "try to take over every meeting," they have "no sense of humor," they're "loud," they "hate men"—and so on. I'd expected some negativity but not a blanket of abuse. It angered me, and when my turn came, I said why. "You claim that lesbians 'hate men,' yet every word spoken tonight has been hateful of women, based on the most tired of stereotypes. No wonder more women don't come to SAGE, no wonder SAGE seems stuck in the separatist ideology of the 1970s."

I went on, trying to control the tremor in my voice, to remind them that LGBT people are a small minority in the country, that despite what differences may exist among us we need to stick together, focusing on the fact that we share a common enemy—the homophobic mindset of the majority of white, heterosexual males (and, alas, some heterosexual women). I also said—aware that I'd never return to this meeting—that I'd found the mixed groups far more satisfying than the all-male ones, and for several reasons: the women as a whole (because of socialization, not genes) were more open, more emotionally expressive, more supportive than most of the men, who tended to deliver set pieces that failed to build on or be responsive to what the preceding speaker had just said, even when they'd just revealed an agonizing experience or feelings of desperation.

Later I thought, we probably need to write this older generation of gay men off. They aren't going to change their attitudes, aren't available for political engagement—let alone working together with lesbians or transgendered people—and are smugly, permanently immunized against the advances in understanding of the past 30 or so years. There are, of course, exceptions—like several of the men in my 75+ group. Yet in total, that's a small number—3 or 4 in the 75+ group versus 5 or so in each of the 50+ and 40+ all-male groups. Finally, I put my faith, such as it is, in the younger generation, where categories are under scrutiny and challenge, and where homophobia and the stereotyping of women are (among the best of the young) considered passé, irrelevant.

Not surprisingly, I've been going to fewer meetings and am beginning to feel that I want to ease out altogether. Sad. I was so enthusiastic and grateful at first. We'll see.

JANUARY—MARCH 2007

Mixed group: Before the session began, as we were chatting away in a circle of chairs, Ann, new to the group, turned to me and said,

"You're Martin Duberman, aren't you? I recognize you from the photo on the *Stonewall* book jacket." My heart sank. I nodded yes and tried to change the subject, but she turned to the women sitting between us and started to recite my resumé. I quickly put a finger to my lips as a way of imploring her to stop. She did, but then after the meeting she confessed, her eyes all pixie-bright, that she'd already told several other people about me as well.

I asked her to *please* not tell anyone else and tried to explain why: I'm in these groups for my own nourishment, not to win some sort of applause. I want to be reacted to like anyone else, as someone with the usual range of problems and anxieties, not as some separate category of being: a WRITER. In reality I'm not a widely known figure — had Ann announced my name to the whole group, I suspect 18 of the 20 wouldn't have the foggiest idea who I was; and outside of the gay world, it would usually be 19 out of 20. I've always had conflicted feelings about being treated as someone "special." I don't minimize my accomplishments, and can certainly take pleasure in their being acknowledged. But what usually follows is isolation, plus a stopped-ear attitude to hearing about any problems I might be experiencing. I'm somebody *so* fortunate that I couldn't possibly have any legitimate grounds for anxiety or complaint.

Just before today's meeting started, Tim, the social worker leading the meeting came over to me and said in a loud voice, "I just found out who you ARE!" Uh-oh, I thought, Ann's been busy despite her promise. I signaled Tim to pipe down, uncertain whether it's more grandiose to stifle or promote these signs of recognition, and he proceeded to sit next to me and give me a sales pitch about doing "an event" for SAGE.

His attentions, overheard by several group members, did freeze me up during the discussion. Not that it was one of the better meetings. My own suggested topic, "Do we feel the national LGBT movement is headed in the right direction?" seemed mostly to puzzle people.

Few had any reaction, reflecting, I think, their disinterest in politics. When I tried to flesh out the topic, mentioning gay marriage and gays in the military versus QEJ's agenda, not a single person had heard of QEJ and there was no dissent from the view that gay marriage should be at the top of the agenda, that we were entitled to "equal citizenship." Everyone agreed with Barry's view that health-care, homelessness, poverty, et al., were every citizen's concern and weren't specific LGBT issues that the movement should take up. I let it go; I like Barry, and have done my share of combat for the week.

Most of today's discussion centered on the topic of friendship. Are LGBT people "better" at friendship than straight people—simply because they've all too often (in the face of social and family rejection) had to form and rely on networks of friends? I used to believe that, and had found it a source of comfort. But I no longer do. Not after the disappointments and disappearances of the last few years. I've belatedly learned that friendship, like everything else, is imper-manent. Friends move, die, change emotionally, shift their focus of interest. Maybe my expectations have always been too high. I do feel a certain amount of obligation should be a part of any intimate friendship: even when you're not in the mood, you show up when a friend's in trouble. High expectations are probably fatal in a shallow culture like ours, where fear of intimacy is greater than the capacity for it and (in a place like New York) where ambition and greed are the primary motivators. When I have found intimacy, it's almost al-ways been with women. I don't believe gay men are any better than straight men at friendship—which is to say: not very good.

Arlene's attitude is one I *wish* I had. She spoke of people hav-ing different definitions of what friendship means and she's glad to keep a relationship going if there are at least some periods of deep connection.

The 75+ group. I'm going to fewer and fewer meetings, in tandem with more and more people telling me they know who I am (no, dammit, you know the titles of my books). With *Kirstein* coming out next month that sort of deference can only increase. Besides, I'll be extra busy with promotional bunkum—and that will probably mark the end of my attendance. Today did nothing further to endear me to SAGE. Social worker Tim sat in on the session and began it with a stern, prissy lecture. Someone who'd attended only one or two of our meetings had complained to him that we talk "much too much" about sex, and sometimes used "bad language."

Tim then distributed a flyer, "Group Guidelines," setting out SAGE's policies. Among the more offensive lines: "Disruptive behavior will not be tolerated"; "No cross talk is permitted"; "Do not speak out of turn." Are these admonishments for a group of mature adults, or for delinquent teenagers? Most conversations worth having occasionally involve passionate interruption and several people talking at once—and yes, even a few naughty curse words are spoken. SAGE should concentrate on empowering seniors, not monitoring their behavior or trying to turn them back into children.

A week later, Tim showed up in the mixed-gender group, with a new set of chastisements. He sternly lectured us on the unpleasant reputations we're getting for arguing with each other (at what age is it no longer permissible to have dissenting opinions?), which in my experience of this group has in fact rarely happened. He went on to announce that the staff had decided to reduce the group to 12 people (from about 30), on a first-come first-served basis, and to add a second facilitator as well.

Our benighted seniors, bless 'em, promptly raised hell. Several pointed out that they come fairly long distances to attend, and others that they had physical disabilities; to make the trek and then be told that the day's "quota" had been filled would be grossly unfair. Quite a few said they wouldn't bother to try. Besides, I added, it made no sense to reduce the group's size *and* add an additional facilitator;

are we so unruly that it takes two young adults to control an aging dozen?

Tim "reminded" us, his face red with indignation, that SAGE is *not* a democracy. It's a corporation, and it hands down policy from above. But couldn't it be argued, if one is willing to accept his patronizing view of things, that as dues-paying members we're analogous to stock-holders—and therefore entitled to a vote. Oh well, one more bit of nonsense pushing me out the door.

Mixed-gender group. The topic: "Do you regret not having children?" Almost everyone spoke; the topic took up the entire session. When my turn came, I talked about never having wanted children until the last few years. Spoke of regret at the lack of continuity, of memories embodied: no one, with the deaths of Tedda and Flo [*my loving aunts*], ahead of me, no real connection with any of the younger generation of relatives behind me (I've reached out but they haven't reached back). I do feel I've missed out on one of life's major experiences, that raising children is central to the development of one's own character—like consistently putting the needs of others first, like having constant practice in how to give and not get.

Only some half dozen people insisted they had no regrets at all about being childless. Polly's position struck me as the weirdest: "children are too expensive; the idea of pregnancy has always filled me with horror: something rolling around in your body is like science fiction." Brenda denied ever having the slightest desire for children: "a child must come first and that can ruin a relationship." Radical Fairy Jeff: "I *hate* kids, besides it's selfish to have children in this over-crowded world." Mary, who was "drunk half my life," never wanted "to get tied down"; if "I thought about it I might feel sorry, but I don't believe in looking back."

The most poignant response was from Marge. Not only did she express deep sadness at never having had children, but in retrospect feels remorseful about her whole life: "I've always chosen the wrong women as partners. I have no family, nowhere to turn to for support, no career to look back on for comfort. My life's amounted to nothing, and now it's almost over. A life wasted." Her brutal honesty was chilling. Though I barely know her, I said that she struck me as a warm, generous and kind person, her goodness marking the best possible sort of life.

Many in the group fell silent, probably, like me, filled with sadness at Marge's revelations. But those who did talk acted, shockingly, as if Marge had never spoken. Perhaps they had to get away, and in a hurry, from comparable feelings she'd set off in them. Jeff and Francine, both in their healthy sixties (Marge is 83), launched into sunny accounts of feeling happier than ever before in their lives, fulfilled and content. Perhaps so, but it seemed to me a bizarre, even (unintentionally) cruel response to Marge's pain. But maybe I'm simply showing off here my superior "sensitivity." Whatever. Marge is still left stranded.

Mixed-gender group. The topic, "Are we [*gay people*] born or bred?" created a near riot. Every single person, some 30 in all, came down, and vehemently, on the side of *born*. But they didn't answer the actual question, substituting instead descriptions of their earliest *behavioral* memories: "As far back as I can remember, I was always attracted to the other little girls, and never to boys." But our memories, I argued, rarely go back to the critical first two years, when basic patterns are set.

There was also universal agreement that in order to demand our rights and insist that our identity (itself defined as innate, not cultural) is genuine, we have to maintain the view that we were "born this way." My counter-argument that various "environmental" factors—*perhaps* in conjunction with some sort of genetic pre-disposition—were important in producing one's sexual orientation, had no takers and was generally scoffed at. Joanne insisted that the biological explanation is *politically* preferable because it makes clear that we have no choice in the matter and therefore can't be told (à la Jerry Falwell) to mend our evil ways.

That may be the politically preferable position (I'm not sure), but how about the claims of evidence? Besides, environmental factors can also imprint sexual orientation early on, making it no more subject to willed change than are genetic or hormonal determinants. Also, it's politically *un*desirable to argue that we're genetically Other. We should be arguing that everyone (Kinsey, plus Masters & Johnson provide the needed evidence) has an intrinsic capacity to respond erotically to individuals, not genders. The true culprit is exclusivity—the assumption that one is either gay *or* straight. Our goal should be the liberation of same-gender erotic impulses among those who behaviorally are exclusively straight, and opposite-gender impulses among those exclusively gay.

My views were received kindly—in the way one gently pats the head of an idiot child. Silly of me, I suppose, to expect that I'd find any sympathy for recent queer theory views—the fluidity of desire, the disservice of oppositional categories of erotic attraction—to a generation imprinted by a model of homosexuality that emphasized the fixed nature of our Otherness. But I can't disguise my opinions, short of being mute.

Anyway, sitting uncomfortably in a room full of fellow oldsters isn't going to do it for me.

I keep hoping for a place to land, a sustainable community. The dream, improbable though it is, persists.

✵   ✵   ✵

Index